BARACK & MICHELLE

The Love Story

Christopher Andersen

MAINSTREAM
PUBLISHING

EDINBURGH AND LONDON

This edition, 2010

First published in the United States of America in 2009
by HarperCollins Publishers, 10 East 53rd Street, New York, NY 10022

First published in Great Britain in 2009 by
MAINSTREAM PUBLISHING COMPANY
(EDINBURGH) LTD
7 Albany Street
Edinburgh EH1 3UG

ISBN 9781845966089

A catalogue record for this book is available
from the British Library

Typeset in Caslon and Requiem

Printed in Great Britain by
CPI Cox and Wyman, Reading, RG1 8EX

1 3 5 7 9 10 8 6 4 2

For my First Lady, Valerie

She is my rock – the one person who keeps it real.

Barack

Barack and I complete each other –
as partners, as friends and as lovers.

Michelle

PREFACE

They exploded onto the national scene in 2004 and within four short years captured the ultimate political prize. In so doing, they became a First Couple like no other: he the biracial son of a free-spirited Midwesterner and her brilliant but troubled Kenyan husband, raised in Hawaii and Indonesia and elected the first black president of the *Harvard Law Review*; she raised on Chicago's hardscrabble South Side by working-class African American parents who sacrificed so she could achieve her own dreams of an Ivy League education and a job at one of America's top law firms.

By the time they claimed the White House in one of the most hotly contested presidential races in modern history, Barack and Michelle Obama were seen by millions around the world as the new Jack and Jackie Kennedy – brilliant, attractive, elegant, youthful, *exciting*. Accompanied by their two young daughters, Malia and Sasha, the Obamas would arrive at 1600 Pennsylvania Avenue with the promise of a new Camelot all but assured.

Given the obvious historic significance of what they accomplished together, the marriage of Barack and Michelle stands as one of the great personal and political partnerships of all time. Seemingly overnight, they somehow managed to obliterate barriers that had stood for centuries – and to accomplish this phenomenal feat with humour, grace and dignity. By the time he was sworn in using Abraham Lincoln's Bible, Barack and Michelle Obama were indisputably the First Couple not only of America, but also of the world.

Whatever inexplicable forces drew these two remarkable people together also propelled them to the summit of power and prestige. And these same forces enabled them to overcome the strains that, for a time, threatened their marriage.

Like so many of the presidents and first ladies who went before them, as individuals each was a mind-spinning tangle of contradictions. He was the supremely confident overachiever whose fatherless childhood left him deeply scarred emotionally, the product of an exotic multicultural upbringing who yearned for roots and a sense of his own racial identity, the prep school alumnus agitating in the hood, the would-be reformer who owed his meteoric political rise in part to a famously corrupt political machine. She was the dutiful daughter who was grateful for the sacrifices her parents made to get her into Princeton but hated every minute there, the young corporate lawyer indulging her taste for the finer things but searching for meaning in her life and her work, the wife and mother who despised politicians but outperformed even the most seasoned of them as she helped her husband win the presidency.

Not since Franklin Delano Roosevelt has a president faced an economic crisis like the one waiting for Barack Obama when he entered office. And like Eleanor Roosevelt, Michelle Obama would be called upon to be her husband's strongest ally as he met this challenge head-on. Now, as Barack and Michelle take their first bold steps into history, it is important to understand what it was that shaped them as individuals and the crucibles – both public and private – that would come to define their marriage. For theirs is a stirring, against-all-odds saga of hope and commitment, and – above all else – an inspiring, intriguing, uniquely American love story.

My wife was mad at me and we had this baby . . .
It wasn't a high point in my life.

Barack

------∞∞∞------

Oh, no. I did not sign on for *this*.

Michelle

------∞∞∞------

There were a lot of stresses and strains . . .

Barack

I

SEPTEMBER 2001

There was something different about the screams this time. They were more piercing, more frantic and insistent than the sounds that usually rousted Sasha's parents from slumber in the middle of the night. As usual, it was Michelle who climbed out of bed first and made her way to Sasha's room while Daddy stayed in bed, hoping that his three-month-old daughter would quickly be lulled back to sleep.

It quickly became clear that the baby would not be consoled. Barack finally threw back the covers and, still half asleep, plodded down the hall to investigate. 'Jeez, Michelle,' he asked as he walked into the baby's room, 'can't you get her to stop?' Michelle, who stood by the crib gently cradling Sasha, whirled around and shot her husband a withering glance.

It was a look he had grown accustomed to since the birth of their first daughter Malia in 1998, and never more so than in the few months since Sasha's arrival. Michelle was a graduate of both Princeton and Harvard Law School. She had worked for one of the top law firms in the nation, and then for the office of Mayor Richard Daley of Chicago before signing on with a non-profit organisation called Public Allies. She was beautiful and brilliant and yet, like so many other young working mothers, she was the one who was expected to bear most of the parenting burden.

In truth, Michelle's anger had reached boiling point a year earlier, after Barack overrode her strong objections and ran in the Democratic primary against popular four-term incumbent Congressman Bobby

Rush. Obama had been elected in 1996 to represent Chicago's gentrified, racially integrated Hyde Park neighbourhood in the Illinois State Senate – a feat he accomplished by using legal challenges`to keep his rivals off the ballot and then running unopposed. After three years, he was impatient to move on and felt confident he could unseat Rush.

A Chicago native, Michelle knew then what lay in store for her husband. She warned him that he was not ready to challenge Rush, a founder of the Illinois Black Panther Party who had earned respectability as an alderman and ward committeeman before being elected to the US House of Representatives. Barack, a lecturer at the University of Chicago Law School, had a white mother, an Ivy League education and no roots in Chicago's black community. In other words, Michelle only half jokingly pointed out to her husband, he had 'zero street cred'. Barack's colleague in the state senate Donne Trotter was even more blunt. He described Obama as 'a white man in black face. There are those in our community who simply do not see him as one of us.'

The gruelling campaign had meant long absences from the family, but Barack did what he could to placate Michelle. In the middle of the congressional primary campaign, Barack kept his promise to take Michelle and then 18-month-old Malia to spend the holidays with his grandparents in Hawaii. When Illinois Governor George Ryan begged him to return for a key vote to make illegal gun possession a felony, Barack reluctantly broached the subject with Michelle. Malia had come down with a cold, and she worried about subjecting the ailing toddler to a long flight. 'We're not going anywhere,' she told him. 'But,' she added icily, 'you just do what you have to do.'

Barack got the message. Unwilling to further anger his wife, he refused to return to Illinois for the crucial gun-control vote. Rush, whose 29-year-old son had been shot to death on the South Side not long before, hammered away at his opponent's unwillingness to interrupt his vacation to cast a vote that would save young black lives.

Not surprisingly, Barack went down to crushing defeat – and Michelle wasted no time reminding him that she had told him not to run. It wasn't losing the race that annoyed her – although she had indeed repeatedly warned him that he would – but the realisation that Barack seemed to be willing to put politics ahead of family.

This was a nagging concern she wasn't afraid to share with him directly – and repeatedly. 'You only think about yourself,' she would say to him again and again in a tone dripping with disdain. 'I never thought I'd have to raise a family alone.' Barack, convinced that whatever time he devoted to his career would ultimately benefit his wife and daughters, shrugged off the criticism. His characteristically cool, detached demeanour had cost him votes in a black community that viewed him as aloof. It was a facet of Barack's personality that frustrated Michelle as well.

'Barack just doesn't seem to care *what* I think,' a frustrated Michelle complained to her mother, Marian Robinson. 'He can be so selfish – and I just can't get through to him that we're supposed to be in this *together*.' She went so far as to question whether, after eight years of marriage, their days as a couple were numbered.

For his part, Barack was also fed up with reprimands that he felt were 'petty and unfair'. He was a devoted husband and father, and as far as the election was concerned, it was her insistence that he spend more time with the family that led him to miss the key gun-control vote – perhaps more than any other single factor, the one thing that cost him the election.

Barack also thought it odd that Michelle complained about being saddled with most of the childcare responsibilities, since for years she had been heartbroken over the fact that she might not be able to conceive. 'It was,' said her long-time friend Yvonne Davila, 'hard for her to get pregnant.' So hard, in fact, that when Davila became pregnant she was reluctant to tell her friend for fear of hurting her feelings. When Michelle finally arrived at Davila's home one day and announced she was pregnant with Malia, Davila burst into tears.

Michelle became pregnant with Sasha soon after the disastrous congressional election, but the marital bickering continued unabated. While Barack sorted through the wreckage of his first big defeat in search of a way to salvage his political career, his wife seethed.

Michelle's anger over what she viewed as Barack's insensitivity to her plight wasn't the only issue that was coming between them. The 2000 congressional campaign had left Barack, now 38, more than $60,000 in debt – this on top of the huge student loans that they both still owed. With his credit cards maxed out, Barack faced some grim economic realities. 'He was very dejected' following the 2000 campaign, said his friend Abner Mikva, a former federal judge and Illinois congressman. 'And he was thinking of how else he could use his talents.'

In the face of running a household, raising two small children and trying to find ways to make ends meet, such soul-searching struck Michelle as self-indulgent. Even though her mother was on hand to help, Michelle felt overwhelmed – and she let her husband know that she felt he was not holding up his end of the bargain. 'It's "me first" with him – that's how it is with all men,' she said. 'For women, "me" comes in about fourth . . . That's not healthy, and that's not the way I'm going to live.'

'I love Michelle, but she's killing me with this constant criticism,' he confided to Madelyn 'Toot' Dunham, the white grandmother who raised him. 'She just seems so bitter, so angry all the time.' For the first time he wondered aloud, as Michelle did to her mother, if they were going to make it as a couple.

For a time, it looked as if he might consider making adjustments, especially in response to Michelle's pleas that he get job that paid 'real money'. At one point, Barack was up for a $300,000-a-year position as director of a non-profit organisation. He was so nervous that he might actually get the job – a job he didn't really want – that his hands were trembling as he prepared for the interview.

Much to Michelle's consternation, Barack didn't land the lucrative position. To make matters worse, he decided that what he really needed to do following his bruising defeat at the polls was hop on a plane for the Democratic National Convention in Los Angeles. When he got to LA, he went straight to Hertz to pick up a rental car – and was promptly informed that his American Express card had been declined. After an hour of cajoling over the phone, he managed to convince American Express to authorise his car rental. 'Needless to say,' he later conceded, 'it was all very embarrassing – and depressing.'

Things weren't much better once he got to the Staples Center, where Barack was turned away because he didn't have a floor pass. After several frustrating days of trying and failing to secure access that would allow him watch convention delegates nominate Al Gore as their candidate, Obama flew back to Chicago.

Now he was faced with the daunting task of catching up on his work as a senior lecturer at the University of Chicago Law School – work that he had let pile up during the nine months he spent trying to unseat Bobby Rush. 'Michelle is furious,' he told a friend. 'She was angry that I went to LA and even angrier when I told her I never even got inside the convention. She thinks I'm being a fool – not just a fool, but a lazy fool.'

Indeed, Michelle was at the end of her tether. Barack's long absences had left her feeling abandoned; even though the congressional campaign was over, it looked as if her husband was not about to change his ways. If anything, he seemed more restless than ever.

Michelle sought advice from the man she trusted most – the man who married them, who counselled Barack in many matters and who baptised their children: Reverend Jeremiah Wright of Trinity United Church of Christ. Wright defended Barack's political ambitions and counselled Michelle to be patient. The reverend stressed that Barack was obviously devoted to his wife and family, and that his absences were more in the nature of a sacrifice – a sacrifice aimed at making a better life for his family.

It was an argument she had heard many times before. After all, Michelle had given her blessing when Barack, who was in the middle of his first campaign for the Illinois State Senate, had joined Wright and others in Louis Farrakhan's 1995 Million Man March on Washington – ostensibly an affirmation of the African American male's commitment to his family and his community.

While Barack repeatedly referred to the Reverend Wright as a 'mentor' and a 'father figure' during this period, Michelle had ties to the reverend that were just as close. Michelle was the Obama who played an active role at Trinity United, who occasionally helped out with services on Sundays and who, when her girls got old enough, made sure they attended Sunday school. If there was any one person other than her mother who Michelle would listen to, it was Reverend Wright.

But not this time. 'Barack seems to think he can just go out there and pursue his dreams,' she told her mother, 'and leave all the heavy lifting around here to me.' One resident in their Hyde Park apartment building recalled coming upon the young couple as they quarrelled in a hallway. 'She was really dressing him down and he was shaking his head and obviously as angry and fed up as she was,' the neighbour said. 'They both shut up the minute they realised someone else was there.'

Now, on this chilly morning in early September 2001, all those questions had vanished. At this moment, Barack and Michelle were asking themselves only one thing: what was making their infant daughter so agitated, and what should they do about it?

Two hours passed before they finally phoned the family paediatrician. He listened calmly to Michelle describe the symptoms and then told them to bring Sasha to his office at 6 a.m. – he would be there to examine her.

By the time they arrived at the paediatrician's office, both Barack and Michelle were exhausted. Sasha had essentially cried non-stop for nearly four hours, and now they were frantic to discover why. When he was finished examining Sasha, the doctor uttered words that would remain with Michelle and Barack for a lifetime. 'I think she may have spinal meningitis,' he told them. 'I think it's important that we get her to the emergency room right away.'

Neither Barack nor Michelle had time to dwell on the terror inherent in the word *meningitis*. Instead, they flew into action. She scooped up the baby and walked briskly to the parking lot, where Barack slid behind the wheel of their car and sped straight to the nearby University of Chicago Medical Center.

Once inside, they sat at their daughter's bedside and watched as doctors performed the necessary tests. Squeezing each other's hands and blinking back tears, Sasha's parents listened to her screams as an emergency-room doctor performed the one procedure that would reliably provide them with the answer they needed: a spinal tap.

The news was not good. 'She does have meningitis,' the attending physician told them, 'but I think we caught it early enough. We'll start her on intravenous antibiotics right away.'

There was still a chance that the meningitis had progressed further than the doctors had thought. She could die, or at the very least be rendered deaf or suffer brain damage. While Michelle's mother looked after three-year-old Malia, Barack and Michelle stayed at the hospital for seventy-two hours straight, taking turns sleeping on a cot in Sasha's room as the nurses and doctors came and went, monitoring her vital signs and periodically checking the IV line that delivered the life-saving antibiotics to her tiny veins.

Whatever the differences and tensions between them, whatever the doubts and anxieties they had been entertaining about their marriage – none of this mattered now. As Barack would later remember, 'My world narrowed to a single point, and . . . I was not interested in anything or anybody outside the four walls of that hospital room – not my work, not my schedule, not my future.' Michelle later described the three days of waiting as 'a nightmare – the kind of thing you hope and pray will never happen to a child of yours. Any other parent would understand how desperate we felt, and how it brought us closer together.'

At the end of the third day, the doctors told Michelle and Barack that Sasha had turned a corner. The antibiotics had worked and the meningitis was in full retreat; their baby was out of danger. Barack and Michelle, who, Barack said, in previous months had 'little time for conversation, much less romance', reacted to the news with a tearful embrace. 'Thank God,' he said, reaching out to shake the doctor's hand. 'Thank God.'

For the next few weeks, Michelle stayed home from work so that she, along with her mother Marian, could keep a watchful eye on Sasha while she made a complete recovery.

As if he needed another soul-jarring reminder of the fragility of life, Barack – and the rest of the civilised world – got it on the morning of 11 September 2001. Obama was driving to a state legislative hearing in Chicago when he heard the news that a plane had slammed into one of the Twin Towers of New York's World Trade Center. He assumed at first, as did millions of Americans, that it was merely a tragic accident. It was not until later, when he walked into his legislative meeting in the State of Illinois Building on North LaSalle Street, that he was told that the first plane was in fact an airliner and that another passenger jet had subsequently struck the second tower. No sooner had he arrived than he, along with everyone else, was ordered to evacuate the building immediately.

Barack telephoned Michelle at home, where she was watching the terrifying events unfold on television. 'Oh my God,' she said. 'Are you seeing this? You don't have any friends working there, do you?'

In fact, Barack, who had spent five years in New York – first as an undergraduate at Columbia University and as a research associate at a small publisher of financial newsletters – really had no idea if any of his old friends were near the World Trade Center that day. He began working the phones, tracking down his college buddies and co-workers to make sure they were safe.

While Michelle tried in vain to grasp the sheer magnitude of the destruction, Barack focused on the quotidian tasks that each of the victims went through that day – how they got up, drank their coffees and kissed their spouses goodbye before heading to work, completely unaware of the horror that awaited them. It was the notion that no one is really safe, that anything can happen in an instant, that weighed most heavily on Barack.

When he got home that evening, Barack hugged Michelle and Malia, then picked up Sasha and cradled her in his arms. Along with Sasha's meningitis scare, this latest reminder of life's fragile nature brought the Obamas closer together than they had been in years. 'How can we argue about all this small stuff?' Michelle asked her husband. 'We have so much to be thankful for.'

The lesson was short-lived. As was the case in most households not directly touched by the tragedy of 9/11, the petty concerns of everyday existence soon resumed their place at centre stage in the lives of the Obamas.

Things had clearly reached a crisis point in the Obama marriage. Barack believed that his political commitments required him to spend long periods away from home. Those absences seemed likely to grow even longer since he was not about to give up a burning ambition to achieve higher office. Michelle's criticisms were 'unfair' and 'short-sighted' he repeatedly claimed. And even though they faced financial pressures, his job teaching at the University of Chicago Law School made it possible for them to keep up the mortgage payments on their modest but comfortable condo at 5450 SE View Park, not far from the university campus. 'We have a good life and I'm trying to make it even better,' he argued. 'How can she find fault with that?'

No matter. Michelle refused to budge. Out of what she would later describe to one friend as 'a state of desperation', Michelle delivered an ultimatum to her husband: if Barack couldn't find a way to pursue his political dreams and at the same time make more time for his family, then he would have to choose between the two. 'That's the way it's got to be,' she said. 'I'm not doing this by myself.'

Long before Michelle met Barack, his character had, in fact, been shaped by two strong women. Now, as he stood at a crossroads in his married life wondering whether he would have to give up politics for the woman he loved, Barack's thoughts drifted back to his childhood in Honolulu – and the young woman with long dark hair whose real name was Stanley but who called herself Ann.

'Barry!' He could hear his Kansas-born mother's flat Midwestern twang as clearly as if she were standing in front of him. 'You are a responsible young man. You know what you've got to do.' Then, just as clearly, he could see his mother kneel down to kiss her little boy, wipe the tears from her eyes, pick up the suitcase that always seemed to be waiting by the front door – and leave. Again.

I've got relatives who look like Bernie Mac and
I've got relatives who look like Margaret Thatcher.

Barack

Because of his childhood, he was the ultimate outsider.

Jerry Kellman, an early mentor of Barack's

I inhaled. That was the point.

Barack

2

On the surface, they seemed about as well suited to each other as two people could possibly be. Both were young, tall, athletic and toothsomely attractive. They exuded a confidence that bordered on cockiness. They were witty, direct, scrupulously well-mannered and hard-working. They were devoted to their families and unerringly loyal to their friends. They were both products of the Ivy League (he earned his bachelor's degree at Columbia University, she earned hers at Princeton) and even went to the same law school – Harvard.

Yet their backgrounds could scarcely have been more different. Where Michelle Robinson and her older brother, Craig, grew up in the same South Side Chicago apartment their mother lived in for over 40 years, biracial Barack experienced a rootless childhood that left him wondering just who he really was – and where he really belonged. It was precisely that thirst for stability that led Barack to the supremely grounded Michelle.

The restlessness that defined Barack's early life stretched back at least two generations – to his white grandfather Stanley Armour Dunham, the man he would affectionately call 'Gramps'. The son of a roustabout who worked among the oil rigs in and around El Dorado, Kansas, eight-year-old Stanley came home from school one day to discover his mother's body hanging from a shower rod – a suicide that everyone in town chalked up to her husband's rampant infidelity.

Whether it was through the shock of finding his mother's body or the mere fact that he had inherited his own father's wild streak, Stanley was soon branded incorrigible. Expelled from high school after striking the principal, Dunham spent the late 1930s as a self-styled hobo, riding the rails from Detroit to San Francisco.

It was back on home turf in the oil boom town of Augusta, Kansas, that Stanley, then 22, met 18-year-old Madelyn Payne, the restless, fresh-faced daughter of a Standard Oil office manager and a former schoolteacher. Madelyn's parents were straight-backed Methodists who disapproved of drinking, smoking, card-playing and dancing. Not that that kept Madelyn from sneaking off whenever she could to hear Benny Goodman, Glenn Miller and Tommy Dorsey play at Wichita's Blue Moon Dance Hall. 'All the big bands came,' recalled Madelyn's classmate Nina Parry. 'It was wonderful – and nobody had more fun than Madelyn.'

Madelyn, who boasted to anyone who would listen that she counted a full-blooded Cherokee among her ancestors (not to mention several slave owners, too, as well as Confederate President Jefferson Davis), was instantly smitten with the lanky young drifter from the proverbial wrong side of the tracks. Her parents, understandably, felt otherwise.

A few weeks before she graduated from Augusta High School, Madelyn and Stanley sneaked off during the spring weekend of the annual junior–senior banquet and secretly married. Madelyn continued to live at home and, on the day she was handed her diploma, sprung the news on her unsuspecting parents.

For the next 18 months, the newlyweds managed to scrape by, until the Japanese invasion of Pearl Harbor led Stanley, like most of his male contemporaries, to enlist. Before Stanley shipped out to the European theatre, he was stationed at Fort Leavenworth. It was there, on 29 November 1942, that Madelyn gave birth to a baby girl.

The new father made no effort to conceal his profound disappointment. He had wanted a son and was convinced right up until the end of his wife's pregnancy that a son was exactly what he was getting. Clearly unwilling to concede defeat, he persuaded Madelyn to go ahead with plans to name the newest member of the Dunham family after him. The name on her birth certificate: Stanley Ann Dunham.

While Stanley was stationed overseas, Madelyn took a job on the production line at Boeing's B-29 plant in Wichita. As soon as he was discharged from the service in 1945, Stanley did what millions of other veterans did at the time: he decided to enrol in college on the GI Bill. The Dunhams headed to the West Coast, where Stanley attended the University of California at Berkeley for six months before dropping out. Guided by Stanley's insatiable wanderlust, the Dunhams returned to Kansas. There he found a job managing a furniture store on El Dorado's dusty Main Street while Madelyn helped make ends meet by working as a cashier in a local restaurant. Soon they were on the move again – first to Texas, where they bounced from one dusty hamlet to another.

It was in one of those Texas towns that Stanley Ann experienced racial hatred at first hand. One afternoon, she and a young black girl were playing in the Dunhams' back yard when a mob of local schoolchildren approached, hurling rocks and racial epithets. Madelyn chased them off, and when her husband called the children's parents the next day to protest, he came to the sobering realisation that the rock-throwing youngsters were just aping their parents' prejudices. Black children and white children, he was told pointedly, were not to play together.

The Dunhams returned to Kansas, where – despite the markedly less racist atmosphere – little Stanley still had to withstand the inevitable teasing over her name as she moved from one school to the next. The Dunhams' only child was studious and – perhaps because the constant relocating made her feel like the perennial outsider – something of a loner. More apt to spend her time reading than seeking new friends, Stanley Ann withdrew into her own solitary world. Whatever anxieties she may have been experiencing manifested themselves in a childhood case of asthma.

Stanley Ann had not yet turned 13 when, in 1955, the Dunhams packed up and moved again – this time to Seattle, where the Boeing-dominated local economy was in the midst of a post-war boom. As soon as they arrived, Stanley landed a job as a salesman at Standard-Grunbaum Furniture at the corner of Second Avenue and Prince Street. The store's groan-inducing slogan: 'First in Furniture, Second at Pine'.

The Dunhams moved into an apartment in Seattle's Columbia City neighbourhood, and enrolled Stanley Ann in Eckstein Junior

High School. The next year they moved to Mercer Island, situated in the middle of Lake Washington, just opposite Seattle. On Mercer Island, they rented Unit 219 of Shorewood Apartments, a sprawling new complex for upwardly mobile families. Determined to stay in the workforce, Madelyn started commuting to nearby Bellevue to work as an escrow officer at a small bank.

Even before she boarded a school bus on the first day of school, Stanley Ann made an impression on her fellow Mercer Island High students. 'I know, I know,' she told classmate Elaine Johnson after they met while waiting for the bus. 'It's a boy's name, and no, I don't like it. I mean, would you like to be called Stanley? By my dad wanted a boy and he got me. And the name Stanley made him feel better, I guess . . .'

In fact, Stanley Ann made no secret about the resentment she harboured towards her overbearing father. Stanley Sr could be scathing in his criticism of his daughter: he berated her for being too timid, for not being excelling at sports, for getting a single B on her report card even when the rest of her grades were all As. 'He was hard on her,' remembered Stanley Ann's friend Maxine Box. 'He picked on her.' As a result, she developed a nervous habit that set her apart from the other girls: Stanley Ann 'cracked her knuckles,' recalled Box, 'and I mean *constantly*'.

Stanley Dunham, whose temper was described by friends and family members alike as 'explosive' and 'violent', did more than merely pick on his daughter. Given to explosive outbursts, he was 'a door slammer, a yeller and a thrower' a neighbour said. Worse, 'there were bruises on Stanley Ann's arm from where he grabbed her. He would slap her when she talked back. But a lot of kids got punished that way back then, well into our teens.'

Whenever she could, Madelyn, who had turned quiet and serious as she shouldered more of the financial responsibilities for the household, protected her daughter from Dunham's stinging words. Still, Stanley Ann learned to defend herself – at least from the verbal abuse her father routinely dished out. 'He had a sarcastic sense of humour,' recalled Box, 'and she could give it right back – and then some.'

'Stannie', as she became known to her tight circle of friends, soon gained a reputation as a superb student. 'She was very intellectual and above all of us,' said Box, 'not just thinking about boys and clothes.' She also possessed a cutting wit. 'She had a really ironic sense of humour – sort of downbeat – and she was a great observer,' remembered another classmate, Iona Stenhouse. 'There was an arched eyebrow, or a smile on her face about the immaturity of us all. I felt at times that Stanley thought we were a bit of a provincial group.'

Not that Stannie's high school years weren't filled with the sleepovers, sock hops, poodle sweaters and football games that were staples of an adolescence lived in 1950s America. She listened to the Kingston Trio and Ricky Nelson and watched *American Bandstand*, but she also discussed jazz and beat poetry with like-minded friends at Seattle coffee houses like the Encore and Cafe Allegro, and caught foreign films at the city's only art-house theatre, the Ridgemont.

Stanley Ann 'never dated the crew-cut white boys,' said her friend Susan Blake. 'She had a world view, even as a young girl.' Another pal, Chip Wall, agreed that Stanley Ann 'was not a standard-issue girl. You don't start out life as a girl with a name like Stanley without some sense you are not ordinary.'

Mercer Island High School itself was anything but ordinary. The year before Stanley Ann enrolled there, John Stenhouse, then chairman of the Mercer Island School Board, testified before the House Un-American Activities Committee that he had been a member of the Communist Party. At the same time, teachers Jim Wichterman and Val Foubert routinely ruffled feathers by challenging their students to question authority and societal norms. While English teacher Foubert assigned such controversial texts as Ayn Rand's *Atlas Shrugged*, William Golding's *Lord of the Flies*, J.D. Salinger's *Catcher in the Rye* and Margaret Mead's writings on homosexuality, philosophy teacher Wichterman led classroom discussions on Camus, Sartre, Kierkegaard and Karl Marx. The hallway connecting Foubert's and Wichterman's classrooms was dubbed 'Anarchy Alley'.

'I had them read *The Communist Manifesto*,' Wichterman recalled, 'and the parents went nuts. They didn't want any discussions about sex, religion, or politics.' As for Stanley Ann, Wichterman remembered that 'she'd question anything: What's so good about democracy? What's so good about capitalism? What's wrong with communism? She had an inquiring mind.' Fellow student Jill Burton-Dascher agreed: 'Stannie was intellectually way more mature than we were and a little bit ahead of her time, in an off-centre way.'

The Dunhams were not part of the inevitable campaign to have Wichterman and Foubert fired. At a time when the overwhelming majority of their neighbours supported Dwight Eisenhower's election to a second presidential term in 1956, they backed Democrat Adlai Stevenson. 'If you were concerned about something going wrong in the world, Stanley would know about it first,' Chip Wall said. 'She was a fellow traveller . . . We were liberals before we knew what liberals were.' Box agreed: 'We were all questioners. It was the feeling of the whole school. We were on the debate team. We knew about current events.'

The chain-smoking, whiskey-drinking, bridge-playing Dunhams also turned their backs on their Midwest Methodist and Baptist upbringings. By the time Stanley Ann was 16, the family was attending Sunday services at the East Shore Unitarian Church in Bellevue. At the height of the McCarthy era, its congregation was so outspokenly left-leaning that East Shore Unitarian soon became known throughout the region as 'the Little Red Church on the Hill'.

Although Stanley Ann and her father both delighted in ruffling Establishment feathers, they were not close. 'He was always welcoming to the kids,' Box said, 'but he embarrassed Stanley because he tried too hard' to impress her friends. Indeed, Stanley Dunham was more than faintly reminiscent of the Willy Loman character in *Death of a Salesman*, and while his brand of back-slapping affability – replete with knowing winks and off-colour jokes – may have seemed merely entertaining to strangers, it left his daughter feeling nothing less than mortified.

Stanley Sr 'always tried to get a rise out of people,' agreed schoolmate Susan Blake. 'It seemed like every time her father opened his mouth, she would roll her eyes.'

The tensions between the two Stanleys often erupted into full-blown arguments in front of her friends. 'He would belittle her with incredibly sarcastic remarks, and she would snap back right on the spot – she always stood up for herself,' said Box. 'But it was awkward for the rest of us to have to watch. Stannie's mother was very no-nonsense and would tell them to both grow up and stop being silly – she was sort of the mediator – but there was a lot of tension in that family. I wouldn't have wanted to grow up dealing with a man who was as egocentric as Stannie's was.'

When she was sixteen, Stannie managed to escape for two months to Chicago, where family friends hired her to take care of their children during summer vacation. Flush with her new-found feeling of independence, she went to a downtown art-house theatre to see the film *Black Orpheus*, a 1959 retelling of the classic Greek myth of Orpheus and Eurydice.

Set among the crowded, cliff-hugging *favelas* of modern-day Rio during Carnaval, *Black Orpheus* was written, produced and directed by a white Frenchman. The Portuegese-speaking, all-black cast portrayed characters who were exotically beautiful, sensual and childlike in their naivety. The film, which Stanley Ann would revisit many times over the years, might seem condescendingly racist by later standards, but at the time it offered her an enticing first glimpse of a culture vastly different from her own and would have a profound influence on the way she viewed both the Third World and people of colour.

Stanley Ann's Chicago sojourn opened her eyes to a world of new possibilities. As expected, nearly all of Stanley Ann's friends had applied to the University of Washington. She did not. One afternoon several months before graduation, she opened an official-looking envelope, carefully unfolded the letter inside, then read it and reread it before squealing with delight. Stanley Ann had received early acceptance at the University of Chicago – her ticket out of Seattle and away from her domineering dad.

Stanley Sr had other ideas. Stanley Ann was too young to be on her own, he insisted. Besides, he was packing up his family and moving again – this time to take a higher-paying job selling furniture at a store in Honolulu.

Stanley Sr made the announcement over dinner one night, and with his customary flair. 'Hawaii!' he proclaimed. After five rain-soaked years in the Pacific Northwest, Stannie's father argued, it was 'high time we all get some sun'. Besides, Hawaii was far more than America's newest state – a status it had achieved just the year before – it was the new frontier. 'It's *paradise*, for Christ's sake!' he bellowed in the face of his daughter's reluctance to pull up stakes and relocate yet again. 'Everyone wants to live in Hawaii!'

Everyone but Stannie. She told Maxine Box that she wanted to stay put – if she couldn't go to the University of Chicago, then at the very least she wanted to join her friends at the University of Washington in Seattle. There were loud arguments between father and daughter – fights that sometimes turned violent – but ultimately Stanley Ann had no choice but to resign herself to yet another move as her father pursued an elusive dream of success. 'Remember me,' Stannie wrote wistfully in Maxine's high school yearbook, 'when you are old and grey.'

The Dunhams' only child went along to Hawaii, but not without making it clear that she was no longer willing to live in her father's looming shadow. From now on, she declared, there would be only one Stanley in the family. Henceforth, she was to be called, simply, Ann.

The Dunhams arrived in Honolulu in the summer of 1960 and rented a roomy three-bedroom house near the University of Hawaii's Manoa campus. Ann enrolled there in the autumn of that year and, as one of the few undergraduates who didn't seem to have roots in the islands, kept mostly to herself. 'She was the shy, timid girl in the corner,' a fellow student said. Another student, Neil Abercrombie, recalled that Ann 'was a scarcely out of high school. She was mostly kind of an observer.'

In her Russian class, Ann was soon observing a dynamic young graduate student from Kenya named Barack Obama. The first African to enrol at the University of Hawaii, Barack – he pronounced his first name with the emphasis on the first syllable, as in *barracks* – Obama was already a campus celebrity of sorts. He gave newspaper interviews and spoke at local schools and churches about his upbringing on the shores of Lake Victoria as a member of the Luo tribe. 'He had this magnetic personality,' Abercrombie said. 'Everything was oratory for him, even the most commonplace observation.'

Audiences were fascinated to hear that Obama's father, Onyango Obama, had enlisted in the British colonial forces and travelled to Europe, India and Zanzibar, where he converted from Christianity to Islam, tacked 'Hussein' to the front of his name and enthusiastically embraced polygamy. Barack Obama, who was the biological son of Onyango's second wife but was actually raised by Onyango's third wife, told rapt listeners that he had been raised a Muslim but now considered himself an atheist. He also described how he attended village schools and herded goats for his father before being accepted to an exclusive Christian boarding school run by the Anglican Church. As part of the 'educational airlift' programme started by Kenyan nationalist leader Tom Mboya and designed to provide Western educational opportunities for young Africans, 23-year-old Barack received a scholarship to study global economics at the University of Hawaii.

One fascinating titbit that Barack Obama chose not to share with his audiences – and certainly not with his fellow students – was that he had been married at the age of 18 in a tribal ceremony to a woman named Kezia. When he left to attend school in Hawaii, Obama left a pregnant Kezia behind with their infant son.

Ann – Obama called her 'Anna' – was soon smitten with the engaging young African, and it became clear he was attracted to her. 'I think she was attracted to his powerful personality,' Abercrombie mused, 'and he was attracted to her beauty and her calmness.'

Before long, Ann brought her African boyfriend home for dinner with her parents. Both Stanley and Madelyn could not help but be impressed by the affable, articulate, supremely confident young economics student who smoked a pipe and vowed he would return to his country to help 'shape the destiny of Africa'. But the obvious physical affection between Ann and their guest clearly rattled Madelyn. 'I was feeling protective, I guess,' she later recalled of that first meeting. Ann 'was so young,' she went on, 'I just didn't want to see her get hurt. People can be so cruel.'

If there was any place in America where interracial dating seemed unlikely to raise hackles, it was Hawaii. Here native Hawaiians mingled with Chinese, Japanese, Portuguese, Filipino, European and mainland American immigrants – and one in five white women married Asian men. Yet one ingredient was conspicuously absent from Hawaii's fabled melting-pot. In 1960, less than 1 per cent of the state's population was black.

At the time, interracial marriage was still illegal in 23 states. Hawaii, Ann pointed out to her concerned parents, was not one of them. However open-minded they may have considered themselves, the Dunhams were not happy when Ann told them she intended to marry the charming young man from Africa.

If the Dunhams were distressed at the news, the prospective groom's father, Hussein Onyango Obama, was downright livid. In a lengthy letter to Stanley and Madelyn, the most senior Obama railed against the idea of a biracial union. He did not, he stated flatly, want the Obama blood 'sullied by a white woman'.

Ann, who had actually started sleeping with Barack just a couple of weeks after their first meeting in September 1960, made the case for marrying Obama more compelling when she announced in late October that she was pregnant. Whatever the Dunhams' feelings about the perils of interracial marriage, these were trumped by a desire not to see their only child become an unwed mother.

On 21 February 1961 – a Thursday – Barack Obama and Ann Dunham were reportedly married in a civil ceremony on the island of Maui, although there are no official records showing that a legal ceremony ever took place. There were certainly no witnesses – no family members were present and none of their friends at the university had the slightest inkling that they were even engaged. 'Nobody was invited to the wedding,' Neil Abercrombie said. 'Nobody.' (Their only son, also named Barack, would later concede that the circumstances of his parents' marriage were 'murky', 'fragile', 'haphazard' – a 'bill of particulars that I've never quite had the courage to explore'.)

When Ann wrote to her friends back in Seattle with the news that she had dropped out of college after a single semester, married an African man and was expecting a baby, they were understandably surprised. 'Shocked – *very* shocked – is more like it,' said Maxine Box. 'I can't think of anything she said or did that would lead to such a radical thing. We could see Stanley, with her good grades and intelligence, going to college – but not marrying and having a baby right away.' As for marrying a black man: 'At that time, you practically crossed the street if you saw a black man and a white woman,' Box explained. 'Black and white didn't go together at that time.'

Certainly it would have complicated matters even further if Ann and her parents had been made aware of Barack's still-extant marriage to Kezia, or the two young children they shared. For now, Stanley in particular took pride in the fact that his new son-in-law was a highly educated man of the world who could speak authoritatively on a wide range of subjects, from the global economy to his own experiences travelling throughout Africa and Europe.

Even a born storyteller like Stanley could not help but be struck by Obama's thundering voice. 'It was a deep, resonant bass with a timbre you could not forget,' Richard Hook said of his friend's voice. 'Barack would walk into a room and say, "My name is Barack Obama" . . . and everyone in the room would instantly look up. Everyone wanted to know who he was.'

Pake Zane, who had also known the senior Obama in Hawaii and later visited him in Kenya twice, agreed that Obama's voice was 'startling and at the same time incredibly seductive. He had the same sort of deep tone in his voice that the actor James Earl Jones has, only much louder. He also had a hint of British accent, very Oxford-sounding.' As for his appearance, Pake recalled that Obama was 'not a large man, but he carried himself like a king. And he was one of the blackest people I've ever met – almost this beautiful shade of purple.'

Even friends had to concede that Barack's cocksure manner 'rubbed a lot of people the wrong way at first'. 'He did not lack for self-importance,' Abercrombie said. 'He was a self-involved, egotistical, vivid person . . . But we forgave him that because he was so genuine. People always liked him. They just thought, "Well, that's Barack."'

Although he had been known to thoroughly disarm hate-spewing bigots with soothing calm – one bar patron who started out calling Barack a 'nigger' ended up feeling so guilty after Barack gently lectured him on the evils of intolerance that he gave Barack a hundred dollars in cash on the spot – Obama could also be impulsive. On one occasion,

Barack drove a visiting fellow African up the road that wound through Oahu's Windward peaks to Nuuanu Pali Lookout, the site of a fierce battle won by King Kamehameha I. It was while standing on the edge of the precipice and marvelling at the canyon stretched out before them that the visitor asked to take a puff from Barack's favourite pipe – and accidentally dropped it over the side.

Mortified, the visitor apologised and promptly offered to buy Obama a new pipe. But that wouldn't do. Obama wanted *his* pipe, and when the visitor refused to climb over the railing and climb down the face of the cliff to get it, Barack grabbed him by the waist and lifted him over the railing. It was only after a frantic Ann interceded that Barack put the terrified man down.

Barack's driving proved equally terrifying. An unrepentant speed demon who often absent-mindedly reverted to driving on the left-hand side of the road, Obama racked up more than his share of traffic tickets and fender-benders. 'You really took your life in your hands,' Pake Zane said, 'when you drove with him.'

Obama's recklessness aside, Stanley, like nearly everyone else, could not help but be impressed by Barack's larger-than-life persona. Madelyn was more circumspect. She did not entirely trust her son-in-law when he claimed to have Ann's best interests at heart. 'I am a little dubious,' she later said, 'of the things people from foreign countries tell me.' Nevertheless, she suggested that Ann and her husband move into the Dunhams' roomy house so they could all await the new baby's arrival together.

On the afternoon of 4 August 1961, Barack drove his pregnant wife the eight miles from their bungalow at 6085 Kalanianaole Highway due east to Honolulu's Kapiolani Hospital for Women and Children. Founded in 1890 by Queen Kapiolani, known as 'the Queen who loved children', the hospital was originally called the Kapiolani Maternity Home and was intended strictly for native Hawaiian mothers.

After just two hours in labour, Ann gave birth to an 8 lb 2 oz. boy. In keeping with the tradition established by Stanley's father, Stanley, they named the baby Barack Hussein Obama.

While her new husband went back to the University of Hawaii to finish his studies, Ann devoted herself entirely to the care of little Barack. From the very beginning, Stanley and Madelyn called their grandson 'Barry' – ostensibly to distinguish him from his father Barack, but also to ease the path towards social acceptance by Americanising the child's name. 'It was hard enough to have to deal with the obviously charged issue of having a black grandson back in the early 1960s,' said one of their Kansas relatives. 'To have to constantly explain his African name – that was too much. Besides, "Barry" just sounds so nice and friendly. It was a very popular name back then . . . "Barack" always seemed harsh – kind of threatening, even.'

The following June, Barack graduated from the University of Hawaii with a degree in economics. He intended to eventually return to Kenya and lead his generation in building a new, modern Africa. On graduation day, he was interviewed by the *Honolulu Star-Bulletin*. Barack contrasted the more accepting behaviour of whites in the islands with whites in other parts of the world and praised Hawaii as a model for promoting harmony among various ethnic groups. He said nothing of his wife and son.

Before he could return to his homeland, however, Obama needed to earn his PhD in economics in the US. The prestigious New School in New York City offered him a full scholarship – enough money to make it possible to bring both Ann and their infant son with him. Harvard also offered Obama a scholarship, although one that would not afford him the luxury of bringing his young family along.

Ann was thrilled about the New School offer and was excited about the prospect of moving to New York. Her hopes were dashed when Obama decided instead to accept the Harvard offer. 'How,' he asked her, 'can I refuse the best education?'

Yet there were others who agreed with Ann, most notably Kenyan nationalist Tom Mboya, who had become something of a mentor to Barack. Although Obama never mentioned his wife and child to Mboya in his letters, Mboya had been told of their existence and chastised Barack for abandoning them.

No matter. Late that July of 1962, Obama departed for Harvard – alone. He did not even stay to celebrate his son's first birthday. 'I know he loved Ann,' Abercrombie insisted. 'But I think he didn't want the impediment of being responsible for a family. He expected great things of himself and he was going off to achieve them.'

At Harvard, Obama rented an apartment just off Central Square and quickly made his presence known. Regardless of his avowed feelings for Ann and little Barry, Barack soon began dating Ruth Nidesand, a tall, blonde American teacher from an affluent New England family. Nidesand's money enabled Barack to move in certain social circles in Cambridge and to indulge his growing fondness for expensive suits, silk ascots and Johnnie Walker Black Label scotch. 'He would shout in that big, deep voice, "Waiter, another double!"' recalled his friend Leo Odera Omolo. Soon, Barack was known to his drinking buddies as 'Mr Double Double'. Later, Barack would actually take to calling himself 'Dr Obama'. In fact, while he did earn a master's in economics from Harvard, he never pursued a doctorate.

Ann continued to write to Barack and send him photos of their son. Even Obama called his son 'Barry' when he showed those photos to his new friends and fellow graduate students at Harvard. Even though she was blissfully unaware of her husband's infidelity, Ann made the decision not to follow her husband to Massachusetts. 'She was under no illusions,' Abercrombie observed. 'He was a man of his time, from a very patriarchal society.'

At her mother's urging, Ann filed for divorce in January of 1964, charging 'grievous mental suffering'. Barack did not contest the action; by that time, he was planning to return to Africa with his new love, Ruth Nidesand. The following year, he and Nidesand would marry and go on to have two sons. But the relationship would not be without its tense moments, since Barack Sr was still married to his first wife, Kezia. However open-minded Ruth may have been, she was not about to allow Kezia and her two children by Barack to move in. So Barack, a willing polygamist, merely visited his first wife periodically. The inevitable result: two additional children with Kezia.

Back in Hawaii, Ann had plans of her own. A full year before starting divorce proceedings, she had resumed her studies at the University of Hawaii. While she attended classes – and made ends meet with the help of food stamps – her parents took care of little Barry. One of his earliest words would be 'Toot' – short for *tutu*, the Hawaiian word meaning 'grandparent' – and the name by which Madelyn Dunham would be known by her adoring grandchildren. Barry bestowed a somewhat less imaginative nickname on Stanley. To Barry, Stanley Sr would always be, simply, Gramps.

To help offset some of the family's mounting bills, Toot went back to work – this time as a secretary at the Bank of Hawaii. She was soon promoted to teller and then to assistant loan officer, bringing in enough extra cash to easily support both Ann and her baby.

Barry's early childhood – spent primarily in the company of his doting grandparents – was nothing short of idyllic. He learned to snorkle at Hanuama Bay on Oahu's south-east coast, tagged along when Gramps went spear-fishing with his Portuguese sailor friends in Kailua Bay, enjoyed the *lomi-lomi* salmon and roast pig served at neighbourhood luaus, and cooled off on sweltering summer days by downing 'shave ice' – Hawaii's answer to the snow cone.

Mom, meanwhile, had fallen in love with yet another foreign student – this time an Indonesian man named Lolo Soetoro. The fact that *lolo* was Hawaiian slang for 'crazy' meant raised eyebrows whenever Soetoro was introduced to anyone on the islands, but he took it in his stride. In fact, the compact, dark-haired Soetoro was as softly spoken and unflappable as Barack Sr had been flamboyantly self-assured. Lolo was not above engaging in a little horseplay with Ann's young son on the Dunhams' living room floor or laughing at Gramps's cringe-making jokes over endless games of chess.

Barry was an outgoing, slightly pudgy six year old when his mother sat him down and told him she was going to marry Lolo and that they were going to move six thousand seven hundred miles away to Indonesia. It would be their first journey outside the country, and Ann, clearly wondering if this was the right thing to do, wept as she broke the news to her son. As far as Barry was concerned, it was perfectly fine as long as his mother loved Lolo. 'Do you love him, Mom?' he asked point-blank. She did, she told him tearfully as she swept him up in her arms.

Lolo returned to Indonesia earlier than he had expected – summoned, as were all Indonesian students studying abroad, by the new military government that had toppled Indonesia's long-time dictator, Sukarno.

Many of these students, viewed as a potential threat by the new right-wing regime, were imprisoned or executed. Unbeknownst to Ann, Lolo was immediately drafted by the Indonesian army and sent to fight guerrillas in the jungles of New Guinea.

It would be nearly a year before Ann and Barry finally joined Lolo in Indonesia – a year during which the once easy-going Lolo seemed to have undergone a dramatic change. Now stuck in a low-paying job surveying roads for the Indonesian army, he was prone to binge drinking and long, sullen silences.

For the moment, however, it was enough just to cope with their exotic new surroundings. Barry and Ann moved into Lolo's small, flat-roofed bungalow on a dirt road just outside Jakarta at 16 Haji Ramli Street, where cockatoos, dogs, chickens, ducks, baby crocodiles and even a pet monkey named Tata roamed the back yard. The absence of paved roads, electricity and indoor plumbing scarcely fazed the boy, who viewed everything as an adventure.

When the children in his neighbourhood viewed the foreigners in their midst suspiciously, Barry climbed atop a wall that separated his house from his neighbour's, where he cawed and flapped his arms like a giant bird. 'That got the kids laughing,' recalled Kay Ikranagara, a friend from that period, 'and then they all played together.'

At first, he was teased about his weight – the other kids called him 'Fatty' in Indonesian – and about his colour. The only black many of these children had ever seen, he was also routinely referred to simply as 'Negro' – an appellation that, according to another friend, Bambang Sukoco, did not seem to bother him.

He even became accustomed to the periodic lashings he received at the hands of the nuns at Franciscus Assisi Primary School. He was the school's only non-Indonesian student; the children of most foreigners went to Jakarta's International School, but Ann and Lolo lacked the money for tuition.

Ann's son was enrolled at Franciscus Assisi as 'Barry Soetero' – using his stepfather's surname – and his nationality was listed on official school documents as Indonesian. Since the Catholic school had been in operation for less than a year and needed local children to fill its classes, it made a point of opening up the student body to all faiths.

'At that time,' explained his teacher Israella Darmawan, 'Barry was registered as a Muslim because his father, Lolo Soetoro, was Muslim.' Former vice principal Tine Hahiyari and third-grade teacher Effendi also recalled that Barry was registered as a Muslim, which determined what weekly religion class he attended. 'Muslim students were taught that religion class by a Muslim teacher, and Christian students were taught by a Christian teacher,' Effendi said. 'Barry was definitely Muslim. He studied the Koran.'

Occasionally, Barry went with his stepfather and his friends to Friday-night prayers at the local mosque. 'We prayed a lot but not really seriously – just following actions done by older people in the mosque. But as kids, we loved to meet our friends and went to the mosque together and played,' said one of Barry's close friends at the time, Zulfin Adi. According to Adi, Barry often wore a sarong to the mosque.

Barry quickly discovered he liked to tell people what to do. On his first day at school, he commanded his fellow students, '*Baris!*' ('Make a line!'), then '*Siap grap*' ('Get ready') and finally '*Tegap!*' ('Stand straight!'). Barry then reviewed the line and, once he was satisfied it was straight, allowed the students to march into the classroom. 'Sometimes I had to tell him to let the other kids do it,' said Israella Darmawan. Her nickname for Barry: 'Little Curly-Haired One'.

Because he was a full head taller than any of the other children in class, Barry also helped Darmawan clean the blackboards. Although he was one of her brightest students – 'especially at mathematics' – it was Barry's instinct for leadership that most impressed his teachers at the time. 'He always wanted to be number one, to be at the front. Psychologically, he wants to be in charge.' Nor was he above informing on his fellow students. 'Whenever they misbehaved,' third-grade teacher Cecelia Sugini said, 'Barry would tell me to make them stop.'

This sense of righteous indignation extended to the playground. Whenever the other children tried to cheat during games of marbles, Barry would stand up and yell '*Kamu curang, kamu curang!*' ('You cheat! You cheat!'), recalled Zulfin Adi. 'We could never cheat him. We did try, but he always found out.' Adi described his friend as 'resolute'.

41

Barry, he said, 'never hesitated to stand up to defend his rights'.

Given Barry's take-charge personality, Darmawan was not surprised at his response when he was asked to write an essay on the theme 'What I Want To Be When I Grow Up'. 'I,' Barry wrote in the opening line, 'will become president.' At the time, Darawan said, it was hard to tell from the essay if he intended to become president of the United States or Indonesia. 'He was an Indonesian citizen at the time,' she recalled. 'His father was Indonesian. His sister was Indonesian. He spoke Indonesian. There was no reason to think that he meant anything other than becoming president of Indonesia.'

It had taken less than a year for Barry to essentially master Indonesia's language and customs. What he found more daunting – even frightening – were his countless encounters with human misery. Beggars, some disfigured by leprosy, others missing limbs, accosted him on the street or came to the house pleading for money or food.

Understandably, Ann, who had a penchant for bursting into tears at the slightest provocation, found herself weeping on a daily basis. Initially unable to turn down any of the beggars who appeared on the doorstep – 'Your mother has a soft heart,' Lolo observed – Ann eventually learned to be more selective.

Ann soon began teaching English to Indonesian business executives at the US embassy in Jakarta. The yawning chasm between this tiny elite and the rest of the country's vast population was a fact of Indonesian life Ann was unwilling to accept. When Lolo joined that elite – landing a job at an American oil company and quickly advancing through its ranks – Ann grew even more indignant. Proud of his attractive American wife, he insisted that she accompany him to cocktail parties and other company functions, but she refused.

With the birth of Barry's half-sister Maya in August of 1970, Lolo hoped that Ann would become less restless and more resigned to her role as a wife in Indonesian society. Certainly she had no quarrel with Lolo's attitude towards her son; in every way possible, he treated Barry as his own.

Still, Ann felt isolated and alone. Moreover, she knew that this was neither the childhood nor the future she had in mind for her son. 'You are not an Indonesian,' she reminded Barry frequently. 'You are an American. You have American values. Don't ever forget that.' Accordingly, during these years abroad she went to great lengths to ensure that Barry never lost his command of the English language and the American idiom. Each day before dawn, she woke Barry up to drill him with lessons from an English correspondence course, then headed off to her job at the American embassy. 'She would be totally exhausted,' he recalled. 'But it was very important to her that I never lose sight of who I was, and where I fit in in the scheme of things.'

That also meant reinforcing Barry's black heritage by having him read books about civil rights leaders like Martin Luther King and listen to recordings ranging from Harry Belafonte and Mahalia Jackson to Sam Cooke, Aretha Franklin and Stevie Wonder. 'Every black man was Thurgood Marshall or Sidney Poitier, every black woman Fannie Lou Hamer or Lena Horne,' Barry would later recall. 'To be black was to be the beneficiary of a great inheritance, a special destiny.'

To Ann, it was also important for Barry to view his absent father as a role model. She preferred to overlook the fact that Barack Sr would go on to father numerous other children (for a grand total of eight) with his various wives and lovers in Kenya. Instead, she stressed Barack Sr's intellect, his idealism and his commitment to bettering the lives of his fellow Africans. 'Your brains, your character,' Ann told her son, 'you got from your father.'

In fact, Barack seldom even bothered to inquire about his American family, much less seek to have direct contact with his son. No matter. The boy was willing to accept whatever his mother told him about his father as gospel – for now.

Barry's mother had done such an effective job of building up Barry's self-esteem that he was nine before it ever occurred to him that being black was anything but a blessing. It was then that he came across a magazine article about a black man who had tried to chemically lighten the colour of his skin and ended up horribly scarred. In one life-altering moment, the young boy realised for the first time that there might be something *wrong* with being black – that it was a condition that some people found so onerous that they would go through painful, expensive treatments to turn themselves white. Seeing the photos was 'violent for me,' he later wrote. 'My stomach knotted. Did my mother know about this?'

Barry said nothing to his mother, or to anyone, at the time. But he would remember that this was the moment when he began to harbour serious doubts about where he really fitted in as a biracial child.

After two years at Assisi, Barry transferred to a public school; this one, like all public schools in Indonesia, was Muslim and incorporated in its regular curriculum teachings from the Koran. 'At the Catholic school, when it came time to pray,' Barry later said, 'I would close my eyes, then peek around the room. Nothing happened. No angels descended. Just a parched old nun and 30 brown children, muttering words.' At 'Muslim School', as he later referred to the public school he attended, the teacher sent a note home to Ann complaining that Barry misbehaved by making faces during Koranic studies. Ann took Barry aside and admonished him to simply 'be respectful', but declined to punish him as the teacher requested.

'My whole family was Muslim,' Barry's sister Maya later said, 'and most of the people I knew were Muslim.' It was a situation that did not sit entirely well with Ann. Barry's mother, whose own deep spirituality belied a distrust of all organised religion, did what she could to drum Western ideals of equality, democracy and fairness into her son's brain. She also tried to imbue both her children with a sense of the spiritual. 'Our mother was fascinated by all things lunar,' Maya recalled. 'She called herself a "Lunatic", and would take us out in the middle of the night to gaze at the moon if it was particularly full or bright.'

The lessons Barry learned from his stepfather were of a more practical nature. When a schoolmate tossed a rock at Barry and left him with a goose egg on the side of his head, Lolo produced two sets of boxing gloves and taught his stepson how to defend himself. 'Men,' Lolo told Barry, 'take advantage of weakness in other men.'

Yet Ann's son preferred the role of peacemaker. Once again, he accomplished this simply by telling his peers how to behave. They invariably complied. 'If his friends were having arguments, he'd become a mediator,' recalled Harmon Askiar, one of Barry's Jakarta neighbourhood playmates. 'He would grab one friend's hand and grab the other friend's hand and force them to shake and be friends again.'

After three years in Indonesia, Ann told her ten-year-old son that his time there was about to come to an end. The owner of the furniture store that employed Stanley Dunham in Honolulu was an alumnus of Hawaii's elite Punahou prep school, and Gramps had asked if he couldn't pull some strings to get Barry accepted.

Founded in 1841 by American missionaries, Punahou (Hawaiian for 'new spring') was more than just the islands' answer to such prestigious mainland schools as Andover, Exeter, Groton and Hotchkiss. Punahou actually offered a first-class private school education from kindergarten straight through high school. By 2009, it would grow to include more than 3,700 students, making Punahou the largest independent school in the US.

Not surprisingly, competition to get into the middle school and high school classes was especially fierce. Even children from some of Hawaii's wealthiest and best-connected families had to settle for being placed on a waiting list. Somehow Gramps not only got Barry bumped to the head of the line, but he also managed to wrangle young Obama a full scholarship.

Race also played a significant role in Barry's selection. Out of a student body that included Caucasians, Asians, Hispanics and numerous combinations of these groups, there were only four blacks at Punahou when Barry enrolled there. 'The school had essentially been all-white until the 1960s and had always had this elitist reputation,' said a former teacher at Punahou. 'By the 1970s there was a lot of pressure to be more inclusive. Barry was biracial, but he was also someone who had spent years in Indonesia. Not that it mattered that much back then, but we were told he was a Muslim. It was all very exotic and appealing to the powers-that-be at the school.'

Exotic was something Barry desperately did not want to be. On the first day of school, teacher Eric Kusunoki struggled with Obama's first name while calling the roll. 'Is *Bar*-ack here?' he asked. When the new student said to him, 'Just call me Barry,' Kusunoki nodded.

'He didn't say it like he was exasperated or anything,' Kusunoki said. 'He just corrected me.'

Despite the fact that it was Gramps's influence that managed to pave the way for Barry's entrance into prep school, the economic power in the Dunham family had shifted to Toot. While Gramps had given up the furniture business to sell life insurance over the phone – an inherently frustrating and at times demeaning job he soon discovered he was not particularly well suited to – Toot had gradually climbed up the corporate ladder to become the first female vice president of the Bank of Hawaii.

It was an opportunity for her son that Ann could not pass up – not even if it meant that she would be separated from him. On a hot day in August, she and Maya waved goodbye from the gate as an airline employee took Barry's hand and led him towards the plane that would take him home to live with his grandparents. He turned to see his mother's lower lip tremble, as it so often did as she fought back tears, although even at this young age he suspected such displays were primarily for public consumption. However, Barack's sister believed their mother's emotional outbursts were genuine enough. 'She cried a lot,' Maya said. 'If she saw animals being treated cruelly or children in the news or a sad movie – or if she felt like she wasn't being understood in a conversation.'

Ann was, in fact, capable of keeping an emotional distance from those around her – including her own children. 'She kept a certain part of herself aloof or removed,' observed one of Ann's close friends in Indonesia, Mary Zurbuchen. 'Maybe in some way this was how she managed to cross so many boundaries.'

At this point, Toot and Gramps would pick up where Ann left off when it came to shoring up Barry's self-confidence. When one of his fellow students at Punahou asked if his African father was a cannibal and others asked to touch his hair – he refused – Barry's grandparents urged him to simply shrug it off. Unlike their daughter, it was clear that they were less interested in stressing Barry's ties to Africa than they were in seeing him blend in. Although Toot declared more than once that she considered Harry Belafonte was 'the handsomest man in the world', her mantra was 'what colour you are just doesn't matter'.

Increasingly, it did matter to Barry. When he befriended the only other black student in his grade – a girl named Coretta – on the playground, the other kids gathered around to tease them for being boyfriend and girlfriend. Embarrassed, Barry shouted for Coretta to stay from him and even gave her a shove. Bewildered and upset, she sprinted away in tears.

In part, Barry, like any ten-year-old boy, objected to being thought of as *anyone's* boyfriend. But he was also distancing himself from the only other person in his class who shared his skin colour. There was a part of him that did not want to be classified simply as black – a lingering result, he would later conclude, of that magazine article about the man trying to bleach his skin. In shoving Coretta, he felt guilty for having committed an act of betrayal.

Barry quickly realised that the often insensitive questions from his peers were not about to abate. Soon, he was embellishing the truth. His grandfather, he told his wide-eyed classmates, was a chief, his father a prince and the family name Obama meant 'burning spear'. (Actually, Kenyatta means 'burning spear'. Unfortunately, the surname Obama is from the Luo word *bam*, meaning 'crooked' or 'bent'. Barack means 'blessed'.)

That first December back in Hawaii, Barry's parents both visited – first Ann from Indonesia, and, two weeks later, Barack Sr from Kenya. For Barry's father, who had just been released from hospital after being injured in a car accident and now walked with the aid of a cane, this visit was intended to provide some much-needed rest and relaxation.

On a stiflingly hot July weekend just two years earlier, Barack Sr had been shopping in Nairobi when he bumped into his old mentor Tom Mboya. 'You are parked on a yellow line,' Barack Sr joked with Mboya. 'You'll get a ticket.' Minutes later, Mboya was gunned down on the street.

Barack, who worked in Kenya's Ministry of Economic Planning and Development, had already infuriated his superiors by publicly criticising his government's economic policies and for complaining that he was working for less capable men than he. Now he risked angering powerful forces in the Kenyan government by testifying at the trial of Mboya's accused assassin.

On the basis of Barack Sr's testimony and that of nine other eyewitnesses, Mboya's killer was tried and hanged. But from that point on, Obama's career – and life – began to spiral out of control. On a visit to Nairobi's Ministry of Economic Planning and Development, American international development expert Clive Gray noticed Obama lurching down a hallway.

'What's the matter with that guy?' Clive asked a ministry staff member. Obama had changed so dramatically that Clive hadn't recognised him at first.

'He is always very intoxicated,' the staffer replied, 'and unable to do his job.'

Although the senior Obama had impressed Gray as 'kind of a loudmouth' when he first encountered him at Harvard, he remembered how much promise the young Kenyan had shown. Looking at him now, Gray could hardly believe this was the man who had vowed to save his country from economic ruin. 'It was,' Gray said, 'very sad.'

Although he did not share the details with either the Dunhams or his son, Barack Sr had been driving drunk when he slammed into a tree and badly fractured his leg. It was only the latest in a series of accidents involving alcohol that left Barry's dad with a permanent limp.

Barry was understandably horrified when he learned his father had accepted an invitation from his fifth-grade homeroom teacher, Mabel Hefty, to speak to her pupils. But by the time Barack Sr had finished telling Barry's class about the wonders, challenges and mysteries of life in Africa – about tribal customs, wildlife and Kenya's own struggle against the British for independence – his son was beaming with pride.

It was, Barry would recall, a 'tortured moment' that ended with 'tremendous relief' that his father had managed to impress teachers and students alike. 'That he's different, but is somehow able to communicate with great confidence a sense of common humanity was actually a great object lesson for me.'

At home, however, Barack Sr's humanity was somewhat less evident. Barry had eagerly anticipated watching Dr Seuss's *How the Grinch Stole Christmas* on television – a holiday tradition in the Dunham household – but instead was ordered by his father to do his homework. 'I tell you, Barry, you do not work as hard as you should,' he said. 'Go now, before I get angry at you.' From that point on, Barry could not wait for his father to leave.

That Christmas visit would last scarcely four weeks. Despite the tensions with Barack Sr and the fact that both his parents were married to other people, Barry would treasure this as the only time he could recall being together with this father, mother and grandparents as a family unit.

What Barry did not know at the time was that his father had pleaded with his mother to return with him to Africa – and to bring Barry and Maya with her. Ann, who was aware that Barack Sr already had at least two wives and half a dozen children waiting for him back at home, declined.

When his father and mother both left – he bound for Kenya, she for Indonesia – Barry tried to accept the separation as 'just the way things were'. But later, he would confess, 'I suspect it had more of an impact than I know.'

Ann promised her son that she would return to return to live with him in Hawaii the following year. In the meantime, his character would continue to be moulded and shaped to a large extent by Toot and Gramps.

Now occupying a modest two-bedroom apartment just ten minutes away from Waikiki, on Beretania Street in Honolulu's Makiki neighbourhood, the Dunhams were going through some trying times of their own. Without the ability to literally pump someone's hand or look that person in the eye as he told one of his over-the-top stories, Gramps quickly discovered that he just wasn't cut out for life as a telemarketer. 'Of course, people were hanging up on him all the time, or making excuses for why they were too busy to see him,' said a family friend. 'It was really killing him slowly inside, making him very resentful – especially towards Madelyn.'

The Dunhams were secure financially – thanks to Toot's steady rise at the Bank of Hawaii. She now earned far more than her husband, despite the fact that the male executives she was training were often promoted ahead of her and invariably paid fatter salaries. It was a commonly seen brand of overt corporate sexism that infuriated her daughter. 'How can you stand it, Mom?' Ann would demand. 'It's not right. It's totally unfair. You should stand up and do something about it.'

Not that Toot could ever be described as a shrinking violet. 'I was afraid of her,' said Alton Kuioka, who was a young trainee at the Bank of Hawaii's loan department in 1969. Kuioka would eventually become the bank's vice chairman. 'She definitely intimidated me. If you were new and learning she was like a drill sergeant.' Another trainee at the time, Dennis Ching, also confessed to being 'totally scared' of Barack's grandmother. 'She was like the grande dame of escrow . . . She gave me a file and said, "You're a college grad. Here, close this." You don't know how to swim, and she throws you in, and you either sink or swim.'

Barry was sensitive to the new dynamic in the Dunham household and the simmering tensions between his grandparents. Fortunately for Barry, his mother left Lolo and returned with Maya to Honolulu, determined to pursue her master's in anthropology at the University of Hawaii. Ann found a small apartment just off the Punahou campus and moved into it with her two children.

To all outward appearances, Punahou was not unlike any small New England college. There were arched windows, broad lawns, indoor and outdoor tennis courts, ivy-covered lecture halls of neo-Romanesque design, state-of-the-art laboratories, an Olympic-sized pool and – to maintain it all – a $180-million endowment. Barry would flourish here academically. 'Barry could whip out a paper that was due the next day the night before,' recalled Suzanne Maurer, whose son Darin was a classmate of Barry's. 'The other kids spent weeks writing the same paper.'

Losing the baby fat that had made him the butt of jokes as a boy back in Jakarta, Barry became one of the lesser stars on Punahou's basketball team – its sole left-handed player.

One of Barry's closest friends at Punahou, Bobby Titcomb, remembered Barack 'dribbling his ball, running down the sidewalk on Punahou Street to his apartment, passing the ball between his legs. I mean, he was into it.'

If he was not the most talented player, he was, said teammate Alan Lum, 'a leader on the court' – in part because of his penchant for enforcing the rules. 'He would call people on it if they were doing something wrong,' Lum said. 'He would question coaches. He was strong and confident enough to ask those questions. I respected him for that.'

Barack's knack for 'calling people out' did not make him any less popular with his fellow students. 'He was the kind of guy,' said classmate Dan Hale, 'who could walk into a room and navigate the cliques.' Although never regarded as a big man on campus, he made friends easily, went to school dances and, like all adolescents, made his first few awkward attempts at dating. Weekends were spent body-surfing at Sandy Beach in East Honolulu or picnicking at Puu Ualakaa State Park on Mount Tantalus, with its sweeping views of Diamond Head, Punchbowl Crater and downtown Honolulu.

Occasionally, Barack would take off hiking with one of his friends. 'We'd go hike up Peacock Flats and camp, just the two of us,' recalled Bobby Titcomb. 'We'd try to get away from everything. We'd basically live on nuts and whatever we could eat on the trail for two or thee days. And we'd talk about how the world could be . . .'

Notwithstanding these periodic soul-searching treks into the wilderness à la Henry David Thoreau, Barack was never regarded as a loner. 'He fit in as much if not more than any other student,' Darin Maurer said. 'He wasn't the most popular kid in school, but he was certainly well liked. I never really saw that he was suffering.' Neither did Alan Lum. 'To always have had that smile on his face . . . and yet to be going through that internal struggle,' Lum said. 'I feel I lost an opportunity to connect with him.'

But Barry was suffering. Beginning with those first embarrassing questions from the other kids and their attempts to touch his hair or rub his head, Barry became increasingly sensitive to the fact that others viewed him differently. 'I began to think,' he later conceded, 'that as a black man being raised by white people, I should belong to both worlds – and yet I couldn't help feeling that I really belonged to neither.'

In the small apartment he shared with this mother and sister, Barry watched *Soul Train* on television and sang along with the Temptations and Stevie Wonder – all a conscious effort, he would later admit, to shore up his own sense of self as a young black American. His mother had always been in his staunchest ally in that endeavour, but when Barry turned 14 she made a stunning announcement: she was returning to Indonesia to do fieldwork for her PhD. She was taking Maya with her, but Barry would be allowed to decide for himself whether he was going to accompany his mother or remain in Hawaii.

Barry chose to stay behind with his grandparents. He had had enough of starting over. As difficult as it was being one of the few blacks at Punahou, he had made friends and was thriving academically. Moreover, Gramps and Toot had always stood by Barry while at the same time giving him considerable control over his own life – actually more autonomy than he had enjoyed while living with his mother. 'We have total confidence,' they liked to tell him when faced with a decision, 'that you will do the right thing.'

For Barry, the 'right thing' meant confronting prejudice wherever it reared its ugly head. While growing up in the racial and ethnic hotchpotch that was Hawaii, Barry still encountered the kind of discrimination inflicted on blacks in less exotic locales. He demanded but never got an apology from a woman in the Dunhams' apartment building who bolted out of the elevator when he stepped into it. At Punahou, Barry reacted to being called a 'coon' by punching a classmate in the face. After he overheard a basketball coach dismiss members of an opposing team as just 'a bunch of niggers', Barry angrily informed the coach that he was 'an ignorant white motherfucker'.

One of his closest friends at Punahou, Keith 'Ray' Kakugawa, believed Barry was perhaps too sensitive to perceived slights. 'He made everything look like it was all racial,' claimed Kakugawa, who was half black, half Japanese and two years older than Barry. During one basketball game being coached by Kakugawa's father, Barry complained that he was frequently benched just because he was black. 'No, Barry, it's not because you're black,' the senior Kakugawa told him. 'It's because you missed two shots in a row.'

'Barry's biggest struggles then,' Keith said, 'were missing his parents. His biggest struggles were his feelings of abandonment. That idea that his biggest struggle was race is bull.'

In truth, Barry did not have to venture outside his own family to encounter evidence of the barriers that still existed between blacks and whites. One morning, as she stood waiting for the bus that would take her to work, Toot was approached by a homeless man asking for money. She tried to ignore him, but the man persisted. So Toot dug around in her purse, pulled out a dollar bill and, with a wan smile, gingerly handed it to him.

Toot had hoped the man would move on to the next victim, but instead he kept his outstretched hand palm-up and asked for more. He was, she later said, 'insistent' and 'menacing'. It was at this moment that the bus pulled up and Toot quickly hopped aboard. As she settled into her seat, she looked back at the homeless man. He never stopped smiling.

Now Toot wanted Stanley to give her a ride to work each morning. The idea of being accosted once again at the bus stop was too much for her. But Gramps knew the real reason behind his wife's anxiety – which he shared with Barack – and he was anything but sympathetic. She would never say anything of the sort to her grandson, but Toot confided to her husband that the homeless man 'was, well, you know . . . He was *black*.'

The sudden realisation that even his beloved grandmother harboured a deep-seated fear of black men pushed Barry over the edge. Toot and Gramps and his mother had always loved him unconditionally, and yet they did not have the answers he needed as a biracial man. He had grown up in a white household, and now, Keith Kakugawa said, Barry 'felt he was not getting a part of who he was'.

Barry got some of the answers he needed from Frank Marshall Davis, a leading black activist and writer of the 1930s and 1940s who eventually settled in Hawaii. Gramps had introduced Davis to Barry in the hope that the older gentleman might give him some insight into what it meant to be a black American.

Barry would later write that he was 'intrigued by old Frank, with his books and whiskey breath and the hint of hard-earned knowledge behind the hooded eyes'. When he told Frank about the panhandler who accosted Toot, Barry was surprised at the old man's answer. Frank told him she was right to be scared because 'black people have a reason to hate'. It was at that moment that Barry felt he might never have really known his family at all. 'The earth shook under my feet . . .' he recalled. 'I stopped, trying to steady myself, and knew for the first time that I was utterly alone.'

Barry continued his journey of self-discovery by plunging into the works of Langston Hughes, James Baldwin, W.E.B. Du Bois and Ralph Ellison. When Barry checked *The Autobiography of Malcolm X* out of the Punahou school library, Kakugawa was taken aback. 'Hold on, man,' he said. 'What you gonna do? Change your name to something Muslim?'

'Well,' Barry replied with a shrug, 'my name is Barack Obama.'

Kakugawa looked at his friend quizzically. 'No it isn't,' he insisted.

'Yes, my name is Barack. Actually, it's Barack *Hussein* Obama.'

'Get off it!' Kakaguwa shot back before the librarian threatened to throw them out.

What upset Kakaguwa most was the fact that, for all his friend's railing against racism, Barry 'seemed about as solidly middle-class American as you can get,' he recalled. 'I knew his dad was African and had taken off when Barry was small, but I had no idea that he had left Barry with an African name. I felt that he had obviously gone out of his way to hide that from me and from the rest of his buddies at the time.'

Indeed, Barry was not yet ready to fully embrace his African heritage by insisting that he be called Barack. But he did find a kindred spirit in assassinated Black Muslim leader Malcolm X, whose unambiguous hatred of 'blue-eyed devils' softened after he visited Mecca and saw whites praying to Allah alongside blacks. Already exposed to its teachings during his four formative years in Indonesia, Barry now wondered if Islam did not provide an orderly framework for racial harmony – and a way for him to reconcile conflicts over his own biracial background.

Barry returned to the Koran for answers and told friends at the time that he was seriously considering joining the Nation of Islam. 'For a while he talked a lot back then about what a great man Malcolm was,' Keith Kakugawa said. 'But the rest of us were just interested in basketball and beer and sex, so he kind of gave up.'

Unable to reconcile his own growing resentment of 'white folks' with his abiding affection for his white mother and grandparents, Barry stopped talking race altogether. 'I learned,' he later explained of this period in his life, 'not to care.'

Barry turned instead to alcohol – and to drugs. At 16, he began sneaking off to drink, smoke pot or snort cocaine ('a little blow when you could afford it,' as Barry later put it) with his new friends. He financed his marijuana and cocaine purchases with money he earned working summers at the Baskin-Robbins ice-cream parlour on Honolulu's South King Street.

Despite the fact that he played on Punahou's basketball team, he was not welcome at the Senior Bench, the stone bench where the jocks, cheerleaders and other 'popular' kids hung out. Nor did he spend time with the theatre people, the nerds or student-leader types like classmate Steve Case, who went on to co-found American Online.

'Barry hung out with the stoners,' said another classmate, who remembered that Obama was among the school's 15 or so 'druggies'. Barry's new group of friends were known to both faculty and students as the 'Bingham Benchers' because they gathered each day on benches outside Punahou's Bingham Hall (named after the first Christian missionary in Hawaii, Hiram Bingham).

'Junkie. Pothead. That's where I was headed,' Barry would later say, admitting that in high school he made plenty of 'bad decisions'. There were several Bingham Benchers who paid a heavy price for those decisions. One was severely injured in a car crash after driving under the influence, one was committed to a mental institution after taking LSD, another barely survived an overdose and yet another was arrested after police pulled him over and found drugs in the trunk of his car.

Keith Kakugawa's plight may have hit closest to home. A track star with Olympic potential, Kakugawa slid into a life of drugs after graduation from Punahou and would end up spending years behind bars.

Barry, who had wisely resisted the persistent efforts of one of his Bingham Bench buddies to get him to try heroin, somehow managed to emerge relatively unscathed. 'You've been very lucky,' his mother said after confronting him about his unsavoury band of pals. 'But your luck won't hold out for ever. Don't waste your life.'

Barry remained unconvinced. On more than one occasion, he drove drunk – 'speeding down a highway with gin clouding my head,' he recalled. There was, he would also admit, more than one occasion when he found himself bloodied in a booze-fuelled fight. Through it all, there were the furtive meetings with drug dealers in public parks and alleyways – encounters during which he risked losing everything if one of those dealers turned out to be what he, like his friends, derisively called a 'narc'.

Conversely, Obama continued to do well on Punahou's basketball team, earning the nickname 'Barry O'Bomber' for his driving jump-shot. Over the years, he had worked his way up the ranks until, in his senior year, he made the varsity team. 'It was rare for someone to make the team in the last year,' said varsity coach Chris McLachlin. 'It's testament to Barry's perseverance that he practised and practised and perfected his game until he was finally given a spot on the varsity team.' Unfortunately, the team was so top-heavy with talent that he often found himself sitting on the bench. At one point, he approached McLachlin as the appointed representative of several benched players. 'He wanted to know what they could do to get in the game, how they could improve,' McLachlin said. 'He was very respectful, much more mature than other kids his age.'

Still, that final year his grades slipped noticeably – though not enough to keep him from being accepted to several major universities in Hawaii and on the US mainland. His final choice – Occidental College in Los Angeles – was unexpected, but Barry had his reasons: he had struck up a friendship with an attractive young coed from the affluent LA suburb of Brentwood who was vacationing with her family on Oahu, and he was hoping to hook up with her once he got to Los Angeles.

The yearbook entry for 'Barry Obama', which featured a photo of him in a short-cropped Afro, reflected those things he considered important at the time: basketball, family and his fellow pot-smokers. Included was a snapshot of 'Barry O'Bomber' on the basketball court with the pidgin-English caption 'We go play hoop'; a photo of his paper-strewn dorm room desk showing a beer bottle, turntable, telephone and tennis trophy as well as Zig-Zag rolling paper and a book of matches under the title 'Still Life' – and, most revealingly, a nod to those who mattered most to Barry at the time. He thanked Toot, Gramps, 'Ray' (Keith Kakugawa) and 'Choom Gang' for 'all the good times'. *Choom* is the act of smoking *pakalolo*, the Hawaiian word for marijuana. Barry signed off with 'LATERS' – slang for 'see you later'.

At his Punahou graduation ceremonies in June 1979, Barry, beaming in his navy-blue blazer and blue-and-gold rep-tie, bounded onstage to accept his diploma to loud cheers from his mother and grandparents. No one was more moved than Toot, who sobbed as she rushed up to Barry after the ceremony and draped an orchid lei around his neck.

Conspicuously absent that day was Barack Sr. It had been eight years since they had seen each other and four years since Barry, weary of trying to forge a bond with his father, had stopped corresponding with him.

It was around this time that Neil Abercrombie was vacationing in Kenya and decided to look up his old University of Hawaii buddy. By this point, Barack Sr, who had been sidelined in the Ministry of Tourism, was depressed and drinking even more heavily than usual.

Barack Sr had always been a menace behind the wheel – drunk or sober. 'He was a terrible driver,' said his friend Philip Ochieng. 'He would get very excited and zoom like Mr Toad.' Now driving under the influence on a more or less daily basis, he caused a series of serious accidents. One of these resulted in the death of another motorist. Inexplicably, Barack was never charged in the case.

On another occasion, Obama himself was struck by a hit-and-run driver and left for dead. 'They tried to kill me,' he told his old friend Pake Zane when Zane and his wife, Julie, visited Barack Sr in Kenya in the 1970s. Obama went on to tell them he had been marked for death by forces within the Kenyan government because, despite the testimony he had given years earlier as a prosecution witness in the trial of nationalist leader Tom Mboya's accused killer, he still knew who was really behind Mboya's assassination.

'It all made him a very angry man,' Zane said. 'He was limping badly, and he would go out every night and get really drunk and really abusive. He yelled at everyone in that booming voice. It was overwhelming – just way too heavy to take. Even his friends couldn't stand to be around him any more.'

'He was a very bitter man,' Abercrombie said of Barack when he last saw him in 1979. Obama felt he had 'not been given the chance to fulfil his destiny and play a major role in the running of his country . . . He was drinking too much. His frustration was apparent.'

The two men talked for hours. Most of that time, Abercrombie sat quietly while a well-lubricated Barack railed against his bosses in government. The only thing that was memorable was what Barack Obama Sr did not say. Not once, Abercrombie marvelled, did Barack Obama ask about his ex-wife or the son who was graduating from high school that year. 'Even for a man as self-absorbed as Barack was,' Abercrombie said, 'I was shocked. How sad for his son . . .'

She was a slight, greying Mexican woman of indeterminate age, and she smiled wanly at Barry and his friends as she trudged down the hallway towards their dorm room at eight o'clock on Monday morning. The students were sitting on the floor, propped up against the wall with beer cans in hand, oblivious to the woman's presence. They had been partying for two days straight and were far too busy praising their own stamina as they passed around yet another joint.

Jackets and shoes were heaped against the front door, making it difficult for the cleaning lady to push her way into Barry's dorm room. Once she did, she wished she hadn't.

'My God!' she cried in Spanish as she surveyed the wreckage – a mind-spinning blur of bottles, cans, pizza cartons, half-eaten hamburgers, Styrofoam cups, Chinese takeaway containers, discarded wrappers, cigarette butts and overturned bowls of potato chips and popcorn. The kitchen sink brimmed with dirty dishes, and the towel-heaped bathrooms, where many a porcelain bus had been driven, were simply indescribable.

Wading through the debris, she held a rag up to her to her nose and mouth to protect against the overpowering stench – a rank blend of cigarette and marijuana smoke, incense, rotting food, urine and vomit. Over the decade she had worked as a maid assigned to clean up the dormitories at Occidental College, the Mexican woman had had no illusions about what awaited her each Monday morning. But there were limits. She wept as she stepped back into the hallway to fetch her mop and pail. Standing there was another maid, who, after surveying the scene, offered to help.

As the two women, neither of whom spoke English, gathered up their cleaning supplies for the assault on Barry's room, they glanced down the hall. They shook their heads in disgust at the sight of Barry and his pals convulsed with laughter.

Just as he had identified with some of the most unsavoury elements in his high school class, Barry wasted no time seeking out the hardest partyers once he arrived at Occidental. For the next two years, he would be unapologetic in his pursuit of getting high.

Towards that end, Obama cast himself during this period as, in the words of his classmate and friend Eric Moore, 'a definite surfer-type'. Barry's carefully chosen uniform of flip-flops, Hawaiian shirts and board shorts – finished off with wraparound sunglasses, a *puka* shell necklace and an ever-present cigarette – was designed to convey the sort of familiar, laid-back persona that Occidental's overwhelmingly white student body would find least threatening.

Rounding out the image of a well-heeled surfer dude cum college man was Barry's used red Fiat – a gift from his grandparents. It also helped that he played intramural sports, including tennis, flag football and water polo. (Barry tried out for but did not quite make Occidental's basketball team.) 'He was an athletic guy,' recalled his freshman roommate Paul Carpenter. 'He was gifted in that regard.' Barry was also 'superbright,' Carpenter said. 'He could get through the coursework in a fraction of the time it took me.'

Classmate Margot Mifflin remembered him as 'an unpretentious, down-to-earth, solidly middle-class guy who seemed somewhat more sophisticated than the average college student. He was slightly reserved and deliberate in a way that I sometimes thought betrayed an uncertainty.'

There were those, however, who saw Barry's 'reserved and deliberate' demeanour as a sign of something else. 'He definitely had a cocky, sometimes arrogant way about him,' recalled another classmate, Robert McCrary. 'He was not open to others.'

Eric Moore agreed with Margot Mifflin that Barry 'was already very polished' by the time he arrived at Occidental. Being biracial, and having grown up in Hawaii and lived for a time in Indonesia, Barry was 'more worldly than the average kid in California,' Moore said. 'But he still wanted to fit in.'

When they first met, Moore, an African American from the mostly white Colorado college community of Boulder, was taken aback by Obama's first name. 'What kind of name is Barry Obama for a brother?' he kidded.

'Actually, my name is Barack Obama,' he replied.

'That's a very strong name,' Moore said. 'Why don't you use it?'

Barry sighed and shook his head. 'It's just too much of a hassle,' he said. 'I don't want to have to explain it every five seconds.'

'Well, screw that Barry shit,' Moore said. 'From now on I'm calling you Barack.'

Obama was grateful that Moore called him Barack, although Paul Carpenter was among many students who never heard him called Barack at all. 'It was always Barry,' Carpenter said. 'And if someone asked him what he preferred, he didn't hesitate to say Barry.' Anne Howells, who taught literary theory at Occidental in the winter of 1980, concurred: 'I asked him if Barack was a Hawaiian name, and he told me it was African. But when I went around the room asking each student what he or she wanted to be called, the only African American in the class did not hesitate to answer. "Barry," he said.'

In truth, this part of sunny southern California, with its tile-roofed, Spanish-style houses, palm-lined streets and sweeping views of the Pacific, seemed comfortably familiar to Barry. Back at Punahou, he was never exposed to anything resembling a slum or a ghetto. At 'Oxy', he was just as shielded from the grim realities of life for blacks in communities like Watts, Compton and South Central LA.

Still, he did set out to build relationships with other African Americans on campus. Soon he was spending most of his time with a handful of other black undergraduates. Unlike the white students and faculty members who called him Barry, his African American friends addressed him as 'Obama'. Wahid Hamid, a wealthy Pakistani who became one of Barack's closest friends at Occidental, was 'not surprised that he decided to embrace that identity because "Barry" could be perceived as trying to run away from something and trying to fit in, rather than embracing his own identity, in many ways, kind of opening himself to who he is'.

Hamid was just one of the many foreign students that Barry went out of his way to befriend during his freshman year. His inner circle at that time included another well-to-do Pakistani named Mohammed Hasan Chandoo as well as Vinai Thummalapally, a native of Hyderabad, India. Thummalapally, who roomed with Barry and Paul Carpenter that first year at Oxy and was six years older than Barry, did a three-mile run with him every morning before classes. As they ran, Thummalapally invariably shared his dreams of opening a successful business back at home in India. Barry made it clear he had no interest in the private sector. 'I want to get into public service,' he told Thummalapally, pausing after each run to reward himself with another cigarette. 'I want to write and help people who are disadvantaged.'

Obama quickly impressed his professors with his new-found social conscience. 'He hung out with the other young men and women who were most serious about issues of social justice,' said Roger Boesche, one of Barry's political science professors.

Boesche was also impressed with Barry's fearlessness when it came to questioning his teachers – a self-confidence that bordered on cockiness. The professor was having lunch at a local restaurant called The Cooler when he looked up to see Barry standing by his table. 'I really think I deserved a better grade than the one you gave me,' he told Boesche point-blank.

'You are really smart, Barry,' Boesche replied. 'But I'm afraid you just aren't working hard enough.'

'I disagree,' Barry pressed on. 'You're holding me up to a higher standard than everybody else in class and that's unfair. I'm being graded on a different curve than everybody else and I'd like to know why.'

Clearly taken aback, Boesche squirmed in his seat for a moment. 'You are capable of so much better, but no, Barry, I gave you the grade you deserved.'

Barry shook his head and walked off, never saying anything to his professor that might be construed as rude or inappropriate. He told Moore, Hamid and his other friends, however, that he was 'really pissed off' about his grade. 'If he thought he was being treated unfairly,' said an Occidental classmate, 'he just wouldn't let go of it. He was a man obsessed. But he never really became outwardly agitated, either.'

However 'pissed off' he may have been, Barry still seemed congenitally incapable of losing his temper. Even when everyone else in the room seemed to be shouting to make a point, Vinai Thummalapally said Obama 'wouldn't get worked up. Other people would be standing, waving their arms around, and Barack wouldn't even change his position on the sofa – and *still* he could make his point. Everybody would just suddenly shut up and listen when he talked.' According to Thummalapally, his roommate 'never swore. Not once can I ever remember him using a cuss-word. Imagine it: an 18 year old who never used profanity.' By the same token, Thummalapally insisted Barry 'was not a nerd. He was not a bore. People were drawn to him.'

Even though as a biracial man he could still easily move from one social circle to another ('He had the benefit of knowing both cultures first-hand,' Eric Moore observed), Barry felt at his most comfortable in the company of other African American students. They understood completely, for example, when Barry he said he suspected his professors were holding him to a different standard because of his colour. In turn, he nodded sympathetically whenever the others griped about the slights and insults they endured on any given day.

It was no small irony that these conversations were the exception rather than the rule. Obama quickly discovered that he and his black friends banded together precisely so they wouldn't have to think about race all the time. The question of race always hung in the air whenever they were in the company of whites. 'To constantly think about race,' he said, 'it's so damned exhausting.' Most of the time,

Barry later said, he and his friends talked about the same things their white counterparts talked about: 'Surviving classes. Finding a well-paying gig after graduation. Trying to get laid.'

As 'progressive' as he and his friends claimed to be, they showed no remorse when the Mexican maids came to clean up their mess after yet another non-stop weekend of partying. That unfortunate disregard for others continued into Barry's sophomore year, even as he and other members of Occidental's Black Student Alliance planned a demonstration demanding that Occidental divest itself of its interests in apartheid South Africa.

The rally, staged opposite the president's office, marked Barry's public speaking debut. Haltingly at first, Barry managed to seize the attention of the lunchtime crowd with a speech that scarcely lasted one minute. For the first time, he realised that the timbre of his voice was not unlike his father's. 'He had this booming voice,' Eric Moore said. 'It helped that people knew who he was because he was so popular on campus, but he also had this commanding presence.'

When that lunchtime crowd cheered and applauded his speech (albeit fleetingly), no one was more surprised than Barry. It was heady stuff for a 19 year old still in the throes of his own identity crisis. 'I knew I had them,' he later wrote. 'The connection had been made.'

No romantic connection, however, had been made with anyone. His infamous parties notwithstanding, Barry did not come close to forging a serious relationship with any female during his first two years at college. According to one Oxy colleague, 'Barry dated girls, but there was no one who came close to being his girlfriend or anything like that. Barry wasn't at all shy, and women liked him, but he seemed too focused on himself to really get involved with someone romantically.'

After two years at Occidental, Barry was floundering. He had no idea of what he wanted to do with his life or where he wanted to settle down. Neither Hawaii nor California – at least the affluent parts of California he had been exposed to – offered him the sort of life experience he longed for. Barry wanted to live in a city – the sort of multinational, multicultural, polyglot urban environment that would stimulate him intellectually and ground him at the same time.

As soon as he learned that Occidental had begun a transfer programme with New York's Columbia University, he signed up. Barry's friend Eric Moore pleaded with him to remain at Oxy, but Barry argued that he needed to make a clean break from his past – and that meant leaving his friends behind. 'I think there was a lot of stuff going on in me,' Obama later said. 'I was starting to work it through. It's hard to remake yourself around people who have known you for a long time.'

Before he made the trip to New York, Barry made another voyage that would, he later said, shape his world view. Travelling to Pakistan with his friend Wahid Hamid, Barry spent three weeks touring the countryside around Karachi. He had already witnessed grinding South East Asian poverty during his childhood years in Indonesia, but he was still shocked by what he saw in Pakistan – particularly the power wealthy landowners had over the lives of the peasants who worked their fields. As the landowners drove by in their Land Rovers and Mercedes, the workers – men, women and children alike – would literally bow down until they passed. 'It was straight out of the Middle Ages,' Barry would later recall. 'The serfs bowing to their lord and master.'

Barry's Pakistan connection would continue even after he arrived in New York. Unable to get into the cold-water flat he had arranged to rent on 109th Street in Spanish Harlem – he would spend his first night in Manhattan huddled with his belongings in an alley – Barry called up the only person he knew in the city for help.

Barry had met Pakistani Sohale 'Hal' Siddiqi a year earlier, when Siddiqi was visiting his friends Hamid and Chandoo in Los Angeles. Now Siddiqi was making ends meet working as a salesman at a boutique during the day and as a waiter at night.

'He arrived dishevelled and without a place to stay,' Siddiqi said. Instantly, Siddiqi recognised something of himself in the homeless African American. 'We were both very lost,' he said. 'We were both alienated.'

Siddiqi took Obama in that first night, helped him move into the Spanish Harlem apartment a few days later and then helped him move out when it turned out the apartment had no heat. Together, they found a sixth-floor walk-up on East 94th Street between First and Second avenues – but there was a catch. In order to secure the lease, they would both have to show they were financially secure. Obama refused to lie on the application – he put down that he was a Columbia University student with no income – leaving it to Siddiqi to falsely claim that he earned a substantial salary working for a high-end catering firm.

Barry, despite his refusal to participate, was fully aware of the subterfuge. 'We didn't have a chance in hell of getting this apartment unless we fabricated the lease,' Siddiqi said. 'So I was the one who had to do it.'

A Park Avenue penthouse it wasn't. Drugs were sold on the stoops of neighbouring buildings in broad daylight and gunshots punctuated the night. The apartment itself was a dark, cramped, postage-stamp-sized one-bedroom with leaky pipes, noisy radiators and paint peeling from the ceiling. There was no money for furniture. The two men slept on mattresses on the floor; the living room couch and chairs were picked up off the street. There were no tables at all. They and anyone who happened to visit them ate from paper plates balanced on their laps.

This spartan existence was all in keeping with Barry's plan. He had actually begun reinventing himself the minute he arrived in Manhattan. Relocating to New York, he said later, 'was a really significant break. It's when I left a lot of stuff behind.' His name, for instance. From this point on, if anyone asked how he wished to be addressed, the answer was always the same: 'Call me Barack.'

This change was not, he later insisted, 'some assertion of my African roots – not a racial assertion. It was much more of an assertion that I was coming of age. An assertion of being comfortable with the fact that I was different and that I didn't need to try to fit in in a certain way.'

Most importantly, Barack now eschewed the alcohol and drugs that had threatened to derail his life – 'the final, fatal role,' he wrote, 'of the young would-be black man.' There would be no more weekend bacchanals, no more Mexican maids throwing up their hands in despair.

For the next two years, Barack embarked on a lifestyle that bordered on the monastic. He fasted on Sundays and for the rest of the week adhered steadfastly to Dick Gregory's vegetarian diet. Gone were the blazers and neatly pressed khakis of his prep school days, replaced by a Navy-surplus peacoat worn with Levis and a turtleneck picked up at the Salvation Army for five dollars. 'I think self-deprivation was his shtick,' Siddiqi recalled, 'denying himself pleasure, good food and all of that.'

Siddiqi made up for his roommate's self-imposed asceticism. He drank, smoked pot and did lines of cocaine with friends in their apartment. He continually offered Barack drugs, and every time, according to Siddiqi, he refused.

For the most part Barack was, by his own admission, leading 'a pretty grim and humorless' life. His routine consisted of getting up and running three miles, attending classes at Columbia, then coming home to spend hours reading. Any free time was spent aimlessly wandering the streets. His exploration of the city – from the stately limestone mansions and brick townhouses of the Upper East Side to Chinatown and the Financial District to the slums of Harlem and the South Bronx – only served to underscore the inequities of American life and fuel his growing despair. He now began to keep detailed journals, which he filled with his observations and his poetry. 'Strange,' he wrote after yet another cab driver drove past him to pick up someone else. 'Don't they see my white relatives?'

When Barack did bother to venture outside the little world he had created for himself, it was to lecture Siddiqi and anyone else he came into contact with about the plight of the world's poor and the failure of Western societies to do anything about it. Predictably, Siddiqi, whose own goal in life at the time 'was to make a lot of money to buy stuff", grew tired of Barack's sermonising.

'Who do you think you are, Barack? A saint?' Siddiqi asked. 'Why are you so serious all the time?' Then he delivered the *coup de grâce*. 'Barack,' Siddiqi said with a sigh, 'you are becoming a bore.'

Perhaps. But Barack wasn't, Siddiqi hastened to add, 'entirely a hermit' during this period. He would invite friends over to the apartment and relax on the floor listening to Van Morrison, Ella

Fitzgerald, Bob Dylan, Stevie Wonder and his new favourite, Billie Holiday. Nor had he given up his principal vice: smoking. 'He'd be sprawled out on the couch,' Siddiqi recalled, 'listening to his music and blowing smoke rings in the air.'

There was something else Barack was not entirely willing to give up. He would join friends for a night out every now and then, and even went cruising some of the East Side's more notorious singles bars with Siddiqi. 'We were always competing,' recalled Siddiqi, who claimed several of his female friends told him they considered Barack 'a hunk'. Although Barack still abstained from alcohol, he and his roommate would, said Siddiqi, 'go to bars and try hitting on the girls. He had a lot more success. I wouldn't out-compete him in picking up girls, that's for sure.'

Years later, Barack would write that during this time he had a year-long affair with a wealthy young white woman who had 'dark hair, specks of green in her eyes. Her voice sounded like a wind chime.' The romance ended, he claimed, after he visited the young lady's stately country home, looked around at the photographs of presidents, senators and industrialists that hung on the walls, and decided he could never be a part of her world. The actual break-up, as Barack would describe it years later in his book *Dreams from My Father*, supposedly took place in the street after he had taken her to see a new play by an angry young black playwright. 'She couldn't be black, she said,' Barack wrote. 'She would if she could, but she couldn't. She could only be herself, and wasn't that enough?'

Barack then observed that even if she'd been black it wouldn't have worked out. 'I mean,' he wrote, 'there are several black ladies out there who've broken my heart just as good.'

No one, including his roommate and closest friend at the time, Siddiqi, knew of this mysterious lover's existence – or could recall Obama's heart ever being 'broken' by a woman, regardless of her race. Not that Barack had taken a vow of celibacy – far from it. 'One-night stands,' a bar-hopping friend remembers. 'That seemed to be pretty much it.'

Neither his mother Ann nor his sister Maya encountered any of Barack's women friends when they visited him that first summer in New York. Thanks in part to Ann's enduring fascination with all things Third World, they hit it off instantly with Barack's free-spirited Pakistani roommate.

The same could not be said for Siddiqi's mother when it was her turn to visit from Pakistan. Having never known a black person, she treated Barack with contempt. 'My mother was terribly rude to him,' Siddiqi admitted. Barack reacted by being 'so polite and kind to her'.

Accordingly, Siddiqi was there for Barack in November 1982 when the call came from Africa that would change Obama's life – and, by extension, world history – for ever. As he so often did, Barack Sr had been out carousing with friends in the honky-tonk town of Kaloleni, this time celebrating rumours that he was soon to be given a big promotion. Having already lost both his legs in another one of his accidents and now walking on crude prosthetic limbs, he was driving himself home but never made it. Veering off the road, he crashed into the six-foot-high stump of a giant gum tree and died instantly. He was 46.

Barack was frying eggs in the tiny kitchen of his apartment when his Aunt Jane, a woman he had never met, phoned with the news. 'Listen, Barry, your father is dead,' Aunt Jane said. 'He is killed in a car accident. Hello? Can you hear me?'

Barack scarcely knew how to react. His father remained a myth to him – 'both more and less than a man' – and because of that he would later say he felt 'no pain, only the vague sense of an opportunity lost'. When he called his mother to tell her Barack Sr had been killed, she cried out in anguish.

Barack Sr was buried in the village where he was raised, Nyang'oma Kogelo. Attending the funeral were several top government ministers, as well as more than 40 members of Obama's extended family. His American son was not among them.

Siddiqi, meanwhile, continued his wanton ways. 'I was partying all the time,' he said. 'I was disturbing his studies.' Barack needed to be free from unnecessary distractions; he had settled on a major – political science, specialising in international relations – and was now heading down the home stretch towards his degree.

Frustrated that Barack would not loosen up, Siddiqi accused him of kowtowing to his white professors. 'Look at you,' Siddiqi sniped. 'You're nothing but an Uncle Tom.' He would deliver this particular zinger on several occasions, and each time his target reacted the same way – with benign indifference.

Indeed, Barack's fabled unflappability was already very much in evidence. One morning, he and Siddiqi were walking Siddiqi's pug Charlie on Broadway when a hulking street person approached them and began stomping on the pavement next to Charlie's head. Siddiqi angrily confronted the homeless man, and as the two men squared off, Barack suddenly stepped between them. 'Hey, hey, *hey*!' Barack said, shoving his face right into the stranger's. The man looked into Obama's eyes and backed down. 'It was an incredible scene,' Siddiqi said. 'Barack could be pretty fearless. He always stood up for what he thought was right.'

Still, Barack could not put up with his friend's undisciplined behaviour indefinitely. By the start of his senior year, he moved out of the East 94th Street apartment and in with a new roommate. 'Barack was really patient,' Siddiqi later said. 'I'm surprised he suffered me as long as he did.'

If he could not always count on friends, Barack knew that the people he considered at the time to be his only real family – his mother, Maya, Gramps and Toot – were there for him. They all showed up in New York when, in June of 1983, he graduated from Columbia University with a degree in political science.

During his waning days at Columbia, he had nurtured dreams of becoming a community organiser – although he was not at all precisely sure what a community organiser actually was or what the job entailed. 'I'll organise black folks,' he told himself. 'At the grassroots. For change.'

For Barack, organising would be no less than 'an act of redemption' – a chance to earn, through shared sacrifice, 'full membership' in the black community. He thought back to the 'sit-ins, the marches, the jailhouse songs' of the civil rights era and imagined himself there – only this time fighting for the social, economic and political rights of a new generation.

In the spring of 1983, Barack fired off scores of letters to black politicians, civil rights organisations, and neighbourhood, tenants' rights and community-action groups around the country. He was a young, black, progressive-minded Ivy League graduate, he told them, and he was eager to do whatever he could for the cause.

He received not a single reply. Undaunted, he decided instead to take a job that would pay the bills while he waited for some discerning activist group to take him up on his offer. He promptly landed a job as a research associate at Business International Corporation, a small publisher of newsletters tracking the activities of corporations operating overseas (a few years later the firm would be acquired by the Economist Group).

Barack would later describe Business International as a leading consulting house where, in order to fit in, he wore a power suit and carried a briefcase. Not so, according to those who worked with him. 'It was a bit like a sweatshop,' said one of his BI co-workers, Dan Armstrong. 'I'm sure we all wished that we were high-priced consultants to multinational corporations. But we also enjoyed coming in at ten, wearing jeans to work, flirting with our co-workers, partying when we stayed late, and bonding over the low salaries and heavy workload . . . Barack never wore a tie, much less a suit. Nobody did.'

Like others who worked alongside Barack then, Armstrong found him to be 'aloof – reserved and distant with his co-workers'. Another BI co-worker, Bill Millar, went a step further. 'I worked next to Barack nearly every day he was at Business International,' said Millar, who had a degree in finance and Wall Street experience. 'I found him arrogant and condescending. He just sort of rolled his eyes if you tried to explain something to him. I'll never forget it.'

Nevertheless, within a few months Barack was promoted to financial writer, contributing articles to one of the firm's key newsletters, *Business International Money Report*. He was also put in charge of editing the company's global reference service, Financing Foreign Operations and given a substantial raise. (He was not assigned his own secretary, however, as Barack would later claim. 'The idea that Barack had a secretary is laughable,' Armstrong said. 'Only the company president had a secretary.')

BI's informal atmosphere aside – a former top executive of the firm called it 'high school with ashtrays' – the fact remained that 22-year-old Barack was the firm's only black executive. All the other African Americans he encountered at Business International Corporation were secretaries, receptionists, mailroom clerks and security guards – the men and women who were indispensable to the entire operation but seldom given the opportunity to rise above their station.

Barack felt more than a little self-conscious about his management position, but he could not afford the luxury of feeling guilty. The women in the secretary pool and the other black staffers were all rooting for him to succeed. Whether he liked the work or not, Barack was, for the time being at least, determined not to disappoint them.

Barack kept toiling away at his Wang computer terminal until he received yet another wake-up call from Africa. This time it was his half-sister Auma, Barack Sr's daughter by his first wife, choking back tears as she delivered more bad news. Their half-brother David, Barack Sr's son by his third wife, Ruth Nidesand, had been killed in a motorcycle accident.

Barack had never met him, but news of his brother David's sudden and shocking death rekindled his desire for 'redemption' through community organising. After a little more than a year laying the foundation for a climb up the corporate ladder, Barack quit his job at Business International.

For the next three months, he worked as a community organiser for Ralph Nader's New York Public Interest Research Group out of the Harlem campus of the City College of New York. He quickly discovered that students – even minority students – were less interested in protesting against the Establishment than they were in joining it. 'A good job in corporate America, a fat paycheck and nice things – that's what they all want,' he told a fellow activist. 'Can you blame them?'

Of course, Barack had willingly given up all those things, and by the late summer of 1985 he was broke. It was then, while perusing a publication called *Community Jobs*, that he spotted a want ad offering a position as a community-organiser trainee in Chicago. Barack answered the ad immediately, sending along his résumé. Within a week he found himself sitting in a Lexington Avenue coffee shop on the Upper East Side with the man who had placed the ad, Jerry Kellman.

The ad was in itself an act of desperation for Kellman, a stocky, not quite middle-aged man who looked like he had spent the night on tumble-dry. Beginning with the campus antiwar movement in the 1960s, Kellman had spearheaded one social protest after another and in the process built a reputation as one of the Midwest's most effective community organisers.

Now Kellman faced his most daunting challenge yet. Chicago was haemorrhaging manufacturing jobs, driving more of the city's urban working class into unemployment and poverty. Unions no longer had the clout they once had, so now Kellman was trying to convince Chicago's powerful black churches to stand up to the corporations on the workers' behalf.

The trouble was, Kellman and his colleagues were white and, for the most part, Jewish. Black pastors on Chicago's South Side were suspicious of their motives. 'Here we were trying to organise in Chicago's African American community,' Kellman said, 'and we didn't have any African Americans on our staff. It did not look good, obviously.'

Before their meeting in the coffee shop, Kellman interviewed Barack on the phone for nearly two hours. 'He was clearly very bright,' Kellman remembered. 'But there are a lot of very bright young people out there. But he was also mature, confident, articulate.'

Kellman was particularly intrigued by Barack's upbringing. 'His father had left the family, his mother wasn't around a lot, he moved from one culture to another – and it all left him feeling like an outsider,' Kellman said. 'Outsiders can do one of two things: they can try to join the mainstream or they can identify with the other outsiders. Barack identified with the other outsiders. That was important.'

Satisfied that Barack was the right person for the job, Kellman came right to the point during their face-to-face meeting. 'I can't break through,' Kellman admitted to Barack. 'So that's why I need someone like you.'

Barack, Kellman later said, 'was looking for the civil rights movement, but it was over. Organising was the closest thing he could find to it.' Barack was also looking to avoid the mistakes made by his father. 'My father was a brilliant man, an intellectual,' Barack told Kellman. 'He returned to Kenya bursting with ambition to do things for his native country, but he didn't know how to turn his ideals into reality. So he ended up just another bitter, broken bureaucrat with a drinking problem. I am *not*,' Barack vowed, 'going to end up like my father.'

It remained to be seen whether Barack was different from so many other young college graduates who had come to Kellman seeking to make a difference. 'The pattern was that people Barack's age who had done well in school, who were Phi Beta Kappa and Rhodes Scholars, would volunteer in the inner city and quickly unravel. They'd burn out in a matter of months. I hoped that his motivation was strong enough so that wouldn't happen to him.'

The pay Kellman was offering – $10,000 for the first year – amounted to less than a quarter of what Barack had been earning as a junior financial writer. No matter. It was the opportunity he had been waiting for. By working shoulder to shoulder with his fellow African Americans in this most American of cities, he would finally lay claim to that elusive sense of self that he had been so desperately seeking.

Barack would also find something else in Chicago – something that had proved equally precious, equally elusive. He would find the love of his life.

I always tease her she had sort of the South Side version of *Ozzie and Harriet*. Or *Leave It to Beaver*.

Barack

I was just a typical South Side little black girl.

Michelle

We knew you would do this 15 years ago when we could never make you *shut up*.

*Michelle's parents, in their 1988
Harvard Law School Yearbook ad congratulating her*

3

'S he's *what?*' Alice Brown asked, the tone of her voice hovering somewhere between anxiety and outright panic. On the other end of the line, Catherine Donnelly was not at all surprised at her mother's reaction. The Princeton University freshman imagined Alice, knuckles white as she gripped the phone, eyes wide with disbelief, her face turning an unsettling shade of crimson.

'Well, like I said, Mom, she seems very nice, quite tall, smart of course, pretty – beautiful, actually,' Catherine answered. 'Her name is Michelle, she's from Chicago . . . and she's black.'

Growing up in Louisiana, Catherine had attended school with a few black students. But the idea of sharing the cramped, sloped-ceilinged dorm room at Pyne Hall with Michelle and another student was something else again. Catherine's mother had grown up in an unabashedly racist southern household, so Catherine braced herself for the worst.

Indeed, the possibility that her daughter might room with an African American during her first year at Princeton was something that Alice Brown had not even remotely considered. A financially strapped single mother who had poured her life into raising Catherine, Alice had always had big plans for her daughter. As far as she was concerned, they did not include a black roommate – much less one raised on the gritty South Side of Chicago by a working-class family.

Like Michelle's family, Alice had made considerable sacrifices for her daughter. Convinced that a private school education would greatly improve Catherine's chances of getting into a top college, Alice took a teaching job at one of New Orleans' most exclusive private institutions so that Catherine could attend tuition-free. When

Catherine was admitted to Princeton, it seemed as if every door was finally open to her. Alice wondered how many of those doors would now slam shut if her daughter was forced to share a room with a black girl. She also wondered if such a person might be a 'bad influence' on Catherine.

'Mom just blew a gasket when I described Michelle,' Catherine would later recall. 'It was my secret shame.'

Alice, who had driven Catherine up from New Orleans, didn't stop there. No sooner did she hang up with her daughter than she marched straight to the student housing office. 'I need to get my daughter's room changed right away,' Alice demanded. 'We're from the South. We aren't used to living with black people.'

When she was told that no other rooms were available, Alice, distraught, called her mother. 'Take Catherine out of school *immediately*,' Catherine's grandmother insisted. 'Bring her home!'

Michelle was blissfully unaware of Alice Brown's reaction or the frantic attempts Brown had made to get her daughter to room with someone else – anyone else – as long, of course, as that person wasn't black. Catherine certainly gave no hint of what was going on behind the scenes. She and 'Miche', as Michelle liked to be called, got along well enough.

'Michelle had these beautiful, long-fingered hands that she used to tell great stories with,' said Catherine, who, like Michelle, was 17 at the time. 'I loved her hands.'

The following semester, however, Catherine jumped at the chance to move out when a larger room became available. When she finally learned, some 27 years later, of Alice Brown's attempts to move her daughter out of their dorm room, Michelle would recall that she and Catherine were 'never close. But sometimes that's the thing you sense, that there's something that's there, but it's often unspoken.' Once Catherine moved out, she and Michelle, who would soon be socialising almost exclusively with the few other blacks on campus, turned the other way when they passed each other on campus.

Catherine would certainly regret what had happened then, as would her mother. 'Michelle early on began to hang out with other black students,' Catherine remembered. 'Princeton was just a very segregated place. I wish now that I had pushed harder to be friends, but by the same token she did not invite me to do things, either.'

Alice Brown's machinations notwithstanding, it quickly became clear to Michelle after she enrolled at Princeton in the autumn of 1981 that she and other minority students were not exactly being welcomed with open arms. Historically, Princeton, with its broad, emerald playing fields and imposing neo-Gothic architecture, was the very definition of resolute eastern elitism. Not even Woodrow Wilson, who was Princeton's president prior to his election to the White House in 1912, believed blacks belonged there. 'The whole temper and tradition of the place,' he wrote, 'are such that no Negro has ever applied for admission, and it seems extremely unlikely that the question will ever assume a practical form.'

It was not until 1936 that a black man named Bruce Wright was admitted to Princeton, and only then because they initially believed him to be white. As soon as the administration realised its mistake, Wright was asked to leave.

By the late 1960s, a handful of African Americans had been admitted into the then all-male university. When Princeton went coeducational in 1969, a smattering of black women joined their ranks. Of the 1,141 students in her freshman class, Michelle was one of only 94 blacks.

As far as most of her white classmates were concerned, Michelle and the other African Americans at Princeton were beneficiaries of affirmative action programmes and did not deserve to be there. It would be commonplace for white students to walk up to blacks and ask them their SAT scores point-blank. 'The implication,' said Michelle's classmate Lisa Rawlings, 'was that I didn't have the scores to get in, I didn't have the grades to get in.'

Princeton itself only fuelled the notion that the bar had been lowered for minority applicants. A few weeks before the school year began, black and Hispanic freshmen were invited to attend special classes designed to help them adjust to campus life. 'We weren't sure whether they thought we needed an extra start,' said fellow student Angela Acree, 'or they just said, "Let's bring all the black kids together."'

Either way, the effect was to isolate minority kids from the rest of the student body. Michelle quickly gravitated to the other African Americans on campus and by her sophomore year was sharing a suite with three other black women. 'I cannot tell you,' Michelle's classmate Lisa Rawlings recalled, 'the number of times I was called "Brown Sugar". Definitely you got the feeling you didn't belong.' Hilary Beard remembered how white students who had never been around blacks before 'would want to touch [her] hair'.

For the most part, however, Michelle and her fellow African Americans on campus were merely ignored. 'The same white kids you were in classes with,' Michelle said, 'would pretend not to know you once class was over. They would just look the other way if you passed them on campus, or even cross the street to avoid you. It happened all the time.'

Angela Acree agreed. 'White kids we knew from class would pass us on the green and pretend not to see us,' said Acree, whose closest friends at Princeton were Michelle and another black student, Suzanne Alele. 'It was, like, here comes a black kid. It was a very sexist, segregated place.'

Michelle might have been less taken aback if her older brother, Craig, who had arrived at Princeton two years earlier on a basketball scholarship, had bothered to warn her. Certainly the mere fact that she was the sister of a Princeton basketball star paved the way for Michelle socially. And Craig was more than generous with his advice when it came to housing and classes and professors.

Craig and Michelle, who bore such a striking physical resemblance that they were often taken for twins, had always been close. So why hadn't he cautioned his little sister about the racism that was pervasive on the Princeton campus? 'We all viewed it as what you needed to do, to do business there,' Craig explained. He hadn't wanted to discourage Michelle – or to cause his parents undue worry – by describing what he and the other blacks on campus had to endure on a daily basis. 'You just,' he said, 'had to put up with certain things.'

Back at home in Chicago, Marian and Fraser Robinson were completely unaware of what their children were going through. 'We had no idea, no inkling,' Marian later said. 'After all, it was *Princeton*.'

To be sure, both children had known nothing but love, support and encouragement growing up in a solid, working-class neighbourhood on Chicago's mostly African American South Side – a world away from Hawaii, Indonesia and Kenya.

In 1964, the same year Barack Obama's parents divorced, 29-year-old Fraser Robinson III landed a job working the swing shift as a 'station labourer' with Chicago's water department. That meant he essentially worked as a janitor at the city's water-treatment plant, mopping, scrubbing and scraping virtually every surface, cleaning the bathrooms, taking out the refuse, flushing drains and doing whatever else it took to make his demanding foreman happy – all for $6,000 a year.

He was thrilled to get the job. Once a gifted high school athlete who excelled in boxing and swimming, the affable, energetic, relentlessly upbeat Fraser had just been diagnosed with multiple sclerosis. Although the symptoms at this early stage of the disease were all but imperceptible, he knew that he would need the kind of steady employment with health benefits and a pension that the city government could provide.

For Marian Shields Robinson, news of her husband's water-company job came none too soon. Sweethearts since high school, where she had been a standout in track, Marian and Fraser wed in 1960. When their son, Craig, was born two years later, she quit her job as a secretary at the Sears Roebuck Catalog Company to take care of the baby. Now that she was pregnant again, Marian, 26, worried that she might have to return to work to make ends meet.

On 17 January 1964 – just three days after Fraser started his new job – Marian gave birth to a healthy baby girl. They named her Michelle LaVaughn (after Fraser's mother) and, as originally planned, Marian continued staying at home as a full-time mom.

The Robinsons breathed a collective sigh of relief knowing that Fraser's salary could pay for their small apartment on South Park (later Martin Luther King Drive) in a solidly black part of the city. But that security came with the price. Having grown up the son of a government worker in Chicago, Fraser Robinson III knew all too well that Mayor Richard Daley's fabled Democratic machine made sure all city jobs were doled out exclusively through an elaborate system of bribery, nepotism and patronage.

It helped that Fraser was a committed Democrat. He volunteered as precinct captain – a powerful position on the grassroots level and an essential cog in the well-oiled Daley machine. There was one Democratic precinct captain in each of Chicago's fifty wards, and it was his job to keep the party faithful happy. The Daley machine may have been one of the most violent, corrupt and notoriously racist in modern American history, but no matter. As long as people like Fraser Robinson were there to make sure their streets were cleared of snow and the garbage was collected on time, Democrats, regardless of race or ethnic origin, would continue to vote Democratic.

African Americans, however, were particularly vulnerable to the pressures brought to bear by these foot soldiers in Richard Daley's political army. Entire families could easily be intimidated by law enforcement, threatened with eviction from public housing or told that whatever government payments they might be receiving would grind to a halt. 'The Negroes always vote for us,' Daley once said in an infamous slip of the tongue, 'because they know what'll happen to them if they don't.'

By all accounts, Fraser was particularly effective as a precinct captain – a job he could perform, it seemed, without ever resorting to dirty tricks or intimidation. Well dressed and sporting a neatly trimmed moustache, Fraser was jovial, quick-witted and sympathetic to his neighbours' needs. And the more effective he was as a precinct captain, the more swiftly he rose through the ranks at the water department. In just five years, he would be promoted three times, rising to the position of 'operating engineer' at twice his starting salary.

The Daley machine seemed light years away from Friendfield, the South Carolina rice plantation where Jim Robinson, Michelle's great-great-grandfather, was born into slavery around 1850. It was here, in South Carolina's Low Country region north-east of Charleston, that thousands of slaves like Robinson worked the snake-invested fields that produced fully half the country's crop of rice.

All that abruptly changed in the wake of the Civil War. Friendfield's magnificent antebellum mansion was looted, its rice mill burned to the ground, and a smallpox epidemic swept through the region, killing blacks and whites alike.

Like many of the other newly emancipated slaves, Jim Robinson stayed to work the land as a sharecropper. In the 1880 census, he was listed as an illiterate farm-hand and the married father of a three-year-old son named Gabriel. Four years later, a second son, Fraser, was born.

When Gabriel and Fraser were still small, their mother died and their father quickly remarried. His new wife, however, considered her new stepsons little more than a nuisance. At the age of ten, Fraser went in search of firewood when a sapling fell on his left arm, shattering it. His stepmother, convinced that it was just a minor injury, refused to seek medical attention for Fraser. Gangrene set in, and by the time his stepmother did finally summon the doctor, all they could do to save his life was amputate.

Francis Nesmith, the white son of a plantation overseer, soon took Fraser under his wing. Eventually, Fraser moved into the Nesmith house and, though officially listed in the 1900 census as a 16-year-old 'house boy', he was raised alongside Nesmith's own children. While described as being illiterate at the time, Fraser would eventually teach himself to read.

Both of Jim Robinson's sons flourished. Gabriel earned enough money as a labourer to buy his own farm. Fraser married Rosella Cohen, a local woman whose parents had taken the name Cohen from their Jewish slave owner, and they had several children.

To support his family, the one-armed man plied his trade as a shoemaker and earned extra money by working in a lumber mill and hawking newspapers. He always managed to take a few copies home each night so his children could improve their reading skills and learn something about the world in the process.

Born in 1912, Fraser Jr was an outstanding student who excelled in public speaking. Yet after graduation from high school, he found himself scraping by working as a labourer at a local sawmill.

As the economy of the rural South continued its inexorable downhill slide, Fraser Jr and his new wife, LaVaughn, joined the millions of other blacks who fled north in search of a better life.

Fraser Jr would be disappointed. For the next 30 years he toiled as a US postal worker, earning just enough to afford a small apartment in one of Chicago's ubiquitous public housing projects. When he retired in 1974, he and LaVaughn packed up and moved back to South Carolina.

(If Michelle Robinson's family tree seems lacking in variety compared to that of her future husband, it is worth noting that one of her first cousins is a rabbi. Capers C. Funnye Jr converted from Methodism to Judaism and in 1985 founded Chicago's mostly black Beth Shalom B'nai Zaken Ethiopian Hebrew Congregation. The only African American rabbi in the Chicago area recognised by the Jewish community, Funnye also became the first African American member of the Chicago Board of Rabbis and served on the board of the American Jewish Congress of the Midwest. Funnye, like most of the members of his congregation, believes that the original Israelites were black.)

Michelle was six when the family relocated to South Shore, a more affluent neighbourhood that stretched along the southern border of Lake Michigan. Following the passage of the Fair Housing Act in 1968, the neighbourhood had undergone a profound transformation as black families moved in and white families fled. The Robinsons watched as, one by one, South Shore's few remaining white families packed up, waved goodbye and left.

While this quiet exodus occurred without rancour – Marian remembered that there were no harsh words or overtly bad feelings between the whites who fled and the African Americans who stayed – the message was clear. 'How do you think we felt?' a black neighbour said. 'They were nice to our faces, but it was pretty clear we weren't good enough to live next to.'

When Michelle and Craig asked their parents why all their white schoolmates were leaving, Marian and Fraser had no easy answers. They could not deny that racist sentiments had always run deep in Chicago and its suburbs; after being stoned by whites during a peaceful protest there in 1966, Martin Luther King said the racial hatred there was even more pernicious than what he'd witnessed in the Deep South.

Fraser and Marian conceded to their children that, even in their tight little community, racist attitudes still existed. But they also urged their children to shrug it off, to not be defined by what others thought of them and to focus on making themselves the best people they could be. 'You can't grow up being a black kid and not be aware of racial issues,' Craig said. 'Our parents always talked to us about it.'

While South Shore's racial character had changed – by the late 1970s nearly all the white families had vanished – the quality of life it offered had not. When businesses like the local bank and the local supermarket threatened to pull out of South Shore, citizens banded together and pressured them to stay. Precinct Captain Fraser and others with political clout made sure city services were not curtailed as they had been in other black communities, and parents lobbied aggressively for funds to keep their schools among the best in the state.

The undeniable sense of civic pride among the residents of South Shore was mirrored inside the Robinson home on the top floor of a dormered two-storey red-brick bungalow at 7436 South Euclid Avenue. There the Robinsons were crammed into three small rooms occupying less than one thousand square feet. Mom and Dad occupied the sole bedroom, and what would have been the living room was divided with plywood panels into three parts – Craig's room, Michelle's room and, between them, a communal study area.

Notwithstanding the cramped quarters, the Robinsons led a reasonably secure life surrounded by uncles, aunts, cousins and a wide assortment of family friends who dropped in to watch sports on TV, barbecue burgers in the back yard or spend the evening listening to Motown and jazz. Cosseted in this warm and nurturing environment, Michelle was to a great extent shielded from the sting of prejudice and inequality. Even though many in their circle were devoutly religious, the Robinsons were at best infrequent churchgoers. 'We believed,' Marian explained, 'that how you live your life every day was the most important thing.'

Sunday visits to her grandparents, who lived nearby in public housing, opened Michelle's eyes to what life was like for blacks in the rural South. Fraser Jr and Michelle's namesake, LaVaughn, spoke wistfully of Georgetown County in South Carolina, though Fraser never mentioned Friendfield Plantation or that his own grandfather had once been a slave there. Still, Michelle would later recall that Fraser Jr 'was a very proud man. He was proud of his lineage. At the same time, there was a discontent about him.' Indeed, she said, both her father and grandfather were 'bright, articulate, well-read men. If they'd been white, they would have been the heads of banks.'

After Fraser Jr moved back to South Carolina, Michelle was a frequent visitor. The heat, the Spanish moss, the dusty roads and the night-time din of crickets and frogs that made sleeping impossible would all be burned into Michelle's memory. So, too, was the memory of the wrought-iron gate and the road beyond it that the Robinsons always passed without comment – the road that led to Friendfield.

That Marian and Fraser III were willing to forego having a living room so that their children would have their own rooms and a place to do their schoolwork spoke volumes about the premium they put on education. Michelle's parents had both been bright enough to skip a grade in elementary school, and they certainly had the grades to get into a reputable college. But Fraser, who had grown up poor in the projects, did not see college as an option. Although Marian's mother had wanted her to become a teacher, she went to work straight out of high school as a secretary instead. 'That's because being a teacher was her dream, not mine,' Marian said. 'I didn't like being told what to do. I really wanted to be a secretary. I *liked* being a secretary.'

Still, Fraser and Marian wanted the best for their children, and they knew that education was the key. 'The academic part came first and early in our house,' Craig said. 'Our parents emphasised hard work and doing your best, and once you get trained like that, then you get used to it and you don't want to get anything but As and Bs.'

Marian had actually managed to teach both her children to read by the time they turned four, although Michelle baulked at first. 'She thought she could figure out how to read on her own,' Marian said, 'but she was too young to say that, so she just ignored me.'

Michelle 'had her head on straight very early,' her mother recalled. 'She raised herself from about nine years old.'

Well before then, the Robinsons had taken pains to instil self-discipline in Michelle and Craig. The day before they started kindergarten, Marian gave both children alarm clocks. 'You are becoming responsible for your life,' she told them. 'You have to see that you get up and give yourself enough time to eat breakfast and get yourself ready.' But while Craig sprang into action when his alarm went off, Michelle just asked him to roust her out of bed when he was finished using the bathroom. At first, Marian was miffed at her daughter's response. But she quickly changed her mind. After all, she said, Michelle's plan to get as much sleep as possible before the bathroom became available 'was smart. It worked.'

There were plenty of other character-building pursuits for the Robinson kids. Every Saturday, Michelle cleaned the bathroom. She alternated kitchen duties with Craig; he washed the dishes Monday, Wednesday and Friday while she took Tuesday, Thursday and Saturday. Mom stepped in to do the dishes on Sunday.

Their access to television was limited to one hour per day – although somehow Michelle still managed to commit to memory every single episode of *The Brady Bunch* (*The Dick Van Dyke Show* and *The Mary Tyler Moore Show* were also personal favourites). That left plenty of time for trying out recipes in her child-sized Easy-Bake Oven and playing with her Barbies, which included Barbie's African American friend Christie, Barbie's boyfriend Ken, Barbie's pink Corvette and, of course, Barbie's Malibu Mansion.

The Robinsons' one extravagance: driving the 180 miles to White Cloud, Michigan, for a week's stay at Duke's Happy Holiday Resort, a vacation destination popular with African American families in the Chicago area. For the most part, however, they stuck close to home – and each other. There were family games of Monopoly, Chinese checkers and a game involving spoons called Hands Down. 'My sister is a poor sport – she really does hate to lose,' said Craig, who claimed he periodically threw games of Monopoly because he had to let her 'win enough so that she wouldn't quit'.

Michelle was driven to succeed from the beginning. 'She wanted to do the right thing all the time without being told,' Marian said, 'and she wanted to be the best at things. She liked winning.'

Often, the only person Michelle was competing with was herself. Once she began taking piano lessons from her great-aunt, Michelle threw herself into the process with such gusto that she exhausted herself and everyone around her. Michelle would come home from school and, without being asked, go straight to the piano and start practising. Hours later, she would still be at the keyboard pounding away – until her frazzled mom finally ordered her to stop.

A bossy streak also surfaced early on. When they played 'office', Michelle insisted that Craig be the businessman while she played the secretary. Then Michelle, with her chubby cheeks, pigtails and a cute chipmunk overbite, proceeded to take on every responsibility so that in the end her older brother 'had absolutely nothing to do'.

Michelle took charge on the playground as well. 'I wouldn't say she ran roughshod over her friends,' Craig said, 'but she was sort of the natural leader.'

If her friends were willing to let her run things, it may have been because she was always considered one of the smartest kids in the neighbourhood. 'As far back as any of us can remember,' Craig said, 'she was very bright.' Like her brother, Michelle skipped the second grade. 'She didn't ever come home with grades that weren't the best,' Marian said. 'She always wanted to do her best, and I don't think it had anything to do with outdoing someone else. It's within her.'

That drive to succeed, and the values that would guide her, stemmed in part from long conversations over the family dinner table. 'Thinking was the big deal – you had to think,' Marian recalled. 'You want your kids early on to start making decisions on their own. You want them to make good decisions but when they make mistakes you want it to be a learning experience. I think that gives kids a lot of confidence. I really did raise my children by ear, day by day.'

Yet, in the Robinson household, parental authority was strictly observed. With Dad away at work, Mom functioned as chief disciplinarian – a position that sometimes required her to administer the infrequent spanking. Dad never had to resort to anything more than a solemn pronouncement. 'I'm disappointed,' he would say, and Craig and Michelle would flee the room in tears.

'We always felt we couldn't let Dad down because he worked so hard for us,' Craig said. 'My sister and I, if ever one of us got in trouble with my father, we'd both be crying. We'd both be like, "Oh, my god,

Dad's upset. How could we do this to him?"' Agreed Michelle, 'You never wanted to disappoint him. We would be bawling.'

If at times they seemed like stern taskmasters, the life lesson they taught their children was an overwhelmingly positive one. 'When you grow up as a black kid in a white world,' Michelle's brother said, 'so many times people are telling you, sometimes not maliciously, sometimes maliciously, you're not good enough. To have a family, which we did, who constantly reminded you how smart you were, how good you were, how pleasant it was to be around you, how successful you could be, it's hard to combat. Our parents gave us a head start by making us feel confident.'

Confidence was something Michelle had in abundance. Unlike her 5 ft 8 in.-tall mother, who hunched over as a teenager because she was self-conscious about her then taller-than-average height, Michelle would always stand ramrod-straight – even when she grew to her full height of 5 ft 11 in. 'I made sure she didn't do what I did,' Marian said. 'I even walked bent over . . . Michelle didn't carry herself like it was any of her concern.'

Nor did Michelle ever hesitate to speak her mind – a trait that delighted her mother. 'I always resented it when I could not say what I felt,' Marian remembered. 'I always felt, "What's wrong with me for not saying what I feel?" Michelle always had her opinions about things and she didn't hesitate to say so because we allowed it.'

Michelle also displayed a quick temper, occasionally confronting other children when she thought they misbehaved. 'If somebody made noise in class, she'd whirl around and "sssshhh" you,' recalled a fellow student at Bryn Mawr Public Elementary School (later renamed Bouchet Academy). 'If somebody was shoving somebody or being mean, she'd tell them to stop. Michelle always had a strong sense of what was right and wrong, and sometimes she'd be a tattletale.' Observed Marian, 'If it's not right, she's going to say so.'

As insistent as Michelle was about everyone following the rules, she was not above challenging her teachers, particularly if she thought she deserved a better grade. She made no effort to conceal her displeasure when things didn't go her way. When a teacher complained that Michelle was having trouble controlling her anger at school, Marian laughed. 'Yeah, she's got a temper all right,' Mom said. 'But we decided to keep her anyway.'

Marian and Fraser had always encouraged Michelle to ask questions. 'Make sure you respect your teachers,' Marian told her children, 'but don't hesitate to question them. Don't even allow us to just say anything to you. Ask us why.'

At age ten – towards the end of a two-year stretch where, inexplicably, she insisted on eating only peanut butter and jelly sandwiches – Michelle was admitted to the gifted programme at Bryn Mawr Elementary. The following year, she and her gifted classmates were taking biology classes at Kennedy-King College, dissecting rodents in one of the college's labs. 'This is not,' said her friend Chiaka Davis Patterson, 'what normal seventh-graders were getting.'

She may have stood tall, but Michelle learned at about this time that standing out was not always a good thing. With those around her getting far fewer opportunities and often facing hardships at home, Michelle taught herself to, as she put it, 'speak two languages' – one to adults and close friends, another to the general population of students. 'If I'm not going to get my butt kicked every day after school,' she said, 'I can't flaunt my intelligence in front of peers who are struggling with a whole range of things . . . You've got to *be* smart without *acting* smart.'

The local public high school was just one block away from their apartment, but the Robinsons had no intention of sending either of their children there. 'We were always driven and we were always encouraged to do the best you can do, not just what's necessary,' Michelle's brother said. 'So naturally we wanted to go to the best schools we could.'

Craig was dispatched to Chicago's Mount Carmel High, a parochial school that was famous for turning out basketball champions who went on to land athletic scholarships. At 6 ft 6 in., Craig quickly distinguished himself as one of the best players the school had ever seen.

A huge opportunity opened up for Michelle in 1975, when the Chicago Board of Education established the Whitney M. Young Magnet High School in the city's West Loop. Aimed at attracting high-achieving students of all races, Whitney Young – named after the long-time executive director of the Urban League – was supposed to be 40 per cent black, 40 per cent Caucasian and 20 per cent 'others'. As it turned out, it was 70 per cent African American when Michelle arrived. Still, it offered the best college-prep courses available, as well as classrooms and facilities that rivalled those of any prep school in the nation. In addition to the usual AP and honours courses, the Whitney M. Young Magnet School had an arrangement with the University of Illinois that allowed Whitney Young students to take courses there for full college credit.

Within months of Whitney Young's opening, Michelle enrolled in the ninth grade. Instead of strolling up the block to public high school, she would have to get up extra early each morning to catch a bus and then a train into the city – a trip that usually took about an hour, sometimes two.

The trek was well worth it. Surrounded by other earnest but friendly overachievers, Michelle fitted right in. She took AP and honours courses, made the honour roll in all four years, earned membership in the National Honor Society, performed ballet in school dance recitals and summoned the courage to speak before hundreds of her classmates when she ran for student council and then for senior class treasurer. (She won that office by a single vote.)

Athletic, long-limbed Michelle might also have been expected to play sports in high school – basketball in particular. After all, her brother was already on the fast track to a basketball scholarship. 'As she got older, because she was tall and black, people assumed she played basketball,' Craig said. 'She hated that. She would never do anything because other people think it's the right thing to do.' That extended to all varsity sports. 'Telling her to do something – that's the best way to get her *not* to do something,' Craig added. 'She didn't want to play just because she was tall and black and athletic.' Sniffed Michelle: 'Tall women *can* do other things.'

When it came to her brother's basketball career, he had no bigger fan than Michelle. Before Craig played in a game, he recalled, 'Michelle would play the piano just to calm me down. It usually worked.' Michelle was so close to her brother, however, that she would walk out of a game if his team was losing because she could not bear to watch.

With her megawatt smile, her almost regal bearing and a casual wardrobe usually consisting of jeans worn with a crisp white shirt, Michelle cut a striking figure at school. The fact that she was one of the tallest girls at Whitney Young also made her stand out.

Perhaps her closest friend during this period was the Reverend Jesse Jackson's daughter Santita, who had grown up in a slightly more upscale part of South Shore and met Michelle in 1977 when they were both 13. Later, when they got their driver's licences, Michelle and Santita car-pooled together.

'Michelle was pretty much liked by everybody,' said one Whitney Young alumnus who knew both young women. 'Michelle and Santita were really tight. Santita wanted to be a singer, and Michelle, well, you knew she wanted to do something big with her life. So it seemed to the rest of us that they belonged together – two special people.'

She may have favourably impressed her peers, but, surrounded as she was so many academic superstars, Michelle made little impression on most of her teachers. When she did manage to grab their attention, it was often as a result of her desire to right a wrong she felt had been done to her.

One afternoon, Michelle took a typing test and hammered out enough words per minute to warrant being given an A. When her teacher gave her a B-plus instead, Michelle objected. She pointed to the chart on the wall that clearly showed she deserved an A. But the teacher refused to acknowledge the mistake and Michelle refused to back down. 'She badgered and badgered that teacher,' her mother recalled. In the end, Marian ended up calling the school. 'Look,' she warned the beleaguered typing instructor, 'Michelle is not going to let this go.' Michelle got her A.

But what really impressed her fellow students was the fact that, in the words of her classmate Norm Collins, Michelle 'seemed to conquer everything effortlessly'. In reality, Michelle usually struggled with tests. 'She was disappointed in herself,' said Marian, who believed she had a psychological block when it came to tests because 'she was hard-working and she had a brother who could pass a test just by carrying a book under his arm. When you are around someone like that, even if you are OK, you want to be as good or better.'

In stark contrast to the situation at many private prep schools across the country, alcohol and drugs were by all accounts not widespread at Whitney Young during Michelle's time there. Most extracurricular fun outside of sports revolved around such quaint 1950s-era activities as dances, carwash-fundraisers and the occasional frenzied food fight. 'Compared to what was going on in other schools,' said a Whitney Young alumnus, 'we were a pretty tame bunch.'

As popular as Michelle was among the girls at Whitney Young, her sunny disposition and toothsome good looks meant that she also seldom lacked for male attention. Unfortunately for the boys who pursued her, Michelle was 'difficult to impress', her mother said. Agreed Craig, 'She didn't suffer fools.' As a result, he added, 'Michelle never really had any serious, long-term boyfriends.'

The reason for Michelle's hard-to-get act was obvious to anyone who witnessed the relationship she had with her father. She watched her father set the bar impossibly high as he struggled each day with the debilitating symptoms of multiple sclerosis. 'My dad was my dad,' Craig said. 'And so she had a definite frame of reference for a guy. She had an imprint in her mind of the kind of guy she wanted.'

Michelle bristled when Craig joked that she was looking for someone who didn't exist. What she was looking for in a guy, she said, was intelligence, hard work 'and some guts'. 'In my house there were no miracles,' Michelle later said. 'All I saw was hard work and sacrifice. My father did not complain and went to work every single day.'

In the middle of her junior year at Whitney Young, Michelle did start going out with a family friend she'd known since she was a toddler. 'I grew up with Michelle and Craig,' David Upchurch said. 'We were neighbours, and our families were close.'

Not coincidentally, Upchurch – tall, athletic, and already sporting a moustache at 17 – bore more than a passing resemblance to Fraser Robinson. But even though the couple dated on and off for the next 18 months, nothing serious would come of it. Apparently Upchurch failed to live up to her dad's formidable example. 'Michelle and I really liked each other,' Upchurch said, 'but you know how some high school boys are. We're not ready to be responsible and we screw up. I was a screw-up, plain and simple!'

Even then, he said, 'Michelle knew what she wanted. She was off to college. I didn't take my future seriously, and I couldn't stand in her way.'

Before they parted ways, Upchurch did take Michelle to the senior prom. In keeping with her growing reputation as something of a fashion plate, Michelle wore a floor-length beige silk gown with a plunging neckline and a provocative slit up the side.

Her family's modest means aside, Michelle developed a taste for the finer things early on. She was adamant, however, that her parents not be faced with footing the bill.

'What's that?' Marian asked one afternoon, eying the stylish leather purse slung over her teenage daughter's shoulder. Marian reached over to touch it. 'Is that a Coach bag?'

'Yes,' Michelle answered matter-of-factly. 'I bought it with my babysitting money.'

'You bought a *Coach* bag with your babysitting money?' she asked, flabbergasted. 'How much was that?'

When Michelle told her the purse cost nearly $300, Marian chided her for her extravagance. 'Yes, Mom,' she explained calmly. 'But you're going to buy ten or twelve purses over the next few years, and all I need is this one.'

Surveying the pile of old purses on the floor of her closet, Marian later came to the conclusion that her daughter had been right. 'She did have that purse for quite a while, and I . . . didn't.'

Money was no object, however, when it came to her children's education. When Craig had to choose between going to the University of Washington on a full scholarship or paying full tuition at Princeton University, his father was adamant that he choose the Ivy League school. 'Go to the best school,' Fraser told both his children. 'Don't worry about the money. We'll find a way.'

As much as he loved basketball, Craig had his eye on a Wall Street career. So for him, the choice was obvious. 'No disrespect to the other schools,' Michelle's brother mused, 'but Wall Street doesn't happen if I'm not at Princeton. Sorry . . .'

Over the next two years, Michelle visited Craig at Princeton and dreamed of some day joining him there. But back at Whitney Young, she received little encouragement. 'Every step of the way,' she said, 'there was somebody there telling me what I couldn't do . . . No one talked to me about going to Princeton or Harvard – or even going to college.' Told by counsellors that her SAT scores and her grades weren't good enough for an Ivy League school, Michelle applied to Princeton and Harvard anyway.

'Princeton, the Ivy Leagues, swoop up kids like Craig,' Michelle said. 'A black kid from the South Side of Chicago that plays basketball and is smart. He was getting in everywhere. But I knew him, and I knew his study habits, and I was, like, "I can do that too."'

It didn't hurt, of course, that her brother was already a student there – not just any student, but one who was on his way to being one of the leading scorers in Ivy League history. Undoubtedly aided by her status a 'legacy' – an applicant who is related either to a current student or an alumnus – Michelle was admitted to Princeton in 1981.

With Fraser Robinson scarcely pulling down $35,000 a year from his job at the water-filtration plant, Marian went back to work after Michelle graduated from high school. The money she earned as an administrative assistant in the trust division of a bank would go almost entirely towards paying the roughly $14,000 annually it was costing to send Craig to Princeton. Now that Michelle was going there too, the cost was doubled – the sum total being more than their father's gross annual income. Michelle's college education would have to be financed almost entirely with student loans.

Given the magnitude of her parents' sacrifice, Michelle was not about to complain to them about the racist attitudes she was encountering at Princeton. 'She didn't talk about it,' Marian said. If her daughter 'did feel different from other people, she didn't let it bother her'.

In truth, Michelle was deeply troubled by the way she and other black students were treated. 'I sometimes feel like a visitor on campus,' she later wrote, 'as if I really don't belong. Regardless of the circumstances under which I interact with whites at Princeton, it often seems as if, to them, I will always be black first and a student second.' Consequently, said Michelle, her undergraduate days 'made me far more aware of my "Blackness" than ever before'.

Princeton's social hierarchy, built around its elite eating clubs, only served to alienate Michelle and her African American friends even more. Functioning like fraternities and sororities, these elegantly appointed clubs were housed in imposing mansions along the campus's main thoroughfare, Prospect Avenue.

Even if she had been admitted into an eating club, Michelle knew she would have been uncomfortable there. Instead, she divided her time between the less exclusive and decidedly more affordable dining facilities in Stevenson Hall and the Third World Center, a social club set up by the university expressly for non-whites on campus.

Although some students baulked at its name – 'We were Americans, not foreign exchange students from some underdeveloped country,' said one – the Third World Center, housed in a nondescript red-brick building, was one of the few places where Michelle could feel at home in the company of other African American Princetonians.

Michelle and her African American friends agreed that they only felt truly comfortable when they could go home and spend time with family. The next-best thing was congregating with other blacks on campus – all but a handful of whom admitted to feeling the same social ostracism Michelle was experiencing. 'The Third World Center was our life,' said Michelle's pal Angela Acree. 'We hung out there, we partied there, we studied there.' Classmate Laurent Robinson-Brown concurred: 'We were each other's support system.'

Michelle, who majored in sociology with a minor in African American studies, took an active role at the TWC, serving on its board and at one point running its after-school programme for the children of Princeton's maintenance and lunch room crews. Michelle's countless hours of self-imposed practice on the piano paid off when she played for children at the school each afternoon. Jonathan Brasuell, who was a second-grader at the time, would recall a quarter of a century later how Michelle played the *Peanuts* theme for him. 'I could not go through a week,' he said, 'without hearing that.'

The TWC also gave Michelle an opportunity to vent as a member of its Black Thoughts Table, a no-holds-barred discussion group on

Kenyan Barack Obama Sr abandoned his
wife and son before the boy's first birthday,
leaving Barry to be raised by his mother
Ann and his maternal grandparents. On a
beach near their home in Hawaii, Stanley
Dunham frolicked with his only grandson.
Half a world away, Michelle Robinson,
shown here at five, was growing up on
Chicago's South Side.

By age nine, Barry was living in Jakarta
with his Indonesian stepfather Lolo Soetoro,
his mom and his baby sister Maya. Back in
Hawaii the following year, Ann and Barry
were visited by Barry's dad for the first
– and last – time.

An emotional Michelle threw her arms around her husband after he delivered the 2004 Democratic Convention keynote address that would put him on the national map. Three months later, the family watched as election returns came in, then celebrated his election to the US Senate from Illinois in a blizzard of confetti.

After a three-year courtship, Barack and Michelle were married on 3 October 1992.

Campaigning in Iowa in August of 2007, Barack and Michelle delighted locals with an impromptu dance, then at the State Fair in Des Moines paired off with Sasha and Malia to compete in carnival games. Riding the bumper cars with Sasha, Barack said, prepared him for the debates with his Democratic primary rivals.

On the campaign trail in June of 2008, Barack and Michelle exchanged knowing glances at a rally in Saint Paul, Minnesota, and as they were introduced by Ohio Governor Ted Strickland in Columbus, Ohio. Several weeks later, a *New Yorker* cover intended to poke fun at rumours swirling about them backfired, igniting a firestorm of controversy.

Vacationing in Kailua, Hawaii, in August of 2008, Barack strolled the beach with Malia and Sasha.

The candidate and his wife beamed while they cast their votes at Chicago's Beulah Shoesmith Elementary School. That evening, the family waved to an emotional crowd of more than 200,000 gathered in Grant Park to celebrate Barack's historic victory.

Ensconced at Washington's Hay-Adams Hotel, the president-elect and his wife got up early to send Malia and Sasha off on their first day at Sidwell Friends School.

Malia and Sasha looked on proudly as Daddy took the oath of office as 44th president of the United States – an oath that, because of a mistake by Chief Justice John Roberts, would have to be repeated in private the next day. In between, the new commander-in-chief danced the night away with his First Lady at no fewer than ten inaugural balls.

Although they left for a quick trip to Chicago just three weeks after taking office, the Obamas now considered 1600 Pennsylvania Avenue home. On 22 February 2009, the nation's hostess dazzled guests at her first formal White House affair, the Governors Ball.

After hesitating at first, Marian Robinson, a constant presence in her grandchildren's lives, agreed to move into the White House to help out. Grandma joined Malia and Sasha in the East Room to hear the all-female a cappella group Sweet Honey in the Rock.

In the midst of the nation's most severe economic crisis since the Great Depression, Michelle joined students from Washington's Bancroft Elementary School to break ground for the White House Kitchen Garden on the South Lawn.

During the Obamas' first trip abroad as
First Couple, Michelle shattered centuries
of English tradition when she and Queen
Elizabeth put their arms around each other
– the first time anyone could remember
Her Majesty being physically affectionate
towards anyone, including members
of her own family. On that same trip,
thousands turned out to greet them
in Paris, Berlin and Prague.

At one of ten inaugural balls held in
Washington, the Obamas beamed as
they danced to their appropriately titled
theme song for the evening, 'At Last'.

the topic of race. She also joined a group called the Organization of Black Unity, which had as its unofficial headquarters the Third World Center. Among other things, the Organization of Black Unity arranged speakers and programmes aimed at Princeton's small African American population.

Michelle had plenty of complaints about the way things were done at Princeton, and not all of them had to do with race. She was a vocal critic of the language programme. 'But you're teaching French all wrong,' she told one of her teachers. 'It's not conversational enough.' Craig winced when he heard what Michelle had said. 'All you can do,' he said, 'is pretend you don't know her.'

Eager to contribute to fundraising efforts at the Third World Center, Michelle took part in two fashion shows. In one, to benefit the TWC's after-school programme, she modelled a canary-yellow Caribbean peasant skirt. For a 'Secret Fantasy'-themed show to benefit the Ethiopian Relief Fund, she walked down the runway in a sleeveless red velvet ball-gown.

Raising awareness was one thing, but rocking the boat was quite another. There were student protests against apartheid and over Princeton's investments in South Africa. Not only did Michelle decline to take part in any of these demonstrations, she did not show up when her South Side neighbour Jesse Jackson appeared on campus to speak.

Like many other students, Michelle did not want to risk being arrested at one of these events. 'Remember, most of us black students had no social safety net,' said classmate Hilary Beard. 'You had an opportunity to change the arc of your life and you were not going to mess it up.'

Besides, race was not the only thing that separated Michelle and her friends from Princeton's in-crowd. Far from it. 'Of course it was different not being black,' she said. 'It was also different not being filthy rich. At the end of the year, these limos would come to get kids, and me and my brother would be carrying our cardboard boxes down to the train station.'

Although there was no shortage of students at Princeton receiving some sort of financial aid, the university was still populated to a large extent by the sons and daughters of the well-to-do. As a group, they summered on Nantucket or in the Hamptons, competed at crew, lacrosse or tennis, and paid hefty fees to park their Jeeps, Land Rovers and Porsches on campus. They often knew how to land the largest suites in the most desirable residence halls, and their parents would often spare no expense in decorating them.

Around campus, Michelle did what she could to keep up appearances. 'Michelle was always fashionably dressed, even on a budget,' Angela Acree said. 'You wouldn't catch her in sweats, even back then.' But when it came to their living conditions, Michelle and her three roommates had few options. 'We were not rich,' Angela Acree said. 'A lot of kids had TVs and sofas and chairs. We didn't. We couldn't afford any furniture, so we just had pillows on the floor, and a stereo.' To make matters worse, Michelle and her three roommates had to walk down three flights of stairs to use their dormitory's only bathroom.

Michelle's stereo would prove to be a magnet for other African Americans on campus, many drawn to hear her extensive collection of Stevie Wonder records. Music was just one more thing that separated the races at Princeton. While the vast majority of the student body leaned heavily towards the whitebread likes of Van Halen, Hall and Oates, The Police, Blondie and Billy Joel, Michelle's group preferred R&B, Motown, reggae and rap.

'The white people didn't dance – I know that sounds like a cliché – and they also played a completely different kind of music,' Acree said. 'Whereas we were playing Luther Vandross and Run-DMC.'

Michelle never allowed such distractions to get in the way of work; unlike so many college students, she did not wait until the last minute to write a paper or cram for an exam. 'She was not a procrastinator,' Acree observed. Instead, Michelle did her work in advance so that she would not be facing down a deadline the following day. But within the narrow confines of their sparsely furnished dorm room – where they felt free to be themselves – Michelle and her girlfriends traded gossip and, Acree said, 'giggled and laughed hysterically'.

For Michelle, romance would not figure into the Princeton equation. Craig Robinson blamed himself. During the two years they overlapped at Princeton, Michelle was to some extent overshadowed by her big brother the basketball star. 'I may have scared them off without even knowing it at the time,' Craig speculated.

In Craig's defence, Michelle actually sent prospective boyfriends to play basketball with her brother. 'You can tell an awful lot about someone by the way they play,' Craig said. 'She wanted me to size them up and report back.'

Whatever the reason, no one asked Michelle out during her freshman and sophomore years. She fared only slightly better in her last two years at Princeton. Once again, the few young men who did ask her out seldom advanced to a second date. If there was a Robinson man to blame for this, it wasn't Craig. 'Dad again,' he said. 'No one could live up to him in her eyes.' Indeed, Michelle still took such emotional sustenance from her father that on visits home from college she unhesitatingly curled up in his lap.

As her four years at Princeton drew to a close, she seemed more torn than ever about her experience there. She addressed the problem head-on in her senior thesis, arguing that, at least for now, true inclusion by whites was beyond the reach of even those African Americans educated at Ivy League universities. Throughout the dissertation, as if to emphasise the significance of racial identity, she capitalised the words *Black* and *White*.

'Earlier in my college career,' she wrote in 'Princeton-Educated Blacks and the Black Community', 'there was no doubt in my mind that as a member of the Black community I was somehow obligated to this community and would utilise all of my present and future resources to benefit this community first and foremost.' But, she continued, 'as I enter my final year at Princeton, I find myself striving for many of the same goals as my White classmates . . . The path I have chosen . . . will likely lead to my further integration and/or assimilation into a White cultural and social structure that will only allow me to remain on the periphery of society; never becoming a full participant.' This realisation, Michelle then explained, only served to strengthen her resolve to do something for her fellow African Americans.

Michelle dedicated her thesis to the important people in her life: 'Mom, Dad, Craig and all of my special friends. Thank you for loving me and always making me feel good about myself.'

Even before her senior year, Michelle had begun to map out a career path for herself. Already adept at networking – she had carefully cultivated friendships with some of the best and brightest at Princeton – Michelle visited the university's career-services office and pored over a list of alumni willing to give career advice.

She ran her slender finger down the list of alumni in the Chicago area and stopped at the name of Stephen Carlson. Noting that he was a partner in the heavyweight corporate law firm Sidley Austin (which boasted of once having Mary Todd Lincoln as a client), Michelle wrote to Carlson. But instead of advice, she asked him point-blank for a summer job.

Unfortunately, summer jobs in law firms were invariably reserved for law school students. But Carlson was so impressed by Michelle's chutzpah that he wrote back with a list of legal aid organisations in Chicago that did hire undergraduates to do research. Following Carlson's lead, Michelle spent that summer working part-time at a legal aid agency not far from her parents' South Side home.

Back at Princeton, Michelle agonised over what to do following graduation. 'The question was, were you a traitor to your race for going to a white-dominated school at all,' mused another black Princetonian. 'Michelle had crossed that threshold in going to Princeton. But she was concerned as she considered law school, is it still an OK thing to do?'

By the time she graduated *cum laude* from Princeton, Michelle had convinced herself that she would need a law degree if she was to make a real contribution to the black community in Chicago. Once again, her parents told her to ignore the cost. 'It would be foolish to go this far,' said Fraser, who now walked with the aid of two canes, 'to get this far in your education and end up going to a second-rate law school.'

When she arrived on the Cambridge, Massachusetts, campus of Harvard University in the autumn of 1984, Michelle stepped into an environment not unlike the one she had just left. The division between whites and non-whites – and between haves and have-nots – was clearly drawn. Once again, the student body was top-heavy with what Michelle disparagingly called 'rich kids' and the law school faculty was straight out of *The Paper Chase* – dour-faced white men in plaid blazers with patches on the elbows, all waiting to pounce on those students unwise enough to show up in class unprepared.

Most galling for Michelle was the continuing assumption that the standards had been lowered to allow her and other black students in. While Michelle had no reason to believe that was the case, other black students acknowledged that it may well have been. Michelle 'realised that she had been privileged by affirmative action,' said her friend and classmate Verna Williams, 'and she was very comfortable with that.'

As she had at Princeton, Michelle became involved in the leading African American organisation on campus – the Black Law Students Association – and wrote for the *BlackLetter Law Journal*, an alternative to the *Harvard Law Review* aimed at minority students. She also signed petitions demanding that there be greater minority representation on the faculty. But beyond that, Michelle demurred when asked to take part in protests or demonstrations that might result in disciplinary action or arrest.

Within the confines of the Black Law Students Association, Michelle was not reluctant to speak out on racial issues. 'We got into big debates on the condition of black folks in America,' Verna Williams said. 'She's got a temper.' When the subject of race came up elsewhere, however, Michelle usually remained quiet. 'She kept her feelings to herself most of the time,' another friend said, 'because she didn't want to be pigeonholed as just another angry black person. She didn't want to be defined solely by her race. Michelle had lots to say about lots of other things.'

That was particularly evident in David B. Wilkins's course on the legal profession. During each class, Professor Wilkins grilled students on how they would behave when confronted with an ethical dilemma. 'Not surprisingly,' Wilkins said, 'many students shy away from putting themselves on the line in this way, preferring to hedge their bets or deploy technical arguments that seem to absolve them from the responsibilities of decision making.' Not Ms Robinson. 'Michelle,' Wilkins continued, 'had no need for such fig leaves. She always stated her position clearly and decisively.'

That ability so impressed Verna Williams that she asked Michelle to be her partner in a mock trial. 'She had incredible presence,' Williams said. 'She was very, very smart, very charismatic, very well spoken.'

A student who possessed these gifts might have been expected to go straight to the *Harvard Law Review*, a traditional path to a Supreme Court clerkship or, at the very least, a job with one of the nation's top law firms. Instead, Michelle chose to spend whatever time she could outside the classroom toiling in the cluttered offices of the school's legal aid bureau.

Like the other students who chose to participate, Michelle pledged to devote a minimum of 20 hours each week to handling the legal woes of the Boston area's poor population. Michelle helped out in the bureau's divorce clinic, worked at hammering out settlements in child custody disputes and fought to obtain various benefits for people who had been denied them. But housing issues consumed most of Michelle's time at the bureau. Having seen so many of her Chicago neighbours struggle to pay the rent, she fought hard for families facing eviction or suffering at the hands of an unscrupulous landlord.

Many of her colleagues who came from more affluent backgrounds were witnessing urban poverty up close for the first time. A few, tired and frustrated, became emotional. Michelle, who had little patience for such self-indulgent displays, waited until she was back in her residence hall to vent her frustration. 'Oh, pul-leeze,' Michelle complained to one of her African American classmates. 'Do you think these people want to hear some rich white girl crying? They've got *real* problems. Give me a break!'

Michelle's legal aid experience was the most rewarding of her academic career and seemed to point to a future in public service. The thrust of the Harvard Law School curriculum, however, was decidedly in the direction of corporate law. Towards that end, she followed Chicago lawyer Stephen Carlson's advice and spent the summer following her second year working for Carlson's high-powered law firm, Sidley Austin.

As she approached graduation, Michelle faced a hard reality: she had massive student loans to repay, and her parents, who had sacrificed so much to send both children to Ivy League schools, were deep in debt. When Sidley Austin, then the fifth-largest law firm in the world, offered Michelle a job with a starting salary of nearly $70,000 (the equivalent of around $100,000 in 2009), she grabbed it. 'The idea of making more money than both your parents combined ever made,' she later said, 'is one you don't walk away from.'

'She came to Harvard Law School with no ambiguity about her race or gender,' said her law school advisor, Charles Ogletree. Michelle had decided that she 'would navigate corporate America, but never forget her father's values or where she came from'.

In the summer of 1988, Michelle moved back into her parents' tiny apartment on South Euclid Avenue and began making the daily commute to Sidley Austin's offices in the Loop. Within a week, she asked to be assigned to the firm's intellectual property group. Compared to such humdrum subdisciplines as antitrust or contract law, intellectual property (along with entertainment and marketing law) involved representing a wide variety of high-profile clients, from TV production companies, clothing manufacturers, radio stations and breweries to record producers, advertising agencies and sports figures.

As a result, the mood was usually upbeat in the intellectual property corridor, where lawyers read scripts as well as briefs and occasionally lunched with celebrity clients. Michelle, however, picked this area of the law over the others for more practical reasons: since there were only a few lawyers assigned to the intellectual property group, she stood a greater chance of making an impression – and advancing more quickly through the ranks.

Michelle was, in a word, ambitious. Not merely ambitious but, said Quincy White, her boss at the time, 'quite possibly the most ambitious associate I've ever seen'. From the outset, she demanded – and got – plum assignments that otherwise would have gone to more senior members of the firm.

When the firm was hired to handle the legal affairs of a beloved children's TV character named Barney, Michelle jumped at the chance. For the next year, she hammered out deals with stations that wanted to air the wildly popular show and oversaw the marketing of stuffed toys based on the talkative purple dinosaur and his sidekick, Baby Bop.

That was not enough for Michelle, however, so once again she complained to her superiors and was handed another plum client – Coors beer. Notwithstanding the fact that the Coors account was considered one of the most interesting, challenging and, of course, visible assignments any lawyer at the firm could hope for, Michelle soon grew restless. No job the firm could give her, White later reflected, would satisfy Michelle's overriding 'ambition to change the world'.

Something was indeed missing from Michelle's life – something that no job could fill. Still living at home at a time when most of her childhood friends had moved on, Michelle seldom socialised with her co-workers and dated only sporadically. Her job at Sidley Austin had become her life.

Meanwhile, the rest of the Robinsons were busy wringing their hands over Michelle's chances of ever having a serious relationship. 'Oh, my god,' Craig told his parents, 'my sister's never getting married because each guy she meets, she's going to chew him up, spit him out.'

Whenever she did go out once or twice with a guy, she ended up, in Craig's words, 'firing him. She'd just fire these guys, one after the other. It was brutal. Some of them were great guys, but they didn't stand a chance.' Once again, Dad was to blame. Marian had given up telling Michelle to stop measuring the men she dated against her father. 'She wouldn't listen,' Marian said. 'She wanted the kind of marriage I had.'

So now it was up to Craig to step in. 'Look, Miche,' Craig said, taking his sister aside after she 'fired' yet another prospective mate. 'You're not going to find guys who are going to be perfect, because they didn't have Dad as a father. So you've got to sort of come up with your own framework.'

'Nope,' Michelle replied matter-of-factly. 'I'm not looking for Dad, but I'm not about to settle, either.'

'But Miche . . .'

'Hey,' she shot back, holding up her hand to silence her brother, 'it's *my* life. You guys have got to stop worrying about me. The right guy is out there, and I'll know him when I see him.'

Hers is the voice I hear inside my head when I make decisions.

Barack

It takes a lot to push his buttons.
He has incredibly low blood pressure.

Michelle

4

He must have driven past Michelle's house a thousand times in his beaten-up Honda without ever knowing it. As soon as he landed there in the summer of 1985, Barack criss-crossed Chicago's South Side in search of African American pastors willing to band together for the common good.

After all, it had been two years since black voters joined together with Latinos and white liberals to send Harold Washington to City Hall as Chicago's first black mayor. Now that Barack had been hired by veteran community organiser Jerry Kellman to bring black churches together as part of his Developing Communities Project, he had little doubt that he would succeed.

Barack had been in Chicago just once before, at the age of ten, when his grandmother had taken him and his half-sister Maya on a month-long whirlwind tour of the US mainland. But he knew from carefully studying the works of Martin Luther King Jr that the South Side of Chicago had been the epicentre of the civil rights movement in the north – the 'capital of the African American community,' Obama proclaimed, as well as 'the birthplace of community organising'.

Chicago was also the home of Saul Alinksy, the leftist firebrand whose 1947 book *Reveille for Radicals* was widely regarded as the bible of the protest movement. Colourful, outspoken and often outrageous, Alinksy believed the only way to effect change was by confronting power – with boycotts, protest marches, sit-ins and strikes. The agitator emeritus believed in a win-at-all-costs approach in the battle for power and that required zeroing in with laser-like focus on one's enemies. Advised Alinksy: 'Pick the target, freeze it, personalise it and polarise it.'

But there was also a more pragmatic side to Alinsky's teachings – one that appealed to the 23-year-old biracial Ivy Leaguer. Alinksy, rightly considered the founder of community organising, advised activists to immerse themselves in the culture and language of the people they hoped to represent. Towards that end, he urged organisers to learn 'the local legends, anecdotes, values, idioms' and listen carefully to their grievances. It was only by bonding with the poor and disenfranchised on a personal level, Alinksy argued, that community organisers could help them acquire the only thing that counted: power.

It was a message that had been not lost on a young Wellesley College student named Hillary Rodham back in the late 1960s. For her trenchant analysis of Alinksy and Chicago's Community Action Program, part of the larger War on Poverty, the future Mrs Bill Clinton received an A-plus.

Hillary so impressed Alinsky that he offered her a chance to work with him after she graduated from Wellesley, but she turned him down. Instead, choosing the same road Barack would choose years later, Hillary applied to several of the country's top law schools. Accepted by both Harvard and and Yale law schools, Hillary chose Yale. 'The only way to make a real difference,' Hillary told Alinsky when he accused her of selling out, 'is to acquire power.'

Jerry Kellman, the battle-scarred community organiser who had lured Barack to Chicago, was another of Alinsky's loyal disciples. In bringing Chicago's black churches under the banner of the Developing Communities Project, Barack would willingly employ Alinsky's methods.'Once I found an issue people cared about,' he reasoned, 'I could take them into action. With enough actions, I could start to build power.'

That Chicago's black churches were a repository of political power was undeniable. But, as Barack soon discovered, the ministers who wielded that power were loath to share it with anyone. Those pastors who deigned to meet with him at all dismissed Barack as a naive young do-gooder. The response at the grassroots level was no less discouraging. As the old Chicago saying went, 'We don't want nobody that nobody sent.'

'Well,' Barack's fellow organiser Mike Kruglik said, 'Barack was somebody that nobody sent.'

Discouraged but not defeated, Barack persevered. Operating out of a cramped office at Holy Rosary Church at 113th Street and Calumet Avenue, he followed Jerry Kellman's explicit instructions to contact 30 people every day. Older black women, understandably, were the first to warm to the skinny young man with the cherubic looks. They called him 'Baby Face'.

'He was a skinny young man,' Jerry Kellman said. 'And in some of the communities he worked, there were a lot single moms, single grandmothers, and they wanted to take him in and feed him and fatten him up. He was an eligible young man. They wanted to introduce him to their daughters and to their granddaughters . . .' According to Kellman, Barack 'found a home' in Chicago and was 'very comfortable there'.

Three women in particular – Linda Randle, Yvonne Lloyd and Loretta Augustine-Herron – became nothing less than surrogate mothers to Barack. 'He was so *young* – most of us had children who were older than he was,' Augustine-Herron remembered. 'It's funny to look back now and realise that even then, when he was just 23, nobody challenged him. We accepted him immediately because he had a way of making you know right off the bat that he really cared. He listened – really listened – which was something none of us were used to.'

Barack pushed his surrogate moms and other community activists to stand up for themselves against landlords and bureaucrats. Towards that end, he would put them through their paces with hours of role-playing so that they could state their case to the appropriate authorities. 'We'd say, "Barack, why don't *you* do this?"' Yvonne Lloyd recalled, 'and he'd say, "No, this is your community, not mine. You all need to this for yourselves, not for me."' When tempers ran high, as they often did, it was Barack who 'told everyone to calm down and stay focused,' Linda Randle said. 'We were all strong women and pretty high-strung anyway. He'd say, "All you're raising is your blood pressure. We'll take the high road." He was always cool, nothing ever seemed to bother him.'

Yet Randle, Augustine-Herron, Lloyd and the others worried about him. 'He worked ten, twelve hours a day,' Augustine-Herron said. 'He never ate anything except salads. We told him he was too skinny, and he'd just laugh.'

They were also concerned that he did not seem to have time for anything except work and his cat, Max. 'He worked day and night,' Lloyd said. 'I don't know if he ever slept.' When he bought a used yellow Datsun 210 hatchback from a Glenview, Illinois, police officer for $500, they had even more cause for concern. The Datsun (Barack said it reminded him of an 'over-ripe banana') was pitted with rust and had a hole in the door that allowed passengers to watch the pavement zipping by.

'All of us would cram into Barack's little car,' Lloyd said, 'and I'd ask, "Why are you drivin' around in this raggedy thing? When are you going to get a real car?"'

'Hey,' Barack always answered with a laugh, 'it gets me from point A to point B, right?'

As eager as they might have initially been to set him up with their daughters and the daughters of friends, the church ladies who were such a large part of Barack's life during this period – he now referred to them as 'my other family' – soon realised that he preferred to keep the details of his love life to himself.

'Barack definitely dated,' Jerry Kellman said. 'But he was just too driven to get deeply involved with a woman.' With one exception: for several months, Barack lived with a dark-haired young white woman who would remain a mystery even to his church moms. 'They were obviously both very private people when it came to that,' Augustine-Herron said. 'They obviously wanted to keep the details of whatever it was they had to themselves.'

For the most part, over the two and a half years he spent as a community organiser, life for Barack was one mind-numbing meeting after another. Lloyd recalled that he was always jotting thoughts down in an ever-present notebook, ostensibly for the purpose of reporting back to his superiors. He also liked to doodle caricatures – usually of dour-looking officials he would draw laughing. A few of his doodles were less charitable – like the ones that depicted certain pastors or intransigent city officials with pointy heads.

To be sure, Barack could boast of a few concrete achievements at community organising during his initial stint in Chicago. The most significant of these was his participation in a very public crusade – actually spearheaded by fellow activist Hazel Johnson – to remove asbestos from Altgeld Gardens, a decaying public housing project that was home to over 2,000 people.

Barack's main assignment – to bring together the black churches as a single, monolithic force for good – did not go quite so smoothly. 'The pastors of these churches were used to running things. They weren't interested in sharing the power and the glory with anybody else,' Randle said. 'You're talking about some pretty big egos.'

One of those who first pointed out to Barack the folly of this approach happened to be the South Side's most flamboyant and influential black clergyman, the Reverend Jeremiah Alvesta Wright. The son of a Philadelphia preacher, Wright had been arrested for grand theft auto at the age of 15, enlisted in the Marines and then served as a Navy corpsman specialising in cardiopulmonary care. In his office, Wright displayed a photo of himself in scrubs tending to President Lyndon Johnson following LBJ's throat surgery in 1966.

Wright went on to earn a master's degree in sacred music from Howard University. Through a combination of bombast and showmanship, the dapper, goatee-sporting minister built Trinity United Church of Christ at Ninety-fifth and Parnell streets into an ecclesiastical powerhouse with over 8,000 congregants.

Wright was one of the first church leaders Barack had approached in his efforts to build a coalition of black churches. The brawny minister, who had placed a 'Free Africa' sign on the church lawn to protest apartheid, had listened patiently as Barack made his case.

'Oh, that sounds good, Barack, real good,' Wright said, his voice tinged with sarcasm. 'But you don't know Chicago, do you?'

Barack looked puzzled. 'You are a minister,' he said. 'Why are you sounding so sceptical?'

'Man, these preachers in Chicago,' Wright told him. 'You are not going to organise us. That's not going to happen.'

'But why—?'

'Barack,' Wright interrupted, 'no, no, no. Not going to happen.'

They were not the words Barack had wanted to hear, but in time he came to appreciate Wright's candour. So much so that, when the time came to determine which church would be appropriate for him to join – a process that involved Barack actually interviewing each pastor – he ultimately chose Trinity United. There was an added advantage to joining Trinity United: it sat just outside the boundaries of Barack's carefully circumscribed organising district. 'Trinity was as close as it could be to the area Barack was operating in without actually being in it,' said Alvin Love, pastor of Lilydale First Baptist Church and one of the local clergyman who worked closely with Barack. 'If he joined my church or any of the others he was working with, it would look like he was playing favourites. He got around that problem by joining Trinity.'

Not that Barack had ever been much of a churchgoer. He had inherited a distinctly laid-back attitude towards religion from his parents and his grandparents, and although he had sampled both the Christian and Muslim faiths as a child, Barack considered himself something of an agnostic by the time he arrived in Chicago.

Now that he had bonded with his fellow African Americans in the City of Big Shoulders, he realised that something was missing. Those wonderful, warm grandmothers and mothers notwithstanding, he still felt emotionally isolated, a person apart. He could never fully share in the black experience, he realised, without belonging to a church.

'Early on,' a confidant later said, Barack 'was in search of his identity as an African American and, more importantly, as an African American man.' Jeremiah Wright 'was instrumental in helping him understand the black experience in America'.

But Trinity United wasn't just any African American church. It was the church of Chicago's black elite. When Oprah Winfrey arrived in Chicago from Baltimore in 1984, joining Trinity was a way for her to connect with the established movers and shakers in Chicago's black community.

What they got was a heavy dose of Afrocentrist, black-liberation theology. Often clad in a colourful dashiki, Wright devoted much of his time at the pulpit to railing against whites in general and the US government in particular. With Ronald Reagan in the White House during his stint in Chicago as a community organiser, Barack often heard Wright blame Reagan's America for many if not most of the world's ills. 'A nation that will keep people in slavery for 244 years will exploit poor people generally,' Wright said, adding that 'all of America's wealth today could not adequately compensate us for centuries of exploitation and humiliation'.

Less than a year before Wright met Barack, the reverend had accompanied his friend Louis Farrakhan, controversial head of the Nation of Islam, to visit Libyan strongman Mu'ammer Gaddafi. Trinity United gave Farrakhan, a virulent anti-Semite who called Judaism a 'gutter religion', praised Hitler as 'a very great man' and described white people as 'potential humans', a lifetime achievement 'Empowerment Award' for his 'commitment to truth, education and leadership'.

In addition to praising Farrakhan in his sermons, Wright denounced his own countrymen as 'war criminals', described America's military as 'some demonic destructive suction tube' and proclaimed that the US had 'committed more war crimes almost than any other nation in the world and we won't stop because of our pride, our arrogance as nation'. To Wright, America was simply 'the greatest purveyor of violence in the world'.

Wright, said Chicago journalist Salim Muwakkil, 'had the reputation of a militant guy who provided kind of a vicarious militance for Chicago's black elites. So they could get a dose of militance on Sunday and go back home and feel pretty good about doing their part for the black movement.'

Barack was intrigued by Wright's message of black empowerment; the pastor's rantings against the 'white power' structure in Washington and the state of Israel – not to mention his defence of Communists in Nicaragua and the Castro regime in Cuba – were met by a chorus of amens every week, and fellow churchgoers remember that Barack chimed in with the rest.

Wright's politically charged sermons weren't the only thing that distinguished him from his fellow black clergymen. While most African American pastors regarded homosexuality as a sin, Wright was an ardent supporter of gay rights.

Trinity United's policy of inclusion undoubtedly appealed to

Barack, as did Wright's passionate take on the black experience in America. But just as important was the calibre of people who flocked to Trinity United each Sunday. The congregation included doctors, lawyers, entrepreneurs, sports figures and recording stars. None shone brighter than Oprah. Although she would apparently not recall it, Oprah first met the fresh-faced community organiser when he walked up to her after services and introduced himself as a big fan. 'Oprah was already a big, big deal,' one church member recalled. 'Barack couldn't take his eyes off her. I think that's when it clicked, you know, like "this is the place where I gotta be!"'

Chicago City Alderman Toni Preckwinkle agreed. 'Not only does it have one of the largest African American congregations in the city,' Preckwinkle said, 'but there are a lot of influential people among the parishioners. It's certainly a good place for a young politician looking to make social connections.' Preckwinkle believed Wright was the deciding factor in Barack's decision to join Trinity United. 'Jeremiah Wright is a powerful speaker and a very charismatic individual.' Barack, she believed, 'could not have helped but be impressed by him'.

Jeremiah Wright was not the only black leader Barack idolised. Mayor Harold Washington had become a bona fide hero to the black citizens of Chicago, and when he died of a massive coronary in November of 1987, they were devastated. Barack was no exception. Depressed and discouraged by his limited success as a community organiser, Barack set his sights on a specific goal: to become the next black mayor of Chicago.

Barack surveyed the political scene and noticed that Washington – and for that matter, most elected officials – had one thing he did not: a law degree. 'I'm not going to accomplish anything significant,' he told Wright, 'unless I get a law degree.'

Aiming for the top, Barack enlisted the help of several influential figures to get him into Harvard Law School. One of Barack's more colourful Chicago associates was Khalid Abdullah Tariq al-Mansour, a radical Muslim who had been a mentor of Black Panther Party founders Bobby Seale and Huey Newton. At al-Mansour's request, Percy Sutton, the respected New York political figure who had once been Malcolm X's lawyer, wrote a letter of recommendation on behalf of Barack. So did Northwestern University professor John McKnight, another disciple of Saul Alinsky who had been impressed by Barack's work in the community.

In February of 1988, Barack received notice of his acceptance to Harvard Law School. Before he left, he returned to Trinity United to hear Reverend Wright give yet another sermon – one that, he would later say, changed his life.

Wright spoke of a painting entitled *Hope*, which depicts a harpist sitting on a mountaintop. On closer examination, Wright continued, the woman 'is bruised and bloodied, dressed in tattered rags, the harp reduced to a single frayed string'. In the valley below, 'everywhere are the ravages of famine, the drumbeat of war, a world groaning under strife and deprivation'.

Although years later he would claim not to have been aware of Wright's more incendiary comments, the reverend used this sermon – Barack's favourite – to denounce the bombing of Hiroshima as genocide, attack the callousness of US government leaders and proclaim 'white folks' greed runs a world in need'. Still, the overriding message of the sermon was one of hope – or, to be precise, the 'audacity' of hope.

'Hope! The harpist,' Wright continued, 'is looking upwards, a few faint notes floating upwards towards the heavens. She dares to hope . . . She has the audacity . . . to make music . . . and praise God . . . on the one string she has left! . . . The audacity of hope! The audacity of hope.'

The sermon, which also drew parallels between American blacks emerging from slavery and the Jews being led out of Egypt, reduced Barack to tears. 'Those stories – of survival and freedom, and hope – became our story, my story,' he later recalled. 'The blood that had spilled was our blood, the tears our tears; until this black church, on this bright day, seemed once more a vessel carrying the story of a people into future generations and into a larger world.'

At another Sunday-morning service, the Reverend Wright would baptise Barack. As moving as Wright's 'Audacity of Hope' sermon had been, Barack would later concede this was a calculated decision

– a matter 'of choice and not an epiphany'. The doubts he had about religion 'did not magically disappear'. By formally joining Trinity United and accepting Wright as his spiritual mentor, Barack embraced a tradition of faith that had sustained the black community through slavery and segregation. He was also signalling to Chicago's African American community that he intended to return and be a part of it.

But first he would have to relocate to Boston and earn that all-important Ivy League law degree. In this new phase of his life, there was no place for the young woman he had been living with. 'It was the one time when Barack seemed to be really stressed,' Loretta Augustine-Herron said. 'He broke it off because he didn't think the situation was fair to her – he didn't want her to put her life on hold for him, which she had offered to do. But Barack was pretty upset about leaving – it seemed to me that he obviously cared for her – and he seemed to be asking if it was the right thing to do.'

Offering what she described as 'words of motherly advice', Augustine-Herron told him, 'Look, if you need to go to Harvard, then go. If she puts her life on hold for you, then the day will come when she will resent you. And if you put your life on hold for her, then the day will come when you resent her. So you're doing the right thing.'

Before starting classes at Harvard, Barack decided to see a bit of that larger world. The year before, Lolo Soetoro, the Indonesian stepfather he had once been so close to, had died of a liver ailment at the age of 51. Like Barack's biological father, Lolo had been disappointed by life and sought to mask that disappointment with alcohol. This latest death in Barack's far-flung family prompted him to once again turn outward, away from America, in search of his identity.

First, he spent three weeks in Europe before deciding it wasn't really where he wanted to be. The maternal side of his family may have been firmly rooted in the soil of England and Scotland, but that was of little consequence to someone the world saw as black. 'It wasn't that Europe wasn't beautiful,' Barack said. 'It just wasn't mine.'

Kenya, however, was Barack's. His subsequent five-week-long pilgrimage to his father's homeland would be a transformative experience for Barack. Not only would he meet many of his Kenyan relatives (including at least five brothers, two sisters, a step-grandmother and assorted uncles, aunts, cousins and stepmothers); Barack would also finally confront the bitter truth about his father.

None of this came quickly. When he first set foot on African soil, Barack had expected to experience a soul-jarring sense of 'homecoming' – an instant and visceral connection with the land of his ancestors. Instead, the grinding poverty he witnessed as he made his way to his ancestral village of Nyang'oma Kogelo – first by all-night train and then via an overcrowded *matatu* (jitney) with bald tyres – left him feeling 'exhausted and numb'.

Gradually, as family members welcomed the young American into their lives and answered many of the lingering questions about his father that had haunted him since childhood, Barack would begin to experience the same stirrings of self-realisation that many of his friends had talked about after they visited Africa for the first time. It was a gradual process, one that by necessity would require a 'span of weeks or months', he would later write, during which time 'you could experience . . . the freedom of believing your hair grows as it's supposed to grow and that your rump sways the way a rump is supposed to sway . . . Here the world was black, and so you were just you.' Coming on the heels of his Chicago interlude, this voyage of self-discovery to Africa would at long last enable Barack to reconcile the two halves of his divided inheritance.

Barack stood out from the crowd the moment he set foot in Harvard Square – and not just because he was the son of a Midwestern white woman and an African man. Barack was, at twenty-seven, five years older than most of his fellow first-year law students. He had also been raised in Hawaii and Indonesia, attended college in California and New York, and worked as a community organiser in one of Chicago's toughest neighbourhoods. As had been the case at Occidental and Columbia, he seemed to possess a kind of quiet confidence and maturity – 'suave and debonair' were the words one female classmate chose to describe him – that impressed students and faculty members alike.

Michelle Robinson had graduated just a few months before Barack arrived at Harvard, and the atmosphere was just as tense. 'There was,' recalled Harvard law professor Laurence Tribe, 'a very rich stew of issues there to greet him.' At the law school, black students continued to press for more minority representation on the faculty, and one professor, Derrick Bell, quit in protest.

Barack stood on the law school steps before a lunchtime crowd to publicly laud Bell for his courage – and kidded the professor about how much he was appreciated for his 'good looks and easy charm'. He also joined the Black Law Students Association, where he called upon his own experiences as an activist in Chicago in urging his fellow African Americans on campus to commit to giving something back to the less fortunate in their communities after they graduated. 'Everybody says they're going to give back,' Barack observed, 'but sometimes there's a mighty chasm between the saying and the doing.'

For the most part, however, Harvard Law was a repeat of Barack's near-monastic experience at Columbia years earlier. Between hastily consumed meals at the C'est Bon sandwich shop in Harvard Square, he hunkered down in the poorly lit law library, a serious, solitary figure poring over case law and statutes well into the night.

Larry Tribe, one of Harvard's best-known constitutional scholars, was so impressed with Barack that he took him on as his research assistant. 'He had a maturity, a sort of level-headedness that was not common for people of his or, for that matter, any age,' Tribe recalled. 'He actually thought carefully before he said anything, and when he spoke, he spoke in complete paragraphs. For the first time in all my 40 years in this profession, I hired him on the spot.'

For a paper Tribe was writing entitled 'The Curvature of Constitutional Space', Barack researched and then analysed Einstein's theory of relativity, the concept of curved space and Heisenberg's uncertainty principal. He also helped with the research on two of Tribe's books – *On Reading the Constitution* and *Abortion: The Clash of Absolutes*.

'Barack didn't come to an issue with a set of pre-packaged ideas. He was entirely open to new approaches, fresh ways of looking at things. Back then, when he was just a first-year law student, I didn't hesitate to tell people that he was amazing – the most all-around impressive student I'd seen in decades.'

Tribe wasn't alone. Michelle's former advisor, Professor Charles Ogletree, marvelled at how the first-year student quickly emerged as 'a moderating influence on the campus by being mature, very much open to a variety of perspectives, but trusted by everyone'. Martha Minow, whose father, Newton Minow, had famously described television as a 'vast wasteland' during his tenure as head of the Federal Communications Commission during the Kennedy era, was another of Barack's professors. She considered him to be flat-out 'brilliant – I don't think I've ever had a student quite like him'.

But it was at the prestigious *Harvard Law Review* – which Michelle Robinson had eschewed in favour of joining Harvard's legal aid office – that Barack would ultimately make his mark. In addition to the racial storms that rocked the university as a whole, and the law school in particular, an ideological battle raged on the *Law Review* between liberals and conservatives. The political environment was 'borderline toxic' said Bradford Berenson, one of Obama's seventy-nine fellow *Law Review* editors and a member of the conservative Federalist Society. 'We stopped short of physical violence, but I remember plenty of raised voices.'

In fact, shouting matches were common at the *Law Review* offices, which were housed on the upper floors of Gannett House, a white-columned Greek Revival building that was the oldest structure on campus. (As if to underscore its less lofty status, the legal aid bureau where Michelle had toiled was located in the building's basement.) Berenson, who would go on to work on the Supreme Court and at the Bush White House, described the politics on the *Law Review* as 'the bitterest [he'd] ever seen in terms of it getting personal and nasty'. Christine Spurell, one of the black writers on the *Law Review* and an outspoken foe of the Federalists, agreed: 'People did a lot of talking and a lot of fighting. By the end, it's like one big, unhappy family.'

Yet somehow Barack remained above the fray, in part by making himself equally accessible to blacks and whites, liberals and conservatives alike. Although he never wavered in his liberal beliefs – the only article he actually wrote for the publication, for example, was a spirited defence of abortion – Barack carefully considered the views of the conservative minority rather than dismissing them outright.

He was also able to bridge the racial divide on the *Law Review*. 'The black kids were all sitting together,' Spurell said. 'Barack was the one who was truly able to move between the different groups and have credibility with all of them.'

Having spent his entire life walking the fine lines between races, cultures, religions and classes, it seemed only natural for Barack to assume the role of mediator and peacemaker. But when he actually made friends with several of the conservatives on the *Law Review*, his fellow blacks were less than amused.

'I don't know why at the time he was able to communicate so well with them,' Spurell wondered, 'even spend social time with them, which was not something I would ever have done . . . I think he genuinely thought, "Some of these guys are nice, all of them are smart, some of them are funny. All of them have something to say." I don't think he had an agenda . . .'

Whether or not Barack had an agenda at the *Harvard Law Review* remained to be seen. He was very clear, however, about his plans for Chicago. 'From the moment I met him, there was never any doubt in my mind that he was interested in going into politics,' said Cassandra Butts, another classmate who became a close friend. 'He only talked about running for one office. He wanted to be mayor of Chicago.'

None of which would have come as surprise to Larry Tribe. 'I saw Barack as an activist, not an academic, and was quite convinced that he would climb through the ranks of whatever political jungle he found himself in,' Tribe said. 'He obviously has the steadiness of purpose and the affability that makes it possible for him to move through a crowd of very sharp elbows without getting jabbed.'

Wrapping up his first year of law school, Barack was eager to get back to Chicago. He needed to reconnect with his spiritual mentor, Jeremiah Wright, and to tend to the many friendships he had made on the South Side. He also needed the kind of summer job that would pay for his stay in Chicago, build his résumé and help him forge the kinds of connections with Chicago's moneyed elite that he would need to fuel his political ambitions. Along the way, he might even find a woman – a true Chicagoan – to help him build the future he sought to pursue.

'Barack Obama?' Michelle asked, one hand planted firmly on her hip. 'What the hell kind of name is *Barack Obama*, anyway? Who names their kid *Barack Obama*?' It wasn't the first time she had listened to a colleague at Sidley Austin rave about the gifted, handsome, suavely urbane Harvard first-year law student who was coming to work there as a summer associate.

It had helped that Martha Minow's father, Newton Minow, was now a senior partner at Sidley Austin. Newton had been instrumental in spreading word of Barack's imminent arrival, going so far as to praise his letter of introduction to the firm as poetic. Soon the firm's rank and file were buzzing about his towering intellect, his exotic background and his equally exotic good looks.

In a less than subtle manoeuvre to bring together two of the relative handful of black lawyers in the five-hundred-lawyer Chicago office, Michelle was assigned to be the new arrival's mentor. She was not amused. She had already pledged to her mother just a week earlier that she was 'not worrying about dating. I'm focusing on me.'

Besides, Michelle insisted, she really didn't have time 'to babysit some guy'. As for the breathless comments from her co-workers, Michelle reacted with characteristic scepticism. 'I figured,' she later said, 'they were just impressed with any black man who has a suit and a job.'

After all, it wasn't as if Michelle hadn't been down this road before. Barack, she said, 'sounded too good to be true. I had dated a lot of brothers who had this kind of reputation coming in, so I figured he was one of those smooth brothers who could talk straight and impress people.'

Before he arrived, Michelle pulled out Barack's bio. 'I've got nothing in common with this guy,' she thought as she read it. 'He grew up in Hawaii! Who grows up in Hawaii? I've never even met somebody who grew up in Hawaii. He's biracial. OK, so what's that about? Hmmm. This guy's going to be a little strange, a little weird, a little off-putting.' She had managed to create in her mind 'an image of this very intellectual nerd'.

Despite her misgivings, Michelle was fully prepared to be polite, professional and as helpful as she could to the hotshot law student everyone was talking about. After all, this was the task she had been given and she took her responsibilities at the firm seriously.

For his part, Barack was attracted to Michelle the moment he stepped into her 47th floor office. He was immediately impressed by her laugh – 'she knew how to laugh, brightly and easily'– her stature – 'my height in heels' – and her beauty. Michelle's first impression: 'He was a lot cuter than I thought he'd be.' And it certainly helped that, at 6 ft 2 in. to her 5 ft 11 in., he was taller than she was.

That first day, Michelle, who at twenty-five was three years younger than Barack, took him out to lunch to get better acquainted. Gazing at him from across the table, she soon realised how much she hated the loud, ill-fitting sport jacket he was wearing. Within a couple of minutes, he took out a pack of cigarettes, offered one to her and, when she declined, began smoking at the table. Watching the cigarette as it dangled from his mouth, Michelle thought, 'Oh, here you go. Here's this good-looking, smooth-talking guy. I've been down this road before.'

But as she listened to him talk about his Kenyan father, his white mother from Kansas and his years in Indonesia, Michelle suddenly 'found him intriguing in every way that you can imagine'. To her surprise, the nerd that she had created in her mind was 'funny and self-deprecating. He could laugh at himself. He was down-to-earth despite his exotic background. We clicked right away.'

Barack was equally fascinated by Michelle's life story, perhaps less exotic but certainly no less compelling than his own. He listened intently as she spoke of her father's courageous struggle with MS, her all-American girlhood in South Shore, the parents who worked overtime to help pay for Michelle and her basketball-star brother to attend Princeton, her experiences doing legal aid work during her years at Harvard Law School.

He had only known her for a matter of hours, but already Barack saw in Michelle both the embodiment of the African American experience and a means to fully share in that experience. Those credentials were further enhanced when Michelle mentioned in passing that Jesse Jackson's daughter Santita had been a friend since childhood.

'Her roots in Chicago went deeper than his roots in Chicago,' Jesse Jackson later said of Michelle and what she brought to the table. 'She comes from a middle-class working family with working-family values and strong church values. She went to public school. And she and my daughter were friends. And so she has roots in Chicago and so she would know people he did not know in the places he would not know.'

Barack's friend Cassandra Butts agreed. The fact that Michelle was 'so rooted in the community,' Butts observed, 'had obvious value.' Jeremiah Wright put it succinctly: 'Michelle is from the 'hood.'

None of which occurred to Michelle at the time. All she knew was that Sidley Austin's newest summer associate was actually interested in what she had to say, and she was flattered. Having spent so much time across restaurant tables from men who talked only about themselves, she seldom got the opportunity to discuss the things that really mattered to her – family, friends, community. She allowed herself to think that maybe, just maybe, 'this guy was special as everybody said he was'.

For his part, Barack was simply blown away. Years later, when recalling these early courtship days to his friend Dan Shomon, he remembered thinking to himself, 'Man, she's hot! So I am going to work my magic on her.'

Michelle's mind, however, was on her responsibility as Barack's advisor at the firm, and not on dating. 'This guy is going to be a good friend of mine,' she told herself. 'I like him. I like him a lot.'

But just to make it clear that she was not in the market for a boyfriend, she told Barack in no uncertain terms that she had big plans, was on the fast track and had 'no time for distractions – especially men'.

Barack found this particularly touching. There was, he later said, 'a glimmer that danced across her round, dark eyes whenever I looked at her, the slightest hint of uncertainty, as if, deep inside, she knew how fragile things were, and that if she ever let go, even for a moment, all her plans might quickly unravel. That touched me somehow, that trace of vulnerability.'

Barack had only been at Sidley Austin a few days when he marched up to Michelle and declared, 'I think we should go out on a date.'

'No, nope,' she told him bluntly. 'Very nice of you, but I'm not really interested in dating anybody right now.' Besides, she told her brother, 'Barack and I are the only two black people in my department and if we start dating it'll just look, well, tacky.'

Michelle found Barack's interest in her 'touching'. She also felt sympathy for the young man who, in spite of the friends he had made during his years as a community organiser on the South Side, seemed awkward and alone. Michelle brought him along to a couple of corporate parties – 'tactfully,' he recalled, 'overlooking my limited wardrobe'. She also tried to set him up with several of her friends. None of those amounted to anything, and for one reason: Barack wanted Michelle.

For over a month, Michelle resisted Barack's advances. He bombarded her with notes, flowers and phone calls, and, on a daily basis, asked her to go out with him. 'He would try to charm her, flirt with her, and she would act very professional,' said Kelly Jo MacArthur, another associate at Sidley Austin. 'We would just laugh because he was undeniably charming and interesting and attractive, and the harder he had to try, the harder he had to try, because the less interested she appeared to be.'

A turning point came when she agreed to tag along with him on a Sunday-morning visit to one of the churches in Altgeld Gardens where he had done some community-organising work. That meeting took place in the church basement and was, like so many of the meetings Barack attended, filled primarily with single African American mothers.

'When he took off his jacket and rolled up his sleeves,' Michelle later recalled, 'it was like seeing him for the first time . . .' As he delivered an impassioned speech about 'the world as it is and the world as it should be', she thought to herself, 'This guy is really different, in addition to being nice and funny and cute and all that . . . To see him transform himself from the guy who was a summer associate in a law firm with a suit, and then come into this church basement with folks who were like me, who grew up like me, who were challenged and struggling in ways that I never would, and to be able to take off that suit and tie and become a whole 'nother person and connect with and feel comfortable in his own skin and to touch people's hearts in the way that he did . . .'

Michelle wondered if she had underestimated Barack. Of course, she had known all along that he was different, even exceptional. But to watch him in the church basement, connecting with the sort of people she had known all her life, made Michelle feel that he was speaking directly to something inside her. 'Barack lived comfortably in those two worlds – his own and mine – and it was impressive,' she said, 'I mean, it touched me . . .' She even allowed herself to think, 'Well, you know, I'd like to be married to somebody who felt that deeply about things.'

It was about the only way Barack *could* impress Michelle. 'He had no money,' she said, 'he was really broke. He was never going to try to impress me with things.' Certainly not his wardrobe, which she described as 'kind of cruddy'. Barack owned exactly seven blue suits, five shirts and half a dozen ties . . . 'I had to really tell him to get rid of the white jacket . . .'

As for his car, Barack was still driving his battered, rusted yellow Datsun 210 hatchback with the hole in the passenger door. 'You could see the ground when you were driving by,' Michelle recalled. 'He loved that car. It would shake ferociously when it would start up.'

From the look in her eyes, Barack could tell that Michelle was gradually changing her mind about him. Emboldened, he asked her out again – and, to his dismay, the answer was still no.

'Why not?' he demanded.

'Nothing has really changed, Barack,' she said, sounding more tentative than she had in the past. 'We work together, and I just don't think dating is the right thing to do. It just wouldn't look right.'

'Who cares?' he shot back, more exasperated than ever. 'I don't think the partners will consider one date a serious breach of firm policy.' He asked her if he'd have to quit the firm before it was all right for them to go out on a date.

'OK, OK, OK,' she said with a loud sigh. 'You wore me down. You win. I'll spend a day with you,' she added, 'but we won't call it a "date".'

'Fair enough,' Barack replied, beaming. 'You won't be sorry.'

It was a sunny, warm Saturday in late July when Barack took Michelle on their 'non-date'. Their first stop was the Art Institute of Chicago, where he impressed her with his 'deep understanding' of Impressionism, the Old Masters and modern art. They stopped for lunch at one of the institute's outdoor cafes, where a jazz group was playing ('That was really sweet,' she would recall), and then strolled up Michigan Avenue. 'We talked and talked and talked.'

From there they went to see a movie at Water Tower Place, Spike Lee's groundbreaking tale of simmering racial tensions in the Bedford-Stuyvesant neighbourhood of Brooklyn, *Do the Right Thing*. The significance of Barack's movie choice was not lost on Michelle. 'So you see, there he was doing his cultural thing,' she said. 'He was pulling out all the stops.'

As they stopped to get popcorn before the film, Michelle realised to her horror that one of her bosses, Newton Minow, was also waiting in line with his wife, Jo. 'Darn it,' Michelle whispered to Barack after they settled into their seats. 'Of all the theatres in Chicago, they had to pick *this* one . . . It'll be all over the office tomorrow . . .'

Minow remembered that Barack and Michelle 'were like a couple of teenagers, both obviously a little flustered that they'd been spotted together. It struck us as kind of sweet,' he said. 'When you saw them it was obvious they belonged together.'

Years later Barack would corner Spike Lee at a reception and tell him, 'I owe you a lot.' It was while watching *Do the Right Thing* that Michelle allowed Barack to touch her knee for the first time.

When the movie let out, Barack had another surprise up his sleeve. He took Michelle's hand and led her across the street to the John Hancock Building, where they were whisked by elevator to the ninety-ninth floor. There, with the lights of Chicago twinkling beneath them, they sipped cocktails – and talked some more. 'By the end of that date,' Michelle said, 'it was over. I was sold. He swept me off my feet.'

A few days later, since they lived not far from each other – Barack in Hyde Park, Michelle with her parents in South Shore – she offered to drive him home after a company picnic. As they pulled up to his apartment building, Barack offered to buy her an ice-cream cone at the Baskin-Robbins at the corner of 53rd and Dorchester.

Sitting on the kerb, trying to eat their ice cream before it melted in the sweltering summer heat, he told her about his summer job as a teenager working at a Baskin-Robbins in Honolulu and, more specifically, 'how hard it was to look cool in a brown apron and cap'. She talked about her high school field trip to France, and how thrilled she had been to actually try out her French on real Parisians. Rather than steal a kiss, he asked for her permission – and got it. 'Mmmm,' he said, 'chocolate.'

It was not long before Michelle brought Barack home to meet her parents – a major achievement in itself, since, as Craig put it, 'almost no one got to the meet-the-parents stage'. Michelle's parents were impressed with how polite and softly spoken her new young man was. He, in turn, marvelled at what he called her idyllic, straight-out-of-the-1950s *Leave It to Beaver* family.

At this point, Fraser Robinson was using a walker to get to the family car and then, with considerable difficulty, driving himself to work each day. Soon he would have to use a motorised cart to get around. Whether he was struggling to button his shirt or brush his teeth – he would give himself two hours just to get ready for work each morning – Michelle's father never succumbed to self-pity. Marian Robinson was equally upbeat, although Barack was sensitive to the emotional toll her husband's illness had taken on everyone in the family.

In fact, Fraser Robinson's MS had a lot to do with Michelle's penchant for perfection – a desire for order that verged on the obsessive–compulsive. Fraser's disease meant that even the most quotidian tasks – dressing, eating, going on a family drive, shopping, dining in a restaurant – had to be mapped out in advance and executed with military precision. These tasks were rendered that much more difficult by the family's desire to never put Fraser in a potentially embarrassing position. 'When you have a parent with a disability,' Michelle explained, 'control and structure become critical habits, just to get through the day.'

Unfortunately, this need to remain in control at all times made Michelle less tolerant of potential suitors – and vice versa.

'He was very, very low-key,' Craig said of Barack's behaviour during that first meeting with the family. 'I loved the way he talked about his family because it was the way we talked about our family. I was thinking, "Nice guy. Too bad he won't last."' How long, Craig wondered, 'is it going to be before this poor guy gets fired?'

This time, when she took her brother aside and asked him to put Barack to the test on the basketball court, Michelle made her feelings known. 'I really like this guy,' she told him. 'Now I want you to take him to play, to see what type of guy he is when he's not around me.' It was, of course, one more rite of passage for anyone who wanted to be part of the Robinsons' world – and a way for Craig to gauge Barack's character.

But, for Craig, this vetting assignment was different from the others. First, he liked the fact that Barack was taller than most of the guys Michelle dated; he knew that his sister felt awkward dating men who were shorter than she was. Then there was the simple fact that Barack impressed Craig 'as the nicest guy. I was very nervous because I liked him a lot,' Robinson said. 'This guy seems like a pretty good guy. I hope he makes it. I was rooting for him.' 'Of course,' he added, 'if he turns out to be a jerk, I've got to be the one to tell her.'

Barack thought he was a pretty decent basketball player and didn't hesitate to say so. But Michelle's brother discovered when they played a five-on-five game that Barack wasn't over-confident, either. 'He wasn't cocky or talking trash,' Craig said. 'Barack was very team-oriented, very unselfish, he's confident – not afraid to shoot the ball when he's open – and he fitted right in.'

However, what most impressed Craig about that first game was that, even though they were on the same team, Barack did not always pass him the ball. 'He wasn't trying to suck up to my sister through me,' Craig said. 'I thought, "You know, I like that."'

Right after the game, Craig called Michelle with his verdict. 'Your boy is straight,' he told her, 'and he can ball.' Still, he wondered if what he said really made any difference at all. 'It the test had proven negative,' he said with a shrug, 'who knows what would have happened.'

Marian and Fraser Robinson were equally delighted to hear that Barack passed Craig's basketball test. There were two facts about

Barack, however, that might have dampened their initial enthusiasm. Michelle and Barack were careful not tell her parents that he smoked – or that his mother was white. 'Mr and Mrs Robinson were very solid, very proud, in some ways quite conservative, black Americans,' said a long-time friend of Michelle's. 'Michelle and Barack didn't want to spring his biracial, multicultural past on them until they came to know and love him as a black man, as one of them.' According to Marian, it would be months before she and her husband learned that Barack's mother was Caucasian and that he had essentially been raised by his white grandparents.

Even Michelle had a hard time absorbing it all. 'Can you believe it?' she told her friend Santita Jackson. 'He's got white grandparents from Kansas!'

She reasoned that they actually had more in common than they realised. 'When there are people who are different from us,' she later mused, 'we automatically think, well, that's nothing like me and we have nothing in common. But we have more in common than not. His grandparents are very much Midwestern, and in that respect the Midwestern value is: work hard, treat people with decency and respect, and do what you say you are going to do, your word is your bond. We're both worried about doing our best,' she said of Barack and herself, 'and doing the right thing.'

Notwithstanding his Midwestern lineage, Barack's family was, as he put it, 'scattered to the four winds'. What he lacked – stability, roots, a sense of place and belonging – Michelle and her family had in abundance. Conversely, he was different, exotic, more open-minded and, in a sense, free-spirited than she had ever been. 'Barack has opened my eyes to a lot of things about the world,' she said. 'No doubt about it – he's a fascinating guy.'

For the rest of the summer, Barack and Michelle were inseparable. They refrained from public displays of affection – 'They were too cool and sophisticated to be hanging all over each other,' said a mutual friend – and tried to downplay their blossoming romance in the office. 'It was cute,' said another lawyer in the intellectual property office. 'Barack would be in her office and they'd be talking in these hushed tones. Then you'd knock and they'd snap to, clearing their throats, pretending to be all business. It was silly, since everybody knew they were an item.'

Actually, Michelle had been far from reluctant to share the good news with her friends. Verna Williams, her pal from Harvard, had often commiserated with Michelle over the sorry state of their love lives. 'Verna! Guess what?' Michelle now told Williams over the phone. 'I've got this great guy in my life. His name is Barack.'

'I could tell this was something different,' Williams later said, 'something special. We had known each other when we dated other guys. You go through this whole "he's not ready for commitment" thing . . . but Barack was none of these things. He was just a good, solid guy.'

He was also someone who was even more driven than Michelle to accomplish great things. 'This brother is not interested in ever making a dime,' she thought to herself. 'I would just have to love him for his values.'

Michelle knew Barack was joking when he teased her about some of the clients she handled, especially Barney and Coors beer. But at the same time, she also felt that her law degree was good for more than just making money.

Both Barack and Michelle wanted to lift their fellow African Americans out of poverty, to give them better healthcare, housing and educational opportunities. Barack had thought long and hard about how to acquire the kind of political power to bring about these changes. He did not want to sound presumptuous or egotistical, he told her, but he had already mapped out his political future. He would share those plans with her, if she agreed to not to discuss them with anyone else.

First, he planned to write a memoir. John F. Kennedy had launched his political career with *Profiles in Courage*, Barack pointed out. What he had to offer was the inspirational story of a biracial American whose journey of self-discovery bridged races, cultures, continents. Michelle was astonished to learn that for years Barack had been taking meticulous notes with the idea of just that kind of book in mind.

Barack had total confidence in his abilities as a writer – in fact, he had told several of his fellow students at Harvard that he might forego legal practice altogether to pursue a career as a novelist. Finding a publisher would not be easy, but Barack had a plan for that, too.

'When I go back to Harvard,' he told Michelle, 'I think I'm going to run for president of the *Law Review*.' Michelle was sufficiently impressed by the fact that Barack, who was only starting his second year at Harvard Law, already had a masthead position on the *Review*. That he might be try to become its first African American president seemed as far-fetched as it was exciting.

Barack explained that the *Review* was in a state of turmoil, that it was sharply divided between liberals and conservatives, and that he was really the only editor who had taken pains not to offend anyone. By his calculations, the balance of power would rest in the hands of the conservatives and their more moderate allies. Barack had made an effort to get to know members of the Federalist Society and discovered that he actually liked some of them. So much so that he was hanging out them as much as he was with his liberal black friends. The conservatives, he explained to a sceptical Michelle, 'are really very nice, and smart, maybe the smartest guys there. And some of them are just fun to be around.'

'Have you told anyone you want to run for president of the *Law Review*?' Michelle asked.

'No, I don't want anyone to know that I'm even interested,' he said. 'I don't want to look too eager.' He stood his best chance to get elected, Barack said, if he appeared to be a last-minute compromise candidate. 'So, please,' he said. 'Don't tell anybody right now – not at the office, not even your family. I don't want it getting back to anyone at Harvard.'

In the middle of explaining his grand plan, Barack took a long drag on a cigarette – his twentieth that day. 'You're gonna have to stop that,' Michelle told him.

'Stop what?'

'The smoking – gotta quit,' she said. Growing up in a household where both parents smoked, as children Michelle and her brother used to pull the tobacco out of their parents' cigarettes and douse it with Tabasco sauce so they would quit. The ploy didn't work, of course, but Michelle was no more tolerant towards smokers than she had been as a little girl on the South Side. 'It's a nasty habit,' she told Barack, 'and it's going to kill you if you don't stop. So I'd really like it if you quit smoking.'

Barack, who had no intention of quitting, rolled his eyes, stubbed out his cigarette and continued. If he could manage to emerge as a peacemaker at the *Law Review* and get himself elected as its first black president, the publicity would be 'enormous'. Although by no means a slam dunk, finding a publisher for his book under those circumstances would certainly be a lot easier.

Once his book had become a bestseller, Barack would return to Chicago, law degree in hand, to pick up where his idol Harold Washington had left off and run for mayor. 'And after that?' Michelle asked, half in jest.

'I think maybe I'll run for the Senate,' he answered without skipping a beat. 'Then president – why not?'

Michelle threw back her head and let out a hearty laugh. 'He's pulling my leg now,' she thought to herself.

'Why are you laughing?' he asked, feigning a wounded look. He certainly appreciated how absurd it sounded. 'Hey, come on, now. Don't laugh. Stranger things have happened.'

That November, Barack returned to Chicago to spend Thanksgiving with Michelle. Since things were obviously getting serious between his sister and the Harvard Law hotshot, Craig, now working as an investment banker on Wall Street, thought it was time to turn up the heat. 'You know,' Craig said, 'I thought I'd do the obnoxious big brother thing and ask him about his future.'

'So, Barack,' Craig said, clearing his throat. 'What do you want to do with your life?'

'Well,' Barack replied with an earnest smile, 'I thought I might like to get into politics.'

'So you might run for alderman or something like that some day?' Craig asked.

'No,' Barack said, shaking his head. 'I was really thinking more on a national scale. Maybe run for Congress or the Senate.' Barack paused for a moment, obviously considering whether he should go on, and Craig was about to jump in when the brash young law student continued. 'Who knows?' he said. 'If I did a good job, I might even run for president some day.'

Craig's eyes darted around the room, hoping that his Aunt Gracie, whose contempt for politicians was legendary, hadn't heard Barack. 'Don't say that too loud,' Craig cautioned his sister's boyfriend. 'Someone might hear you and think you were nuts.'

In truth, Barack and Michelle had not even let on about his more immediate plans to seek a different presidency at Harvard. 'He didn't talk about himself,' Marian remembered. 'He didn't tell us that he was running for president of the *Harvard Law Review*. We never realised that he was as bright as he is.'

It was around this time that Michelle told her parents about Barack's white mother and grandparents. Marian Robinson in particular was 'very surprised' – and 'a little bit worried' about his white relatives and how they would all get along if her only daughter ended up marrying him. At least he's not white, she thought to herself. 'I guess I worry about race mixing,' she explained, 'because of the difficulties, not so much for prejudice or anything. It's very hard.' (As it happened, Craig would marry a white woman.)

Now it was Michelle's turn to meet Barack's family, and to gain some insight into the people and places that shaped the young man she had fallen in love with. Barack had always spent Christmas in Hawaii with Gramps, Toot and – when they could make the journey from Indonesia – his mother and Maya.

Landing at Honolulu International Airport, Barack and Michelle stepped off the plane onto the tarmac and into the bright Hawaiian sunshine. When they had left Chicago nine hours earlier, the city was in the icy grip of a winter storm. 'So you grew up here,' she said, nodding her head. 'Poor guy.'

Hand in hand, they walked towards the terminal and the teenage greeters who would stand on tiptoes to wrap flower leis around both their necks. Once inside the terminal, Barack searched the crowd for familiar faces.

'Barry! Barry!' Gramps shouted. 'Over here!' Barack looked over to see them all smiling and waving – his 18-year-old sister Maya, his grandmother and his mother, clad in a muumuu-like Indonesian batik *daster* and – as was so often the case – crying with joy.

Michelle had been warned that Barry was the name Barack had grown up with, but she was surprised to hear it nonetheless. Gramps gave Michelle a welcoming hug, and Michelle bent down to embrace Ann, Maya and Toot one by one. 'Well, Barry,' Gramps said, nudging Barack, 'she's quite a looker.'

Toot rolled her eyes. She would be no less impressed by Michelle, but for very different reasons. From that first meeting, it was clear to Toot that Michelle was what she called a 'no-nonsense' woman like herself – someone who would support Barry while at the same time grounding him in reality.

Michelle told Toot and the others about Barack's plan to run for office and shared her doubts about seeing such a 'decent guy' in the rough-and-tumble world of Chicago politics.

'He's a dreamer, like his mother,' Toot explained. 'That's why he needs someone like you around.' In the end, Toot would pay the young lawyer from Chicago what she considered to be the ultimate compliment. 'Michelle,' Toot told her grandson, 'is a very sensible girl.'

Ann Dunham Soetoro may indeed have been a dreamer, but Michelle connected with her as well. Barack's mother and sister had just flown in from Indonesia, where Ann was helping to build a microfinance programme that granted small loans to credit-poor entrepreneurs. It was her anthropological research into the ways people actually work that set the guidelines used by the Bank Rakyat Indonesia. Eventually, the microfinance programme Ann helped set up would rank number one in the world, with more than thirty million members.

Now a heavyset woman with frizzy black hair, Ann was, in the words of her friend Mary Zurbuchen, 'a big personality and a big presence'. As a grassroots activist, she was thrilled when Barack became a community organiser in Chicago. As an academic who was still working on her PhD dissertation in anthropology, she was equally delighted when her son enrolled in Harvard Law School and when he made the *Law Review*. 'All of us knew where Barack was going to school,' said another of Ann's friends, Georgia McCauley. 'All of us knew how brilliant he was.'

Ann, unlike her mother, saw no reason to doubt that her son would succeed if he decided to pursue a career in politics. Contrary to what Toot may have thought of her, Ann was not all dreamer. She spoke passionately about her desire to help the world's poor, but her approach – as evidenced by her success with the microfinance programme in Indonesia – was focused, pragmatic. 'She wasn't ideological,' Barack would later say. 'I inherited that, I think, from her. She was suspicious of cant.'

While Toot urged her grandson to aim for a career in international law and, ultimately, a spot on the US Supreme Court, Ann told her son to aim for the White House. If anyone had a shot at being the first black president, she said, it was him.

If Michelle had ever wondered where Barack got his confidence and his seemingly boundless ambition, here was the answer. Barack had been the focus of these people's lives just as she and her brother had been the focus of their parents' lives. 'We're all products of the Midwest, really,' she said. 'There's a lot of Kansas in his grandparents and his mother, and that means there's a lot of Kansas in Barack.'

Perhaps. But Michelle would also learn that, in her words, 'to understand Barack you must first understand Hawaii'. During that first eye-opening Christmas visit to the islands, the 'very sensible' Midwesterner immersed herself in the people, places and things that had shaped the young Barack. He took her to the beaches where he liked to snorkle and body-surf, to the parks and *palis* (cliffs) that were no less beautiful to the locals because they attracted thousands of tourists, to the campus of Punahou prep school to the Baskin-Robbins store on South King Street where he had found it so hard to look cool scooping ice cream. There were also sunset luaus, torchlit hula demonstrations, romantic walks on the beach and Mai Tais at the Royal Hawaiian Hotel on Waikiki.

This was a world as far away from the South Side of Chicago as it could possibly be, and yet what impressed Michelle most were the similarities in their backgrounds. Like Fraser and Marian Robinson, Toot and Gramps were hard-working people who had never gone to college but did not hesitate to make the sacrifices necessary to send their children – and, in Barack's case, their grandchild – to college. The Dunhams' modest two-bedroom apartment in a white concrete building had a tiny balcony, but in most other respects it was comparable to the Robinsons' cramped apartment on South Euclid Avenue.

Barack's family also revelled in the kind of small, reassuringly familiar traditions shared by so many American families. 'From the start,' Maya said, 'Michelle was a ready convert to our lazy and fun Christmas rituals.' These included marathon games of Scrabble, watching TV Christmas specials and the obligatory Christmas-morning package-opening frenzy followed by a brunch of pancakes, cheddar-cheese eggs, papaya and freshly squeezed orange juice.

For Michelle, the Christmas visit to Hawaii yielded other insights into Barack. During the long Thanksgiving weekend he spent with the Robinsons in Chicago, Michelle was touched to see the way he handled an inebriated uncle of hers with compassion and respect. Now that she could see the way he interacted with his grandparents, it became clear to Michelle that Barack had had a lifetime of practice dealing with drinkers. He had shared with Michelle the details of his father's life – how disappointment over the course of his government career in Kenya had resulted in his becoming a hopeless, self-destructive alcoholic. Now she witnessed at first hand the drinking problem that also existed on the maternal side of Barack's family. In addition to the smoking habit they shared with their grandson, Toot and Gramps were both two-fisted drinkers. 'It's one way of coping with life's disappointments,' he explained. 'They've done everything for me. I'm in no position to judge.'

In truth, Barack shared with Michelle the nagging concern that he might be genetically predisposed to substance abuse. It was one of the reasons why, after spending his high school and early college years drinking to excess, smoking pot and occasionally snorting cocaine, he suddenly decided to quit – everything, that is, except smoking.

'You're a runner,' Michelle pointed out. 'You exercise regularly. Don't you see how crazy it is to do all that and then light up a cigarette?'

'Hey,' Barack would answer with a wink. 'You have to keep at least one vice. Besides, I'm not that strong.'

After they returned to the mainland – she to Sidley Austin in

Chicago, he to resume his law studies at Harvard – Michelle and Barack were fully committed to their long-distance relationship. 'We were both determined,' he recalled, 'to do whatever it took to make it work.' As for the smoking: 'I'm working on him,' she told one of her co-workers at Sidley Austin. 'I'm working on him . . .'

For the next two years, they would burn up the phone lines between Cambridge and Chicago. Although he devoted as much as 60 hours a week to his studies and the *Law Review*, there was the odd occasion when Barack could hop on a plane to Chicago for a quick weekend visit. 'It's not something I would have had the maturity to do before,' Barack later said. 'Michelle centred me in a sense. She made it possible for me to really concentrate on what was important in life.'

Just one month after he returned from visiting Hawaii with Michelle, Barack launched his carefully thought-out plan to become the first black president of the *Harvard Law Review*. The mere fact that he was already serving as an editor of the highly regarded publication was impressive enough. The *Law Review* numbered among its esteemed alumni Supreme Court Justices Felix Frankfurter, Stephen Breyer, Antonin Scalia and Ruth Bader Ginsburg; former Secretary of State Dean Acheson; Pulitzer Prize-winning poet Archibald MacLeish; Harvard University President Derek Bok; Yale University President Kingman Brewster; and Elliot Richardson, who at various times served as Secretary of Defense, Secretary of Commerce, Secretary of Health, Education, and Welfare, and Attorney General. The *Law Review* elections were as quirkily arcane as one would find anywhere in academia. In accordance with tradition, the process began on a Sunday morning with the nineteen candidates – including four African Americans – cooking meals for their fellow editors while they cast ballots. At first, Barack was not among those running. Sticking to his plan not to appear eager for the job, he grudgingly agreed to run only after being urged by his friends to do so.

'He was clearly seen as a leader, but at the same time he never put himself out as a leader,' Cassandra Butts said of her friend and classmate. 'He had a very quiet, very calm presence. And his leadership style was such that people were drawn to him and they embraced him as a leader.'

Brad Berenson agreed. 'Barack was very laid-back, much less nakedly ambitious than some of the others on the *Law Review*,' he said. 'He never struck me as one of the strivers. He didn't come across to people as a political operator, which is testament to what a good political operator he really was.' At the same time, Berenson said, 'I never thought that he was disingenuous or two-faced – saying one thing to me and another to somebody else. We were on opposite sides of the political spectrum, but there was no escaping that he was a very, very decent person – a classy guy.'

The balloting continued for the next sixteen hours as one by one candidates were eliminated from the race. By midnight, no clear front-runner had emerged. 'It's late at night and we're trying to figure out how to resolve this thing,' recalled Kenneth Mack, one of the other black candidates, who was out of the running early on. 'Clearly Barack has a lot of support, but it's not resolved yet.'

Then a conservative editor who disagreed with just about everything Barack stood for spoke up. 'We are a divided institution,' he said, 'and what we need is the best person to reach out to all constituencies and lead us forward. That person is Barack.' According to Mack, 'Conservatives marvelled at his use of language and metaphors that resonated with their core beliefs.'

When the votes were tallied and Barack had won, a tearful Mack leapt up and embraced the first black president of the *Harvard Law Review*. The first call Barack placed was to Michelle in Chicago.

'Say hello,' he told her the minute she answered the phone, 'to the new president of the *Harvard Law Review*.'

'You're kidding!' Michelle squealed. 'Oh baby, that's wonderful.' When she told her parents, they were even more surprised. 'But,' Marian Robinson said, 'he never even told us he was running . . .'

Later that day at Sidley Austin, Michelle's fellow attorneys dropped in to congratulate her and sing the praises of their recent summer associate. 'She was glowing,' said one, 'and obviously very proud of Barack. But she kept her cool about it, too. There's a quiet dignity about Michelle – a sense of what's appropriate behaviour in the workplace, and she was still soft-pedalling their relationship to some extent.'

The African Americans editors on the *Review* were jubilant, and even the white conservatives were pleased with Barack as their new leader. 'Conservatives were eager to have somebody who would treat them fairly,' Bradford Berenson said, 'who would listen to what they had to say, who would not abuse the powers of the office to favour his ideological soulmates . . . Somebody who would basically play it straight. Barack fit the bill better than anyone else.' Another conservative on the *Review* echoed that sentiment: 'Whatever his politics, we felt he would give us a fair shake.'

Barack was so even-handed, in fact, that he risked alienating his liberal friends by appointing three members of the Federalist Society to top spots on the masthead, and only one African American. 'Barack took ten times as much grief from those on the left on the *Review* as from those of us on the right,' Berenson said. 'And the reason was, I think there was an expectation among those editors on the left that he would use his position to advance the cause.' Instead, Berenson added, his 'foremost goal was to put out a first-rate publication, and he was not going to let politics or ideology get in the way of doing that'.

As he predicted, Barack's election as the first black president of the *Harvard Law Review* in February of 1990 made national news. He was profiled in the *New York Times* and the *Los Angeles Times*, and told the Associated Press, 'From experience, I know that for every one of me there are a hundred, or thousand, black and minority students who are just as smart and just as talented and never get the opportunity.' In his first TV interview, he observed that his election 'symbolises some progress, at least within the small confines of the legal community. I think it's real important to keep the focus on the broader world out there and see that for a lot of kids, the doors that have been opened to me aren't open to them.'

Leaning against a pillar in jeans, black turtleneck and Bass Weejuns, the collar of his jacket turned up to frame his boyish face, Barack cut a dashing figure on campus. He was, bar none, the best-known and most respected student at Harvard. Seasoned professors gossiped about which Supreme Court Justice he was likely to clerk for, and female classmates joked that Blair Underwood would probably be best suited to portray Barack in the movie version of his life.

For all his successes at Harvard, Barack did suffer one embarrassing defeat. When a panel of coeds charged with screening candidates for a pin-up calendar of black men at Harvard rejected him, Barack was peeved. The reason he didn't make the cut: 'Barack,' one of the judges recalled, matter-of-factly, 'just wasn't hot enough.'

Jane Dystel disagreed – at least in terms of the young man's potential as an author. Spotting the glowing profile of Barack in the *New York Times*, the young literary agent asked him to write up a brief book proposal based on his life. Dystel then submitted the proposal to several editors and a deal with struck with Poseidon Press, a small imprint of Simon & Schuster. He pocketed the first half of the $150,000 advance – a hefty sum for a first-time author – and returned to his law studies with the intention of writing the book between classes.

Understandably, Michelle was thrilled that her boyfriend had landed a lucrative book deal and shared the news with one of her dearest friends, her old Princeton roommate Suzanne Alele. The Nigerian-born daughter of two physicians, Alele was raised in Kingston, Jamaica, and moved to Washington DC as a teenager. At Princeton, the beautiful, bright Alele majored in biology, ran track, managed the lightweight football team and, according to one classmate, 'saved the rest of us from computer catastrophes'.

Alele earned her master's at the University of Maryland and went to work for the Federal Reserve as a computer specialist, but she was always seen by those who knew her as laid-back, fun-loving and not at all concerned about trying to please others. She travelled the world and made a point of urging her friends – especially Michelle – to lighten up.

In February, around the time Barack was elected president of the *Harvard Law Review*, Alele was diagnosed with advanced lymphoma. Four months later, Michelle got the call she had been dreading. Michelle rushed to the National Institutes of Health in Washington and was holding her friend's hand when she passed away on 23 June 1990. Alele was just 25.

'I was confronted for the first time in my life with the fact that nothing was really guaranteed,' Michelle recalled. Although Suzanne's life was cut short, Michelle envied the way her friend had chosen to spend it. 'One of the things I remembered about Suzanne is she always made decisions that would make her happy and create a level of fulfilment,' Michelle said. 'She was less concerned with pleasing other people, and thank God.'

After Alele's funeral, Michelle seriously began to question the path she had chosen. 'If *I* died in four months,' she asked herself, 'is this how I would have wanted to spend this time? Am I waking up every morning feeling excited about the work I'm doing? I need to figure out what I really love.'

She worried that she had 'unthinkingly' taken the 'automatic path' from Harvard to a corporate career. 'I started thinking about the fact that I went to some of the best schools in the country and I have no idea what I want to do,' she said. 'That kind of stuff got me worked up because I thought, "This isn't education. You can make money and have a nice degree, but what are you learning about giving to the world, and finding your passion and letting that guide you?"'

Besides, she began to feel guilty about the material trappings of success. Known as something of a clothes-horse by her Sidley Austin colleagues, she was careful to dress down around less affluent relatives and South Shore neighbours. 'Can I go to the family reunion in my Benz and be comfortable,' she wondered, 'while my cousins are struggling to keep a roof over their heads?'

Despite these mounting doubts, Michelle continued to make her mark in the intellectual property department at Sidley Austin. It would take another, even more personal tragedy to force a change in the course of Michelle's life.

In March of 1991, Fraser Robinson went through his time-consuming daily ritual of getting out of bed, dressing and driving to his job at the water-treatment plant. It had become all the more painful in the wake of a recent kidney operation he had undergone, but Fraser was determined to tough it out.

Fraser never made it to the plant. Unbeknownst to Michelle's dad, he was suffering major complications from the kidney surgery. He died behind the wheel of his car at age 55.

Michelle was devastated, but she was also able to draw inspiration from her father's death. 'He died on his way to work,' Michelle said. 'He wasn't feeling well, but he was going to get in that car and go. That's how we grew up, living your life to be sure that you make the most of it. If what you're doing doesn't bring you joy every single day, what's the point?'

Barack rushed to Michelle's side, and she wept on his shoulder as her father's casket was lowered into the ground. It was then, Barack later said, 'that I promised Fraser Robinson I would take care of his girl.' (Strangely, although Barack would later write that this took place only six months after he met Michelle, he had actually known her for nearly two years by the time her father died.)

Graveside promise or no, Barack had been dancing around the subject of matrimony for well over a year. There was never any question about how he felt. 'I'm hooked, I'm in love,' he told his Occidental roommate Vinai Thummalapally and anyone else who would listen. 'She was highly intelligent, highly educated and gorgeous,' Newton Minow said. 'He was completely devoted to Michelle.' But Barack remained skittish when talk turned to marriage. The issue had become, Michelle conceded, 'a bone of contention between us'.

'Come on,' she would say to him, only half kidding. 'What's your problem? Let's get with the programme here.'

'It's just a piece of paper,' he said, rolling his eyes in exasperation. 'I mean, what does it really mean?'

'Oh, brother . . .'

The debate continued as Barack approached graduation in June of 1991. When Chicago attorney Judson Miner called the *Law Review* offices to offer him a job, Barack's assistant answered, 'You can leave your name and take a number. You're number 647.'

At first, Barack passed on all the offers – including one from Michelle's firm, Sidley Austin. Determined to do something in public service, his first priority was to return to Illinois and take the bar exam. He passed on the first try. (Michelle had failed on her first attempt, but passed on the second.)

That night, Barack took Michelle to celebrate at Gordon, the landmark Chicago restaurant famous for its contemporary American cuisine. Over artichoke-fritter appetisers, they once again launched into their long-running debate over marriage. The argument died down enough for them to enjoy their entrée, but began to heat up again as dessert approached.

'Marriage, it doesn't mean anything,' Barack insisted. 'It's really how you feel.'

'Yeah, right,' Michelle replied sarcastically.

'I mean, come on, Michelle,' he continued. 'We know we love each other. What do we need to get married for?'

She shot him a withering glance. 'Look, buddy,' she said, 'I'm not one of these girls who'll just hang out for ever. That's just not who I am.'

Barack just sat there smirking as Michelle smouldered. In the middle of her tirade, the waiter arrived with Gordon's signature dessert – flourless chocolate cake. On the plate was a small velvet box. 'So I'm sort of stopped in my tracks,' she later said of the moment. Michelle opened the box to reveal a one-carat diamond engagement ring inside.

She looked up in stunned silence at Barack. 'That,' he said, 'sort of shuts you up, doesn't it?'

For once, Michelle was indeed speechless.

It is true my wife is smarter, better looking.
She's also a little meaner than I am.

Barack

⸻❦⸻

I cannot be crazy, because then I'm a crazy
mother and I'm an angry wife.

Michelle

⸻❦⸻

Every high-flying kite needs somebody with their feet
on the ground. And that's Michelle.

Avis LaVelle, friend

⸻❦⸻

I trust her completely, but at the same time she's also
a mystery to me in some ways.

Barack

5

As a senior partner at Sidley Austin, Newton Minow used his considerable clout to promote Michelle's career at the firm. He had grown equally fond of her boyfriend and wasted no time trying to entice him into the Sidley Austin fold as well.

Yet Minow was not really surprised that Barack was now standing across from him listing all the reasons why he was going to have to turn down Minow's generous offer of a job in favour of a life in politics. After all, Minow was no stranger to public service himself; he had been chairman of the Federal Communications Commission in the Kennedy administration and active in the Democratic Party all his life.

'You don't have to explain anything to me,' Minow told Barack after listening to him outline his interest in grassroots activism followed by a run for state, and then national, office. 'You can accomplish a great deal of good in the public sector. I'll do whatever I can to help.'

Barack cleared his throat. 'You may not feel that way,' he said tentatively, 'after you hear the rest of what I've got to say. I suggest,' he added, 'you sit down.'

Minow, nonplussed, eased into the chair behind his desk. Barack sat down opposite him. 'What the hell is this?' he thought.

'I'm taking Michelle with me.'

Minow bounded to his feet and pointed a finger in Barack's face. 'Why you no good son of a—'

'Hold it,' Barack said, raising his hand. 'Now just hold it! You don't understand—'

'Oh, I understand, all right,' Minow shouted. 'I understand perfectly—'

'We're getting married,' Barack said, cutting Minow short.

147

'Oh,' Minow said, 'that's different.' He reached across his desk, pumped Barack's hand and congratulated him enthusiastically. He also reiterated his offer to help in any way could to advance his – and Michelle's – new career in the public sector.

It was only after Barack left that it occurred to Minow that Barack, who did not even work for the firm, had essentially resigned for Michelle. During a legal career that spanned half a century, Minow had never heard of a man acting so explicitly on behalf of his wife, much less his fiancée. This resignation by proxy seemed especially odd given the fact that Michelle had never exactly been hesitant to speak up for herself at the firm.

Although Michelle had not voiced her dissatisfaction to her superiors at Sidley Austin, the sudden deaths of her friend Suzanne Alele and her father had left her more confused than ever about the future. She was well aware that many of her fellow lawyers were happy with the work they were doing. But, she asked, 'were they bounding out of bed to get to work in the morning? No.'

'You just knew that they weren't going to contain her in that law firm,' Michelle's Sidley Austin colleague Kelly Jo MacArthur recalled. Michelle wanted to make a real impact on public policy, but in this she was already deferring to Barack. 'She was talking about him constantly,' another Sidley Austin lawyer said. 'A lot of people brag about their husbands or boyfriends, but this was different. Her tone was almost worshipful. He was going to do great things, she kept saying.'

In the autumn of 1991, Barack was still weighing the many options that were available to him. As the first African American president of the *Harvard Law Review*, he was all but guaranteed a shot at clerking for a Supreme Court Justice. In the meantime, one powerful judge on the US Court of Appeals for the DC Circuit, Abner Mikva, had taken the initiative and approached Barack with an offer to clerk for him in Washington – which Barack promptly turned down. When Barack told Mikva he intended to return to Chicago to enter politics, Mikva thought, 'Boy, has he got something to learn. You don't just come to Chicago and plant your flag.'

Back in Chicago, the brash newcomer sought the advice of the many powerful and politically savvy friends he had made during his years as a community organiser in Chicago – people like the Reverend Jeremiah Wright, the Reverend Jesse Jackson, Mikva and Minow. What they all told him was that, since his election as Chicago's mayor in 1989, Richard J. Daley's son Richard M. Daley held the key to real political power in Illinois.

At Barack's urging, in July of 1991 Michelle sent her résumé to Mayor Daley with a cover letter asking to join his staff. Across the letter someone had scrawled:

This woman is no longer interested in being at her law firm. She wants to be in government and give back.

Daley aide Susan Sher walked the letter and résumé over to Daley's deputy chief of staff, Valerie Jarrett. 'She is made for you,' Sher told Jarrett. 'This is exactly what *you* did.'

A member of Chicago's African American elite – her mother was a noted psychologist and her father an internationally recognised geneticist and pathologist – Jarrett was actually born in Iran, where her father was running a hospital for children in the mid-1950s. As a child, he spoke Persian and French as well as English. After a year in London, the Jarretts returned to the Windy City, where Valerie's father became a professor at the University of Chicago. Yet he continued to do genetic research across the world. As a result, she recalled, 'we would spend summers traipsing across Africa. One summer we went from Ghana to Nigeria to Ethiopia to Uganda to Egypt and then back to Iran.'

After graduating from Stanford and then Michigan Law School, Jarrett went to work for a big Chicago law firm with offices on the seventy-ninth floor of the Sears Tower. 'I would sit in that office and just cry,' Jarrett said. 'Cry my heart out. "I've got to get out of here. This is not what makes me tick."'

Where the deaths of Michelle's father and her best friend led her to re-evaluate her life, Jarrett's self-evaluation was triggered by the birth of her daughter. 'I wanted to do something,' Jarrett said, 'that she would be really proud of me for.'

No sooner had she been handed Michelle's résumé than Jarrett picked up the phone and called her. 'I was just unbelievably bowled over by how impressive she was,' Jarrett recalled of that first conversation. Drawing parallels between her own dissatisfaction with working for a big law firm and Michelle's, Jarrett saw in Michelle a kindred spirit. 'This is why Michelle and I connected,' Jarrett said. 'She felt the same way.'

Later, when they met face-to-face in the office of Mayor Daley's chief of staff, Michelle impressed her even more. 'An introductory session turned into an hour and a half. Michelle was so mature beyond her years, so thoughtful and perceptive and confident and committed and extremely open.'

Michelle was so mature that, before Jarrett realised it, she had essentially turned the interview process on its head. 'She really prodded me about what the job would be like because she had lots of choices,' Jarrett said. 'I offered it to her on the spot, which was totally inappropriate because I should have talked to the mayor first. But I just knew that she was really special.'

Before she could accept the $60,000-a-year job as an assistant to Mayor Daley, Michelle had to talk it over with her future husband. Together she and Barack still owed more than $300,000 in student loans. 'How are we ever going to pay back these loans if I take a 50 per cent cut in salary?' she asked. But Barack was confident that, by combining their incomes, sharing rent and cutting back on living expenses, they would have enough to survive and at least chip away at their debt. Besides, he still had nearly all the money – more than $60,000 – he had been advanced by Simon & Schuster.

Michelle's reticence had less to do with finance and more to do with plunging into the cut-throat world of Chicago city politics. 'She had some serious reservations,' Jarrett recalled, 'about whether she was going to leave the practice of law and leap into the mayor's office in a political environment.'

Remarkably, Michelle then asked Jarrett if she wouldn't mind joining her and Barack for dinner. 'My fiancé wants to know,' Michelle explained, 'who is going to be looking out for me and making sure that I thrive.' So, she continued, 'how about we have dinner and go out and talk this through?'

'Michelle told me Barack wanted to meet me,' Jarrett said, 'so he could figure out if he was comfortable with her going to work for Mayor Daley . . . I can't think of many people you hire who say, "I'd like you to meet my fiancé." But I would have done just about anything to get Michelle.'

So, just as he would engineer Michelle's departure from Sidley Austin, Barack took charge of Michelle's entry into public service. They met at a downtown restaurant for dinner, and from the very outset Jarrett felt as if she would have to prove herself worthy of their trust. 'I knew,' she said, 'that unless this conversation ended well, probably the two of them were going to go home and say, "Well, not so much. Maybe that's not the right move."'

Jarrett, Michelle, and Barack slid into a booth – Barack directly opposite Jarrett. Then, Jarrett recalled, 'he interrogated me in the nicest possible way'. While Michelle listened quietly, Barack quizzed Jarrett on the details of the job, what was to be expected of his future wife, how much power the position actually entailed, how much autonomy she would have, what her access to Mayor Daley would be and – most importantly – what her political exposure would be. Barack wanted Jarrett to promise that, whenever infighting arose, she would 'have Michelle's back'.

Anyone else might have thought Barack's involvement to this degree was highly presumptuous, not to mention an unsettling indicator of the sway he held over his future bride. Not Jarrett. She even seemed to enjoy being grilled by Barack, although she hesitated to even call it that.

'Barack never grills,' Jarrett said. 'That's part of what is so effective about him: he puts you completely at ease, and the next thing you know he's asking more and more probing questions and gets you to open up and reflect a little bit.'

In the same way that she instantly identified with Michelle, Jarrett quickly discovered that she and Barack had much in common. 'That night we talked about his childhood compared to my childhood,' she said, 'and both realised we had rather . . . *unusual* childhoods.'

When they were finished and Jarrett paid the tab, she leaned back in her seat and asked, 'Well, did I pass the test?'

Barack smiled broadly. 'Yes,' he said, much to Jarrett's visible relief. 'Yes, you did.'

Michelle moved into a small office down the hall from Jarrett's and quickly gained a can-do reputation. 'You didn't go to her with a 311 problem,' Jarrett said. 'You went to her with a 911 problem, and she fixed it right away. She's that good.' Avis LaVelle, Mayor Daley's press officer at the time, concurred: 'Michelle was formidable – successful, smart, well liked, someone you paid attention to.'

Barack was never far away. 'She talked a lot about her fiancé, and he visited the office a few times,' said another operative at City Hall. 'Suddenly, she's giving him instant access to the powers that be in the Daley organisation, and all that entails.'

Of all the contacts Michelle made, none would prove more valuable than Valerie Jarrett. A fixture on Chicago's social scene, Jarrett moved effortlessly among Hyde Park's intellectual elite, the rank-and-file Daley Democrats who really ran the city and environs, and the 'lakefront liberals' (aka 'limousine liberals', 'Learjet liberals' and 'latte liberals') who occupied the glittering high rises that lined the shore of Lake Michigan. 'If you were raising money for a homeless shelter, a concert hall or a campaign for the US Senate,' said a City Hall colleague, 'there was nobody better to know than Valerie.'

Just as valuable were the contacts Michelle forged with leaders of the African American business community. Foremost among these was John W. Rogers Jr, the son of Republican powerhouse (and ambassador-at-large in the George H.W. Bush administration) Jewel Lafontant and Circuit Court Judge John Rogers Sr. In addition to founding Ariel Capital Management, he established the first two mutual funds managed by African Americans.

Through Michelle, Barack also met Marty Nesbitt, one of Craig Robinson's college basketball buddies. With the financial backing of billionaire Penny Pritzker, who would later play a huge role in Barack's political career, Nesbitt founded a hugely profitable airport-parking company known simply as the Parking Spot and would go on to head the Chicago Housing Authority.

Michelle had only been in the mayor's office for a few months when Jarrett was picked to head Chicago's Department of Planning and Development. Jarrett brought Michelle with her as the city's new 'economic-development coordinator', a job that put her in close personal contact with the top tier of Chicago's business community.

In her new job, Michelle not only promoted projects that would stimulate economic growth but also put her legal skills to use negotiating contracts between the city and a wide range of business entities. Real-estate developers, bankers, retailers, venture capitalists and union bosses – essentially anyone who sought to start or expand a business within the Chicago city limits – would find themselves sitting across the table from Michelle.

'She was very personable but also very tough,' said one developer who dealt with Michelle during this period. 'She always came in totally prepared, very commanding, and she knew her stuff. She paid a lot of attention to the stuff on the ground – what the impact would be on neighbourhoods, people's lives.'

Michelle revelled in her new-found authority and proved just as take-charge when it came to running her office. Where Jarrett and other managers were understandably reluctant to discipline or discharge a staffer, Michelle did not hesitate to lower the boom. 'I don't mind telling people what they need to know about their job performance,' she said. 'If it's great, I'll let them know. If it's lousy, I'll let them know that, too.'

For the most part, Michelle was, in the words of one City Hall colleague, 'always kind' to the people who worked under her. A favourite ploy was to tell an employee he or she had 'outgrown' the job and needed to 'move on' – usually to graduate school for additional training. 'You were halfway down the hall and feeling pretty good about yourself,' recalled one staff member who was given one of these talks by Michelle, 'before you realised you'd just been fired.'

Barack, who had had to deny promotions to disgruntled minority editors at the *Harvard Law Review*, was proud of what staffers routinely referred to as Michelle's 'tough but fair' approach at work. He was also impressed that she was able to accomplish what she needed to as a manager without leaving a trail of bad feelings in her wake. 'So you just told him he had to move on?' he asked. 'And he was just perfectly fine with that?'

With Michelle entrenched at City Hall and making valuable contacts among the heavy-hitters doing business with the city, Barack was free to continue laying the groundwork for a grassroots power base outside Chicago's political machine.

Towards that end, he became a founding board member of Public Allies, a nationwide non-profit organisation aimed at steering young people away from the private sector and towards public service. Public Allies signed up 18 to 30 year olds to work for a year with non-profit or government agencies providing services to the poor. In exchange, these 'allies' were paid a monthly stipend of up to $1,800 a month plus health and childcare.

Central to the purpose of Public Allies was to create a small army of like-minded young activists on the ground in cities like Chicago, New York, Los Angeles and Washington. By way of grooming this new generation of 'social entrepreneurs', Public Allies conducted a series of seminars and retreats during which Barack and other organisers exhorted recruits to shun 'the money culture'.

Although it was ostensibly non-partisan, Public Allies had a clear agenda from the outset. The young people who joined were urged to agitate for 'social change' through picketing, sit-ins and boycotts. 'Our alumni,' the organisation would soon boast, 'are more than twice as likely . . . to engage in protest activities.'

There was a heavy psychological component to the Public Allies regimen as well. Every week there were 'diversity workshops' during which recruits were required to take part in various exercises designed to break down racial, ethnic, religious and gender barriers. 'You're not going to be able to work together to get anything done,' Barack told a group of new Public Allies recruits, 'if you're fighting among yourselves. You've got to think and act as one if you want effect real change.'

Both happily consumed with work, neither Michelle nor Barack saw any reason to set a wedding date. They were content with the status quo: he maintaining his own apartment in Hyde Park, she staying with her recently widowed mother at her childhood home on South Euclid Avenue.

In early 1992, Toot phoned from Hawaii with the news that Gramps had taken a turn for the worse in his long battle with prostate cancer.

When he died that February, Barack travelled to Hawaii to comfort Toot and attend the funeral. Gramps had served in France under 'Old Blood and Guts' George Patton during the Second World War and, as a veteran, was entitled to be buried at Punchbowl National Cemetery. With his family and a few old friends from his bridge-playing days looking on, a bugler played taps as the American flag that had draped Gramps's coffin was carefully folded into a triangle and presented to Toot.

Later, as the family gathered at Toot's apartment, Barack's mother announced that she had finally finished the PhD dissertation she had been working on for nearly 20 years. She dedicated the opus – a 1,000-page analysis of peasant blacksmithing in Indonesia – to her mother, her doctoral advisor and 'to Barack and Maya, who seldom complained when their mother was in the field'.

Barack returned to Chicago with a renewed sense of urgency. He told Michelle that, having spent so much time at school, he now wanted to 'get on with life' – and that meant starting to get serious about making wedding plans.

Since she had been prodding him to do precisely that ever since he had proposed to her eight months earlier, Michelle's reaction was predictable. 'You're kidding, right?' she asked sarcastically. With the help of Michelle's mother, the couple began planning for their October nuptials. Barack's main caveat: 'Just as long as it's not around election time, that's all.'

He wanted to be unencumbered during the 1992 presidential elections – and with good reason. With Public Allies poised to deploy thousands of young activists into homeless shelters, AIDS clinics, abortion clinics and welfare offices across the country, Barack turned his attention to politics on his home turf.

Arkansas Governor Bill Clinton had hoped to wrest Illinois, a swing state that had gone to George H.W. Bush in the previous election, from the Republicans. Moreover, Cook County Registrar of Deeds Carol Moseley Braun was seeking to become the nation's first African American female senator. Even though the black vote was going to be crucial in the outcome of these contests, the fact remained that the Daley machine had never pushed registration in the city's predominantly black wards.

Barack was determined not to let this opportunity slip through the Democrats' fingers. Starting in April of 1992, he would spend seven months running the local office of Project Vote, a DC-based national voter registration drive aimed squarely at low-income, inner-city residents.

Devising a comprehensive media campaign based on the slogan 'It's a *Power* Thing', Barack enlisted the aid of local churches, college students and some of the Alinksy-inspired activists he had worked with during his community-organiser days to knock on the doors of thousands of homes on the South Side. In addition to helping to train some 700 deputy registrars, Barack often rolled up his sleeves and hit the streets himself, making his face familiar to thousands of potential voters in the process.

While Project Vote was ostensibly non-partisan, there was little doubt in anyone's mind that the overwhelming majority of these first-time voters – by most estimates more than 95 per cent – would register as Democrats. 'It was not very subtle,' said a former Democratic alderman. 'There were these big black-and-yellow posters with "Power!" in bold letters and a big X. The message was definitely one of harnessing black power at the ballot box – it sure as hell wasn't aimed getting whites to sign up.' Confirmed one volunteer: 'We targeted areas where there were blacks and Latinos. Period.'

Project Vote proved to be something of a baptism by fire for Barack, who promptly found himself having to cope with various turf wars between elected officials and grassroots activists. He was determined not to let any of these petty rivalries get in his way. 'He was typical,' said ward chairman Ivory Mitchell, 'of what most aspiring politicians are: self-centred – that "I can do anything and I'm willing to do it overnight."'

Not quite. But in the span of just six months, Barack's army of volunteers registered more than one hundred and fifty thousand black voters. This was enough, it would turn out, to secure the state for Clinton – the first time Illinois had gone Democratic since Lyndon Johnson was elected in 1964 – and a Senate seat for Moseley Braun.

The pay-off for Barack came in the form of valuable new connections made with grassroots leaders, office holders and liberal donors – all connections he actively sought out. Abner Mikva remembered a typical exchange:

'Abner, do you know so-and-so?' Barack would ask.

'Yes.'

'How well do you know him? I'd really like to meet him.'

'He wasn't obnoxious about it – not at all,' Mikva recalled. 'But he certainly wasn't shy when it came to asking for help, either.'

Mikva, like so many others Barack approached for help, obliged by setting up a series of lunches. It was also during Project Vote that Barack met Bettylu Saltzman, daughter of Chicago shopping-mall magnate and former Commerce Secretary Philip M. Klutznick. Saltzman not only touted the nervy political neophyte to her rich and powerful friends as a future president, but she also introduced him to a man who had been chief political consultant to both Harold Washington and the incumbent Mayor Daley: David Axelrod.

Again, it was Barack who sought out the meeting with Axelrod. 'I think he was strategic in his choice of friends and mentors,' Chicago Alderman Toni Preckwinkle said. 'I think he saw the positions he held as stepping-stones to other things.'

At the same time, Barack also had his mind on another important project that was in the works: his upcoming wedding. Michelle had seen the white half of his family during their Christmas trip to Hawaii, and he was grateful that she had had the chance to know Gramps before he passed away. But for Michelle to really understand the man she was going to marry, Barack felt it was important that she meet the people who had shaped his father's life.

In late spring of 1992, Barack took Michelle to meet the other half of his far-flung family – the half-brothers, half-sisters, cousins, aunts, uncles, stepmothers and step-grandmother who lived in Kenya. As they strolled the dirt roads of Alego, the small village on the shores of Lake Victoria where Barack's father had grown up, Michelle was 'deeply moved. Not just to be in Africa, but to be where Barack's family lived for generations . . . it was overwhelming, really.'

In Alego, Michelle proved an instant hit with Barack's relatives. With her statuesque bearing, athletic gait, ebony skin and ready smile, she fitted in easily. It also helped that she made a serious effort to learn Luo, the local dialect. Barack's step-grandmother Sarah, who spoke only a few words of English and communicated with him through an interpreter, was especially impressed with his choice of fiancée. 'She is very beautiful,' Granny said, 'and obviously she has very good taste in men.'

When Michelle asked to see what life was like for urban Kenyans, Barack and his half-sister Auma took Michelle to Nairobi's Kibera district, the largest slum in Africa. This first-hand look at the desperate conditions Africa's poor city dwellers live in left Michelle shaken. 'I cried,' the usually hard-nosed Michelle confessed. 'You couldn't look at those children and *not* cry.'

Before they left, Michelle and Barack invited all of the Obamas to their wedding in early October. A few would actually make it, including Barack's older half-sister Auma, who boasted a PhD in German literature from the University of Heidelberg, and Auma's brother Malik. Also known as Abongo or Roy, Malik had a special assignment – to serve as best man.

On 3 October 1992 – a Saturday – some 130 invited guests filled the pews of Trinity United Church of Christ to see Michelle LaVaughn Robinson wed Barack Hussein Obama. The best man wore a traditional black African gown trimmed in white and a matching cap. The ring-bearers, Michelle's five- and six-year-old cousins, wore little tuxedos with African cloth caps that matched their cummerbunds.

The rest of the men, including the groom, Michelle's uncles and Barack's old friends from Punahou School in Hawaii and his roommates at Occidental, wore white tie.

In keeping with Barack's Kenyan roots and the Afrocentric bent of Trinity United, several in attendance – including Reverend Wright – joined Malik Abongo in wearing traditional African dress. But most, including Valerie Jarrett, Jesse Jackson and the scores of public officials, corporate lawyers, business leaders, activists, academics and community organisers who made up Barack and Michelle's rapidly expanding world, opted for the usual business suits and dressy outfits. Barack's mother, Ann, who had flown in from Hawaii with his sister Maya, wore a knee-length black skirt and an orange silk blouse, Marian Robinson, a floor-length black skirt and a sequined black-and-white top.

Michelle's maid of honour, Santita Jackson, sang as the bride walked down the aisle in a classic off-the-shoulder white silk sleeveless gown worn with long white gloves. As the afternoon light streamed through the cavernous sanctuary's stained glass windows, the Reverend Wright pronounced Michelle and Barack man and wife. Barack would later observe that, despite the emotion of the moment, only his sister Auma cried. Still, Valerie Jarrett recalled, 'it was magical. They were clearly madly in love with each other.'

The reception was held at the South Shore Cultural Center, a majestic, pink-walled, tile-roofed Mediterranean-style villa that had once been an exclusive whites-only country club. For their first official dance as man and wife, they chose Nat King Cole's 'Unforgettable'. Santita Jackson also sang one of Michelle's favourite Stevie Wonder ballads, 'You and I'.

The Obama nuptials stood out from other weddings, Michelle's friend and law-firm colleague Kelly Jo MacArthur observed, 'because people understood that putting the two of them together was like putting hydrogen and oxygen together to create this unbelievable life force. Everybody knew it. We understood that together they were going to be so much more than they would have been individually.'

Barack's church mothers – Loretta Augustine-Herron, Yvonne Lloyd and Linda Randle – were also among the guests. 'We were overjoyed with the choice he made,' said Augustine-Herron, who admitted that Barack's 'other family' had been wondering aloud if anyone would be good enough for their surrogate son. 'Michelle was smart, attractive, fun – right up there on the same level with Barack. And she was so genuinely nice – none of that phoney stuff. When she talked to you, she made you feel like she really cared – just like Barack. She had *class*.'

'It was obvious to all of us that Michelle was the right woman for our Barack,' Augustine-Herron said. 'She is obviously his equal, and he needs to have an equal as his partner in life – someone he can talk to on the same level.' It was also obvious, Randle added, that 'Michelle can stand on her own two feet. The last thing Barack needed was a woman who was high maintenance.'

As they met the wedding party on the receiving line, all three women were impressed by Ann Soetoro. 'Barack's mother was so warm and kind,' Lloyd recalled. 'You could really see there was a lot of her in him. I told her she did a good job of raising her son, and she just nodded and smiled. Of course, later I discovered that Barack's grandmother was probably an even bigger influence on his life.'

The couple honeymooned in California, driving up the narrow Pacific Coast Highway that winds along the coastline from Santa Barbara past Big Sur and Carmel on the way to San Francisco. They made the trip with the windows rolled down – despite Michelle's objections, Barack was smoking more than ever – and whenever he flicked his ashes out the window, Michelle was quick to admonish him. 'Hey,' she said, anxiously looking at the next blind bend in the road, 'both hands on the wheel, buddy.'

When she wasn't gasping at the oncoming trucks that seemed to come perilously close to running them off the road and into the sea, Michelle marvelled at the endless vistas of blue-green water and waves crashing on the rocks below. 'They revelled,' Maya said, waxing poetic, 'in the majesty of the cliffs and the water.'

Back at home in Chicago, Mr and Mrs Barack Obama moved in with Michelle's mom while they looked for a place of their own. Six months later, they paid $277,500 for a two-bedroom apartment on the ground floor of a three-storey condominium complex on South Eastview Park, near the lakefront and not far from the University of Chicago campus in Hyde Park.

The newlyweds gave several small dinner parties at their spacious new condo, which was decorated with paintings, photographs and artefacts from their travels to Kenya and Hawaii. Over simple but elegant dishes like shrimp over pasta, the Obamas would entertainment no more than two or three couples. 'Michelle was charming, gracious, very professional,' Mikva recalled of these evenings. 'It was obvious she was not the kind of woman who would be happy just baking cookies. And of course she was beautiful – strikingly so.'

At the time, there were those among Barack's ever-widening circle of wealthy and influential friends who regarded him as something of a bore. 'Because Barack was so smart,' said their friend Cindy Moelis, a Stanford Law School graduate whose father was president of New

York's Equity Leasing Corporation and a breeder of thoroughbred racehorses. Moelis, who met Michelle when both women were working at City Hall, was married to fellow Stanford Law School alumnus Robert Rivkin, the Harvard-educated son of John F. Kennedy's ambassador to Luxembourg.

'Barack was pretty serious when we were in our thirties,' Moelis said. So sombre, in fact, that she used to poke him and say, 'Come on, let's talk about the last movie you saw.'

According to those closest to him at the time, Barack was preoccupied with one thing: following in Harold Washington's footsteps. Once the November 1992 election was over and both the Clinton and Moseley Brown campaigns thanked Obama's Project Vote campaign for making the difference in Illinois, Barack decided to join a law firm. He was thinking of taking up the offer of Judson Miner, the lawyer who had earlier been told that he was 647th in line. But first he wanted Michelle's opinion. She told him that if he wanted to join a legal outfit that was the diametric opposite of Sidley Austin, he could not do better than the small civil rights firm of Davis, Miner, Barnhill & Galland.

Unlike Michelle, who had appeared in court during her legal aid days at Harvard and occasionally wrote briefs in the civil cases handled by Sidley Austin, Barack would never be involved in a trial or write a brief on his own. Over the nine years he was associated with the firm – which primarily handled discrimination cases and worked with developers of affordable housing projects – Barack worked exclusively as part of a team of lawyers, apparently never taking the lead.

For Barack, who had also signed on as a visiting lecturer at the University of Chicago School of Law, there was far more to Davis, Miner, Barnhill & Galland than the practice of law. His name was Judson Miner. One of the chief legal minds behind the rise of Harold Washington, Miner had served as corporation counsel – the city's chief lawyer – during Washington's tenure in City Hall.

Whatever contacts Barack hadn't already made through Michelle, Valerie Jarrett and the Sidley Austin partners, he now secured through Miner. 'If Judson doesn't know somebody,' Barack cracked, 'then I guess I don't have to know them, either.'

It was just as well. Michelle was again beginning to feel restless in her job as Chicago's economic-development coordinator – a position that, since it catered directly to the business community, was beginning to resemble her old job at Sidley Austin.

Barack had his own reasons for wanting Michelle out of City Hall. With his sights still set on becoming mayor – or perhaps a US senator – both he and Michelle worried that her continuing association with the Daley regime might tarnish the reputation he sought to build as a young reformer. 'You don't have to think evil of Obama or City Hall,' said veteran Chicago activist Quentin Young, 'to realise that could be a liability to a person who is politically on the rise.'

As it happened, Public Allies was looking for a new executive director, and Barack, who still sat on the board, proposed Michelle for the job. Before she took it, he resigned from the board to avoid any appearance of impropriety.

'It sounded risky and just out there,' she said. 'But for some reason it just spoke to me. This was the first time I said, "This is what I say I care about, right here. And I will have to run it."'

As head of the non-profit foundation that was eventually wrapped into the federal AmeriCorps programme, Michelle proved to be even more aggressive – and effective – than her husband had been. Going after millions in contributions from Chicago's long-established philanthropies, she now found herself introduced to a whole new set of movers and shakers – the old-money crowd that wielded tremendous power and influence while managing to stay discreetly below the radar.

Once again, Michelle asserted herself as a tough taskmaster, upbraiding staff members who were not performing to her standards and, in some cases, telling them it was time to 'move on'. Even those who were higher up in the chain of command were intimidated by Michelle. 'Even though she worked for me,' said Vanessa Kirsch, who actually picked Michelle for the job, 'I definitely felt like I worked for her.'

Through Public Allies, Michelle took scores of young activists under wing. 'Each ally was placed with a not-for-profit, about 20 to 30 a year,' said one of those protégés, Craig Huffman. 'When you think of the number of people who got to know who Michelle was, and by extension Barack, that's a whole generation from all over Chicago.'

Not all of the Obamas' time was spent tending to their widening network of sociopolitical contacts. In fact, Barack was faced with another, more pressing deadline. The autobiography he was supposed to turn in to Simon & Schuster in 1991 was now two years overdue, and Barack remained hopelessly blocked.

When the publisher finally cancelled the project in 1993, Barack worried that they would come after him for the $75,000 he had already been paid – half the agreed-to $150,000 advance. But when Barack informed them that he had spent the money – and that both he and his wife were still chipping away at their massive student-loan debt – the publisher agreed not to press the issue.

With only a partial manuscript in hand, Barack turned again to his gravel-voiced agent Jane Dystel, who promptly landed him yet another deal – this time for $40,000 – with the Times Books division of Random House. For months, Barack worked until the early morning hours in what Michelle dubbed 'the Hole', his tiny, cluttered office tucked discreetly behind their kitchen.

'The Book', as he now referred to it, was more than just a vanity project. Drowning in debt, the Obamas needed a massive infusion of capital if they were to stay afloat financially. 'Let's face it,' Michelle told him point-blank, 'one of us is going to have to get a job with a big corporate firm and make some real money or we're going to have to move back in with Mom.'

But Barack had a plan. He was convinced that the book he was working on would become a bestseller, and he was already thinking of a sequel.

'It was like Jack and his magic beans,' she later recalled of those conversations. 'He's like, "Look, honey, I'm going to write these books and we'll be fine," and I'm like, "Yeah, sure, right."'

She had good reason to be sceptical. When he sat down to write what would become *Dreams from My Father*, Barack had filled up scores of legal pads with notes, all in his overarching left-handed scrawl. Beyond jotting down his thoughts and observations over the years, however, he had not really done much writing. At the *Harvard Law Review*, while he was responsible for selecting which articles were sufficiently scholarly to make the cut, his only *Review* article was an unsigned defence of legalised abortion.

Lamentably, Barack had tried his hand at verse. Back during his undergraduate years at Occidental, he published two poems in *Feast*, a student literary journal. Later, in a masterpiece of understatement, he would call these literary efforts 'very bad'. From Barack's poem entitled 'Underground':

> Under water grottos, caverns
> Filled with apes
> That eat figs.
> Stepping on the figs
> That the apes
> Eat, they crunch.

In another poem entitled 'Pop'– the only other known, signed example of his writing up until this point – Barack seemed to be writing about drinking and getting high with an older friend:

> Under my seat, I pull out the
> Mirror I've been saving; I'm laughing,
> Laughing loud, the blood rushing from his face
> To mine, as he grows small,
> A spot in my brain, something
> That may be squeezed out, like a
> Watermelon seed between
> Two fingers.

Desperate to finish the book, Barack and Michelle took a leave of absence from their jobs and decamped to the Indonesian island of Bali so that, as his sister Maya put it, he could 'find a peaceful sanctuary, where there were no phones, to work on the book'. When he returned in early 1994, Barack burrowed even deeper into the Hole in a last-gasp effort to finish the book.

Two months later, with a September 1994 deadline looming, Barack was still stymied. It was around this time that, at Michelle's urging, he sought advice from his friend and Hyde Park neighbour Bill Ayers. Michelle had known Ayers's wife, Bernadine Dohrn, at Sidley Austin, where Dohrn worked as a paralegal between 1984 and 1988. Dohrn's father-in-law, former Commonwealth Edison CEO Thomas Ayers, just happened to be one of the firm's most important clients.

Barack got to know Bill Ayers's father and his brother, John, when all three served on the Leadership Council of the Chicago Public Education Fund. Another mutual friend of Ayers and Barack was Jean Rudd, whose non-profit Woods Fund had provided Jerry Kellman with the money he needed to hire Barack as an organiser back in 1985.

Neither Michelle nor Barack seemed particularly troubled to discover that William Ayers and Bernadine Dohrn had been two of the 1960s' most infamous radicals – leaders of the Weather Underground terrorist group that had set off thirty bombs in the 1960s and 1970s.

After an explosion in the Weathermen's Greenwich Village bomb-making laboratory killed three of their fellow Weathermen (including Ayres's girlfriend at the time, Diana Oughton) and virtually destroyed the neighbouring townhouse owned by Dustin Hoffman, Ayers and Dohrn went underground. In 1973, charges against them were dismissed due to prosecutorial misconduct, but Dohrn remained a fugitive until she finally turned herself in to police in 1980.

Ayers made no apologies for his terrorist past, and in the 1990s still described himself as 'a radical, Leftist, small "c" communist . . . The ethics of communism still appeal to me. I don't like Lenin as much as the early Marx.'

Ayers's radical past didn't seem to bother Chicago's civic leaders, many of whom worked with him on education reform. He worked particularly closely with Mayor Richard M. Daley on reshaping the city's school programmes – an effort that also brought him into contact with one of Daley's assistants at the time, Michelle Obama.

What did interest Barack were Ayers's proven abilities as a writer. Unlike Barack, Ayers had written scores of articles and treatises, as well as several non-fiction books, beginning with *Education: An American Problem* in 1968. But it was the tone Ayers had set in his latest book – *To Teach* (1993) – that Barack hoped to emulate.

The tale of a maverick teacher who takes her students onto the streets of New York to teach them first-hand about history, culture and survival, *To Teach* was written in a fluid, novelistic style. Barack asked for Ayers's input, and Ayers, who like so many in his circle was greatly impressed by the charismatic young activist, obliged.

To flesh out his family history, Barack had also taped interviews with Toot, Gramps, Ann, Maya and his Kenyan relatives. These oral histories, along with his partial manuscript and a trunkload of notes, were given to Ayers. 'Everyone knew they were friends and that they worked on various projects together,' another Hyde Park neighbour pointed out. 'It was no secret. Why would it be? People liked them both.'

In the end, Ayers's contribution to Barack's *Dreams from My Father* would be significant – so much so that the book's language, the oddly specific references, the literary devices and themes would bear a jarring similarity to Ayers's own writings. Even the caveat at the beginning of *Dreams*, in which Barack points out that he uses invented dialogue, embellished facts, composite characters, inaccurate chronology and pseudonyms to create an 'approximation' of reality, resembles Ayers's defence of the inaccuracies in his memoir *Fugitive Days*. In the foreword to his book, Ayers states the book was merely a collection of his personal memories and 'impressions'.

'There was a good deal of literary back-scratching going on in Hyde Park,' said writer Jack Cashill, who noted that a mutual friend of Barack and Ayers, Rashid Khalidi, thanked Ayers for helping him with his book *Resurrecting Empire*. Ayers, explained Cashill, 'provided an informal editing service for like-minded friends in the neighbourhood'.

Certainly none of these authors hesitated to acknowledge their admiration for one another at the time. In his 1997 book *A Kind and Just Parent*, Ayers would cite the 'writer' Barack Obama (along with Muhammad Ali and Louis Farrakhan), as one of the celebrities living in his neighbourhood. In turn, Barack would write a glowing review of that same book for the *Chicago Tribune* and Michelle would host a panel discussion on Ayers's book at the University of Chicago, with Ayers and her husband as the principal speakers.

Thanks to help from the veteran writer Ayers, Barack would be able to submit a manuscript to his editors at Times Books. With some minor cuts and polishing, the book would be on track for publication in the early summer of 1995. In the meantime, he began showing the rough draft to a chosen few relatives.

Toot, for one, was miffed at his portrayal of Gramps as a bitter man, and the tensions that arose in the house when she became the principal breadwinner. And she didn't like the profanity used in the book, particularly one word that described a part of the female anatomy. 'It probably made her a little nervous, having the family written about,' Maya said of their grandmother, 'just because you don't do that in Kansas.'

Toot was also worried about passages where Barry admitted to being a regular user of pot and an occasional user of cocaine in his youth. It was a concern shared by Michelle. 'That stuff isn't going to sit well with the ladies at church,' she warned him – the very women, she pointed out, that he would need once he decided to run for governor or the US Senate.

Barack disagreed, and so did Jeremiah Wright. In recent years, Wright had become increasingly strident in his rhetoric – among other things, praising the likes of Louis Farrakhan, Fidel Castro and Mu'ammer Gaddafi, and attacking Washington for allegedly starting the AIDS epidemic as part of a vast conspiracy to annihilate the world's black population. A number of members of the congregation – most notably Oprah Winfrey – left the church. 'Oprah is a businesswoman, first and foremost,' one long-time friend told *Newsweek*. 'She's always been aware that her audience is very mainstream, and doing anything to offend them just wouldn't be smart.'

Barack, who heard such messages delivered from Wright's pulpit scores of times over the years, apparently did not share Oprah's misgivings. The reverend remained the Obamas' closest and most trusted spiritual advisor. Wright, who had always been candid about his own teenage arrest record, urged Barack to share the details of his marijuana and cocaine use in the book. Not only was it an evocative illustration of Barack's own 'redemption', Wright told him, but it would also speak directly to young men in the black community who had struggled or were struggling with drugs.

Moreover, Barack, who now described Reverend Wright as 'a father figure' to him, had shared his political aspirations with the reverend in detail. Wright reminded him that, despite Barack's contributions to the black community, there were those who remained wary of him. While Trinity United's congregation was more affluent and sophisticated than most, many of those people Barack encountered on the South Side still found the eager young activist too exotic (raised in Hawaii and Indonesia), too well educated (Columbia, Harvard) and too white (raised by his Kansan grandparents, his speech had neither the cadence nor the rich flavour of Chicago's African American community).

Barack had long been concerned that he lacked 'street cred' and had already explained to Michelle that his book offered the fastest and most effective way to remedy the situation. Now that Wright agreed, Michelle dropped her opposition. 'Barack loved and respected Reverend Wright,' said a fellow church member, 'but not as much as Michelle. She had grown up going to church and made that kind of attachment to her pastor. Michelle was in total awe of Reverend Wright.'

Barack also sent the manuscript to his mother in Hawaii. The book's focus on Barack's father, who had abandoned Barack and Ann to return to Africa, surprised her. It was Ann, after all, who – along with Toot and Gramps – had raised Barack and shaped his values. But Ann shrugged it off. 'She never complained about it,' her friend Nancy Peluso said. 'She just said it was something he had to work out.'

Around this time, Ann returned to Indonesia to do more fieldwork and to reconnect with several old friends. She was dining in the Jakarta home of one of them, economist Richard Patten, when she doubled over with a sharp stabbing pain in her stomach. The next day, Barack's mother went to a local doctor, who diagnosed her with indigestion, gave her an over-the-counter remedy and sent her on her way.

The pains in Ann's abdomen persisted, however, and when she returned to Hawaii three months later she visited the doctor again. This time, she was told she had advanced uterine and ovarian cancer.

Understandably, Barack was devastated by the news. That Christmas, he and Michelle flew out to Hawaii as they always did to spend the holiday with Barack's family. Chemotherapy had caused Ann's hair to begin falling out, but the prognosis was hopeful. What really concerned Ann at the time was the possibility that her insurance might run out, leaving her unable to pay for her cancer treatments. 'At a time when she should have been focused on getting well,' he later said, 'my mother was in a hospital bed arguing with her insurance company because they refused to cover her treatment on the grounds that she had a "pre-existing condition".'

Barack returned to Chicago more determined than ever to run for office. He went to his friend Abner Mikva and asked him to put out feelers to see if any office might be opening up. 'He couldn't wait,' Mikva said, 'to get into the ring.'

He wouldn't have to wait long. In early 1995, Illinois Congressman Mel Reynolds was facing charges of having sex with an underage campaign worker. In August, Reynolds would be convicted and sentenced to two years in prison (later he would be sentenced to an additional six and a half years for wire and bank fraud). Reynolds finally resigned his seat on 1 October. But in the meantime, there was a frantic scramble to replace him. One of those most interested in Reynolds's job was fifty-five-year-old African American State Senator Alice Palmer.

This was precisely the opening Barack had been searching for. He had actually paid a visit to his alderman, Toni Preckwinkle, to broach the subject in January of 1995. 'If Alice decides she wants to run for Mel Reynolds's seat,' Barack told Preckwinkle, 'I want to run for her state senate seat.'

His first run for office aside, 1995 would turn out to be an eventful year for the Obamas. On 22 June, Barack was officially named chairman of the Chicago Annenberg Challenge – an Annenberg Foundation-funded grant that was the brainchild of Barack's friend and neighbour Bill Ayers. The Challenge, aimed at promoting reforms in the public school system, would dole out $49.2 million to various experimental projects – including a 'Peace School' where the curriculum centred on a United Nations theme – before shutting down in 2003 because, said the foundation's final report, it had 'little impact on school improvement and student outcomes'.

Five days after Barack's appointment to head the prestigious Annenberg Challenge, Palmer announced she was running for Congress and soon made it clear she backed Barack to succeed her in Springfield. Not long after, Bill Ayers and Bernadette Dohrn hosted a small gathering for Palmer in the living room of their Hyde Park home. Barack was there as well, and while Ayers did not technically launch his political career as would later be suggested, he was likely the first to introduce Barack as a candidate.

Then, on 18 July 1995, *Dreams from My Father* was published to generally positive reviews. Barack embarked on a ten-day national book tour, and although in this first incarnation *Dreams* would sell only ten thousand copies, it added considerably to the author's cachet among Chicagoans.

One of several book parties honouring the novice author was thrown by Valerie Jarrett, who packed her elegant art deco-designed co-op in the Kenwood district of Hyde Park with some of Chicago's wealthiest and most influential citizens. Coincidentally, it was the same week Mel Reynolds was convicted in his sexual assault case. Alice Palmer had already announced her intention to run for Reynolds's soon-to-be-vacated seat, and Jarrett's book party was abuzz with gossip about Barack's impending run to fill her seat.

'Michelle was there,' remembered one guest, 'working the room like a pro while he sat there autographing books.' Her mood changed noticeably, however, when talk of a possible state senate run came up. 'Everyone was buzzing about it, but,' said the guest, 'Michelle was clearly not enthusiastic.'

Indeed, Michelle confided in one long-time friend that the subject had been the source of heated arguments between them. 'It's beneath you, Barack,' she told him. 'It's too small-time. What can you possibly accomplish in *Springfield*?'

But Barack persisted, and Michelle acquiesced. 'I married you because you're cute and you're smart,' she said. 'But this is the dumbest thing you could have ever asked me to do.'

On 19 September, more than 200 supporters showed up at the Ramada Inn Lakeshore in Hyde Park-Kenwood to hear Barack announce his candidacy in the same room where Harold Washington had announced his candidacy for mayor 13 years earlier. 'Barack Obama carries on the tradition of independence in this district,' Palmer said when she introduced him to the standing-room-only crowd. 'His candidacy is a passing of the torch.'

In addition to setting him up with several of her key precinct operatives, Palmer went to her long-time supporters and asked if they would host a series of coffees to introduce Barack to voters. Over the course of the next six months, there would be as many as four per week.

One of the first of these meet-and-greet events was hosted by Rabbi Arnold Jacob Wolf. 'Some day you are going to be vice president of the United States,' Wolf told him.'

Barack laughed. 'Why not president?' he asked.

Another couple who hosted one of these coffees had no such reservations about Barack's prospects. 'This guy,' Martha Ackerman said to her husband, Sam, 'could be the first African American president of the United States.'

It was during this period that, according Barack, his relationship with controversial Syrian-born developer Tony Rezko 'deepened'. Rezko had pushed for legislation to give hefty tax credits to real-estate developers like himself who were willing to build low-income housing in Chicago's run-down neighbourhoods. Rezko hired Davis, Miner to represent his interests, and in the process became friendly with Barack.

While he turned down Rezko's frequent entreaties to go to work for him as far back as his days on the *Harvard Law Review*, Barack did consult him on his political future. He also relied on Rezko for financial support; the developer would become his largest single contributor, paying for a consider chunk of Barack's state senate campaign.

One of Tony Rezko's biggest boosters was Michelle, who had met him during her stint as Mayor Richard M. Daley's economic-development coordinator. The Obamas soon began socialising with Rezko, dining at his Wilmette, Illinois, mansion and even visiting his sprawling vacation home in Lake Geneva, Wisconsin. 'Michelle was impressed with the Rezkos and their devotion to her husband, and she clearly enjoyed their company,' said a Rezko business associate who dined with both couples on several occasions. 'Michelle encouraged Barack to cultivate the Rezkos. I think she liked them even more than he did.'

With his March 1996 primary still five months away, Michelle pressed Barack to take time out to visit his desperately ill mother in Hawaii. Toot and Maya had been keeping Barack apprised of her worsening condition, but Ann kept insisting she was doing fine and responding to treatment. There was no reason, she said, for her son to interrupt his campaign to visit her.

Michelle wasn't buying it. 'Dad always said he was feeling great no matter how bad he really felt,' Michelle reminded Barack. That was precisely what he had said when he went out the door to work that final morning. Michelle still regretted the fact that no family member was with her father when he passed away, and she did not want Barack saddled with the same feelings of remorse.

'I think you ought to take the time to go out and see your mother,' Michelle told her husband, trying to downplay the fact that it might well be the last time. 'You can surprise her. She'll be thrilled.'

Whether or not he was in denial about the gravity of his mother's condition – she had been told at the time of her diagnosis that she had only a slim chance of survival – or actually believed Ann's fervent claims that she was responding to treatment, Barack put off visiting his mother.

Instead, Jeremiah Wright had persuaded Michelle to let Barack to accompany him to Nation of Islam leader Louis Farrakhan's Million Man March in Washington on 16 October 1995. As soon as he returned, Barack approached the alternative news weekly the *Chicago Reader* and offered to share his impressions of the event.

'Historically,' he told the *Reader*, African Americans have turned 'towards Black Nationalism whenever they have a sense, as we do now, that the mainstream has rebuffed us, and that white Americans couldn't care less about the profound problems African Americans are facing. What I saw,' he continued, 'was a powerful demonstration of an impulse and need for African American men to come together to recognise each other and affirm our rightful place in society.'

Less than three weeks later, on 7 November 1995, Barack was back in Chicago working on his campaign when news came that Ann had died. She was 52. As Michelle predicted, he was overcome with guilt. 'I should have been there,' he told her. 'I should have been there . . .' Maya and Toot tried to reassure him that the end had come suddenly, unexpectedly – that they had all believed there would be time for him to say goodbye. But Barack would never forgive himself. 'The single greatest regret of my life,' he would later say, 'was not being there when my mother died.'

Barack and Michelle flew to Hawaii and, along with Toot and Maya, scattered Ann's ashes over the Pacific. 'My mother was the sweetest woman I've ever known,' he would say. 'Everything I am, I am because of her.'

When Michelle and Barack returned to Chicago, they brought with them some of the treasures his adventurous mother had collected over the years – including her childhood arrowhead collection from Kansas and two trunks crammed with Indonesian batiks. Ann's friends would also say something of her lived on her son. 'When Barack smiles,' said Nancy Peluso, a pal from her days in Indonesia, 'there's just a certain *Ann* look. He lights up in a particular way that she did. There is·this thing in his eyes.'

Barack would need all the optimism he could muster. As the primary election for Mel Reynolds's Second Congressional District seat approached, it was clear to everyone that Alice Palmer was going to go down to defeat. Still upset by the loss of his mother, Barack met with a group of veteran black leaders who asked him to release Palmer from her promise not to run for re-election to the state senate.

'We want you to step aside,' one of the men said, 'like other African Americans have done – for the sake of unity.'

At first, Barack did not reject their request. He told the older gentlemen – many of them whom had resisted his earlier efforts at community organising in earlier years – that he would think about it. He hadn't decided what he was going to do.

After Alice Palmer went down to crushing defeat at the hands of Jesse Jackson Jr in the 28 November 1995 congressional primary, her backers again demanded that Barack withdraw from the state senate race so she could reclaim her old seat. 'We don't think Obama can win,' said Northeastern Illinois University Political Science professor Robert Starks. 'He hasn't been in town long enough. Nobody knows who he is.'

This time, Barack refused. 'I've gone out and raised money, opened an office, recruited people, put my name out there,' he said. 'And I'm supposed to take that back because you now want to change the agreement we already had? That just doesn't make a lot of sense.'

Alice was furious that the young upstart she had backed now refused to step aside for her. Armed with an endorsement from the very man who had just beaten her in the congressional race, Jesse Jackson Jr, Palmer dispatched volunteers to collect the signatures from registered voters necessary to get her on the ballot for the March 1996 state senate election. On the 18 December deadline, she filed nominating petitions containing the 1,580 signatures – twice the number required.

Based on his own experience signing people up for Project Vote, Barack knew that in Chicago ('where three out of two registered voters is a Democrat'), politicians took a less than punctilious approach to signing up prospective voters. It also struck Barack that Palmer's volunteers had gathered the necessary signatures in an extraordinarily short period of time.

Barack ordered his campaign operatives – actually called 'operators' in Chicago – to check out Palmer's petitions filed at the Chicago Board of Elections. Comparing the names on the petitions with those on the actual voter registry, they uncovered scores of irregularities – enough to disqualify two-thirds of the signatures.

Palmer argued that, in most cases, the disqualifications hinged on such technicalities as the misspelling of a street name or whether or not an individual printed, rather than signed, his or her name on the petition.

No matter. Palmer was denied a spot on the ballot. Seeing how easy it was to knock one opponent off by challenging her petitions, Barack had his operators check his other opponents as well. By the time they were finished, all of his opponents had been knocked off the ballot. In his first bid for office, Barack ran unopposed.

'To my mind, we were just abiding by the rules that had been set up,' Barack said in defence of what some viewed as an underhanded tactic. Was it fair to deny the voters a choice of more than one candidate? he was asked by the *Chicago Tribune*. 'I think they ended up,' he replied, 'with a very good state senator.'

Michelle could not have agreed more. She was immensely proud of her husband's election victory and stood beaming by his side at all his public events. But, as thrilled as she was that Barack now held elective office, she worried that the manner in which he won might come back to haunt him. Michelle had, in fact, begged her husband not to challenge Alice Palmer's petitions. 'It will just leave a bitter taste in everybody's mouth,' she told him. 'The big Harvard lawyer comes here and uses his legal tricks to knock poor old Alice and everybody else off the ballot. Who the hell does he think he is?'

Moreover, even though she campaigned at his side – showing up in the living rooms of strangers for neighbourhood coffee klatches and charming potential donors like the Rezkos over dinner, Michelle still believed that the state senate would only sidetrack her husband. 'She felt it was just too small-time,' one friend said. 'They both already know so many important people; she just wanted him to go straight to the national stage. Either that or make tons of money.'

As it sank from sight, it soon became apparent that Barack's book *Dreams from My Father* was not going to provide the windfall they had hoped for. Between his salary at Davis, Miner, Barnhill & Galland and hers at Public Allies, they were grossing about $250,000 a year – still not enough to pay off their student loans. 'I worried a lot,' she said of this period, 'about where the money was coming from. Somebody had to.'

Barack floated above such petty concerns. 'There will be plenty of time to make money – lots of it,' he assured his wife. 'Right now is the time to make a difference.' Besides, he like to say with a sly wink as he held up one of his credit cards, 'have plastic, will travel.'

As was the case in many families, the Obamas' household finances were handled by Michelle. While he was three and a half hours away in Springfield, she did the bookkeeping, wrote out the cheques, filled out the insurance forms, even assembled records for tax purposes. Barack was only asked to submit his receipts so he could be reimbursed for legitimate business expenses, and that he did only sporadically. 'It made her a little crazy that he had such cavalier attitude towards money,' an aide said. 'She was very grateful when we'd remind him every once and a while about keeping track of his expenses. But it was something that he had no interest in doing.'

According to his banker grandmother Toot, Barack, like his mother and grandfather, was 'clueless' when it came to handling his personal finances. 'Barry has no head for money,' said Toot, who sympathised with her daughter-in-law's mounting sense of frustration in that department. She even apologised to Michelle for 'not emphasising that more' when Barack he was growing up.

Michelle was also fretting about her husband's personal habits. Barack did not pick up his socks and underwear, and was less than religious about hanging up his clothes at all. He left wet towels on the bathroom floor, cups and glasses scattered about the house, and the toilet seat up. Dirty dishes were left in the sink until Michelle placed them in the dishwasher, and all the laundry, ironing, vacuuming and dusting was left to her. 'And,' she told her mother and anyone else who cared to hear, 'Barack never, ever replaces the paper towels – or the toilet paper.'

Early bird Michelle, who was usually in bed by ten, also resented the fact that he stayed up alone until two in the morning, then slept in. And he snored.

For Michelle, Barack's chain-smoking was particularly annoying. Aside from the obvious health concerns – 'Buddy, did you ever hear of second-hand smoke?' she would tease – Michelle was fed up with the sheer messiness inherent in Barack's nasty habit. Ashtrays brimmed with cigarette butts – which could also be found stubbed out in coffee cups and saucers – and there were cigarette burns in the carpet. The acrid smell of smoke lingered on their clothes, in the drapes, in the upholstery, in her hair. She moved a framed picture on the wall to reveal that the walls of their condo were turning a sickly yellow, along with his teeth and fingertips.

'Michelle is a very meticulous person,' Valerie Jarrett said. 'Whether it's the clothes she wears or her home, she maintains a very high standard.' A standard that her husband, much to Michelle's near-constant frustration, was either unable or simply unwilling to live up to.

Absorbed in his nascent political career, Barack was oblivious to the trouble brewing at home. When Michelle did erupt, it often triggered arguments that seemed to last for days. 'Like a lot of husbands,' said one of her friends, 'Barack couldn't figure out what her problem was. All her complaints about him being a slob – which I heard her call him many times, sometimes joking, sometimes not – well, he thought they were petty. You know, it was "Why are you bothering me with this crap while I'm busy changing the world?"' That attitude 'only made Michelle crazier. She was just as accomplished as he was, and she out there changing the world, too. So why, she wanted to know, was she cleaning up after him?'

Underlying Michelle's dissatisfaction was a deeper, more pressing concern. Not long after their marriage in 1992, Michelle and Barack began trying to start a family. 'When it didn't happen right away,' said Marian Robinson, 'she got a little worried.'

By the time Barack went to Springfield to be sworn in as a state senator in the spring of 1996, Michelle was frantic. When a physician friend pointed out that the stress of working 60 hours a week running Public Allies might have been a factor in her inability to conceive, Michelle quit.

Instead, she took a job as the associate dean of student services and the first director of community relations and community service at the University of Chicago. When she arrived to interview for the job, she startled the dean of student services by announcing that, although she grew up just blocks from the university, she had never set foot on the campus. 'All the buildings have their backs to the community,' she explained later. 'The university didn't think kids like me existed, and I certainly didn't want anything to do with that place.'

Unfortunately for her husband, who lectured at 'that place', most blacks shared Michelle's hostile attitude towards the University of Chicago. Viewed as a bastion of white intellectual elitism smack-dab in the middle of one of Chicago's grittiest minority communities, the university had made little effort to connect with the working-class people who encircled it. 'The University of Chicago is not a brand that helps you,' said Obama's friend and one-time aide Will Burns, 'if you're trying to get votes on the South Side of Chicago' – votes he would need if, say, he wanted to run for Congress.

But for the time being, the votes from Hyde Park would be enough to keep him ensconced in the state senate. When Barack arrived in Springfield, it was with a built-in reputation as, in Burns's words, 'a threat'. Precinct worker Ron Davis agreed: 'He knocked off the incumbents, so that right there gave him some notoriety. And he ran unopposed – which for rookie is unheard-of.'

When he landed at the State Capitol in January of 1997, the high-minded, Ivy League-educated freshman senator seemed like something of a hothouse flower to his backroom-dealing, often literally cigar-chomping colleagues. 'What the hell are you doing here? You don't belong here,' fellow Democrat Denny Jacobs said bluntly. Barack, he said, just 'looked at me sort of strange'.

Corruption was as rampant as ever in the Illinois legislature and, to make matters worse, Republicans controlled the Senate when Barack arrived – and they would continue to control it for the next six years. Since state government was firmly controlled by the 'Four Tops' – the Senate President, the House Speaker and the two minority leaders – run-of-the-mill lawmakers like Barack were held in especially low regard. They were called 'mushrooms' because, as Barack would explain with a laugh, 'We are kept in the dark and fed shit.'

From the moment he set foot in Springfield, Barack was determined not to fall into that category. Right after being sworn into office, he was approached the powerful Democratic leader Emil Jones, a friend from his organising days.

'You know me,' Barack told Jones. 'You know me quite well.'

'Yes? And?' Jones asked tentatively, squinting through a cloud of cigarette smoke.

'You know I like to work hard,' Barack continued. 'So feel free in giving me any tough assignments.'

'Good,' said Jones, who promptly saddled him with legislation on campaign-finance reform. In his caucus, Barack, who assiduously courted his Republican counterparts in search of a viable compromise, was the object of boos and catcalls.

'He caught pure hell,' Jones remembers of his protégé's performance. 'I actually felt sorry for him at times.'

Barack's toughest critics were fellow African American senators who viewed him as a know-it-all snob. 'Just because you're from Harvard,' Senator Donne Trotter would snipe, 'you think you know everything.' Rickey Hendon, whose district was on Chicago's West Side, frequently squabbled with Barack on and off the Senate floor. 'What do you know, Barack?' he asked during one debate. 'You grew up in Hawaii and you live in Hyde Park. What do you know about the street?'

One verbal sparring match on the Senate floor nearly escalated to the real thing. At one point, after yelling at each other for fifteen minutes, the normally unflappable Barack strode over to Hendon's desk with fists clenched. 'I'm gonna kick your ass!' he told Hendon before someone stepped in to break them up.

For the most part, Barack avoided his fellow African American senators from Chicago and instead befriended his fellow legislators – mostly white – from the suburban and rural southern part of the state. In addition to taking up golf ('An awful lot happens on the golf course,' he told his friend Jean Rudd), Barack joined fellow senators and a few lobbyists for their weekly poker game. He quickly proved himself to be a methodical, if cautious, card player. 'I'm putting his kids through college,' complained Republican Terry Link.

One of Obama's earliest allies in Springfield was Jacobs, a self-described 'old-school, backroom politician' and a member of Barack's tight-knit circle of poker players. At first, Jacobs recalled, Barack was 'always asking questions for the sake of asking questions. So I got up and said, "Listen, go learn on your own goddamned time. We're doing business here." And he didn't get ticked. He just listened, and took in the advice, and from then on when he asked a question it was right to the point. That's the thing about Barack: he has a tremendous capacity to grow – to learn and to retain.'

At the urging of his new political advisor Dan Shomon, Barack also decided to test the waters outside Chicago – to see if he would stand a chance with white middle-class voters in the event he tried for statewide office. In order to make him seem like less of an elitist, Shomon played Pygmalion to Barack's Galatea. Gone was Barack's casual uniform – worn with obsessive–compulsive consistency – of a wide-collared black silk shirt, jeans and Bass Weejuns worn with no socks. Now, when he played golf with the local Kiwanis and Rotary Club members, he donned a polo shirt, khakis, golf shoes and a cap.

He made similar adjustments in his food preferences when he was courting 'downstaters': now he drank beer instead of Chablis, used yellow mustard squeezed out of a plastic bottle instead of Dijon, and was careful to order doughnuts, not croissants, when he dropped in to chat with town burghers at the local coffee shop.

More important than these cosmetic changes was the fact that, in the faces of these mostly white middle-class Midwesterners, Barack saw Toot, Gramps and his mother. He understood them just as easily as he understood the inner-city black population he represented, and they responded in kind. 'I learned if you're willing to listen to people,' he reflected, 'it's possible to bridge a lot of the differences that dominate the national political debate. I pretty quickly got to form relationships with Republicans, with individuals from rural parts of the state, and we had a lot in common.'

Back in Springfield, Barack laboured in relative obscurity to get a handful of bills through. Between these efforts and his relentless network building, there was little time left for Michelle.

With Barack away from home in Springfield at least four days a week during the legislative session and lecturing once a week at the University of Chicago Law School, Michelle would only see him weekends. She did what she could to keep busy – up at 4.30 a.m. to work out at the gym, then off to work at the university, lunch with friends, back to work, sometimes dinner with her mother, then home to television, some reading and bed by 9.30 p.m.

When Barack was in Springfield, he and Michelle shared the details of their days apart over the phone. While he said he would 'fall asleep content in the knowledge of our love', Michelle hung up feeling, she told one friend, 'frustrated and sad'.

Unlike Barack, who lived in abject fear of ever leading a humdrum nine-to-five existence, Michelle cherished order and routine. These were the things that had sustained the Robinsons through her father's long illness. But they could not disguise the fact that she missed her husband. 'Michelle was feeling lonely,' Valerie Jarrett told a mutual friend. 'Desperately so.'

The fact that they had been trying to have a baby for over four years now was also weighing heavily on Michelle's mind. She was talking to friends about fertility clinics and adoption when, in November of 1997, a visit to her doctor confirmed the results of a home pregnancy test.

'Hey! You're kidding!' Barack shouted when she broke the news to him over the phone. 'Wow. Wonderful, wonderful.' Barack's first impulse was to share the good news with the one person who, next to Michelle, who meant the most to him. 'Got to call Mom,' he said, reaching for the phone before reality struck. 'Oh . . .'

The life of a political wife is hard.
And that's why Barack is such a grateful man.

Michelle

If I'm a ten, Michelle's an eleven.

Barack

They're very demonstrative.
You'll always pick up a glance between them, a touch . . .

Valerie Jarrett, friend

She's my co-conspirator.

Barack on Michelle

I don't want anybody to think that it's easy . . .
We have a strong marriage, but it's not perfect.

Michelle

6

'Now we have two things to celebrate on the Fourth of July!' Barack declared as he cradled his infant daughter in his arms for the first time. Obstetrician Anita Blanchard, who also happened to be the wife of Barack's close pal Martin Nesbitt, was thrilled that the delivery had gone so smoothly – particularly in light of the fact that Michelle had had such difficulty conceiving.

Barack and Michelle named their first child Malia Ann, a nod to both her grandmothers. Malia is the Hawaiian equivalent of 'Mary', the closest they could come to Marian, and Ann after Barack's mom.

Elated, he kissed his wife and left her to rest in her private room at the University of Chicago Medical Center maternity ward. It was only as he was driving back to see her a few hours later that he realised he was empty-handed. Frantic, he pulled over at the Hyde Park Shopping Center on 55th and Lake Park Avenue and dashed into Joyce's Hallmark card shop.

He walked up and down the aisles for a few minutes before finally approaching the store's owner, Joyce Feuer, and throwing up his hands. 'My wife has just had a baby,' Barack said, 'and I'm visiting her and our incredible daughter in the hospital, and I have absolutely no clue as to what to bring her. Flowers? A card?'

An old hand at such things, Joyce and her sales staff quickly whipped up a gift bag that included pink balloons, a card for Mom and a plush teddy bear. She congratulated Barack as he grabbed the bag, turned and bolted out the door. 'Even for a first-time father,' said the sales clerk, 'he was just over the moon with joy.'

There were plenty of reasons for Barack and Michelle to celebrate Malia's Fourth of July arrival, not the least of which was the simple fact that Daddy was actually on hand to enjoy it. During the summer, he was able to stay in Chicago because the state senate was not in session. Nor did he have to teach any classes, or spend long hours attending meetings, preparing his lectures and grading papers. Michelle was also free; she had taken maternity leave and would not be returning to her job at the university until September.

For three months, they revelled in the joys of young parenthood. They sang to her, rocked her, burped her, dangled keys above her head to get her attention, took countless snapshots ('So many we started to wonder if we were damaging her eyes,' he said) and showed her off to anybody who happened to be in the vicinity. Because Dad was a night owl and Mom was an early bird, she turned in even earlier than usual and he stayed up until 2 a.m. heating up bottles, changing diapers and rocking Malia to sleep. Barack would later remember this period in their lives as 'magical'.

The magic, however, ended with the summer. Once again, Barack was in Springfield four days a week – sometimes more. They hired a babysitter to take care of Malia so that Michelle could return to work, but when she returned home from the office each night she faced the job of caring for Malia alone.

The tensions that had been simmering in their marriage ever since he was elected to the state senate were now boiling over. The phone calls between them were becoming less frequent and more terse. She scolded him for spending so much time in Springfield – where he did not have to cope with 1 a.m. bottle feedings, changing diapers, laundry, housekeeping and – most importantly – a mind-numbing lack of adult conversation and companionship. 'Politics,' she went so far as to tell a local reporter who asked about her husband's nascent political career, 'is a waste of time.'

More to the point, Michelle viewed Barack's state senate career as a *costly* waste of time. 'She still didn't really understand,' Dan Shomon said, 'why he was not at a law firm, where he could be making $700,000 or $800,000 a year or a million or two, and why he was lowering himself to the state legislature.' Observed Abner Mikva, 'They were as poor as church mice, and she was one very unhappy mouse.'

Nevertheless, with a babysitter caring for Malia during the day, Michelle was free to put in her usual eight hours at the university. There, she managed to repeat the success she had had at Public Allies. By pushing undergraduates to go outside their comfort level and volunteer in the community, she started the process of breaking down walls of resentment that had built up over decades.

But when she came home to Malia and no Barack, Michelle felt 'very much alone. It was hard to suddenly be by yourself with a baby,' she said, 'and frankly I was angry.'

It wasn't much better during the few days a week Barack did manage to spend in Chicago. Back to his old schedule, he was either teaching or out at meetings giving the kind of heartfelt speeches that had made Michelle love him in the first place. Only now, Barack's social consciousness no longer seemed so endearing.

Michelle shared her frustrations with her brother, who had given up his career on Wall Street to coach the basketball team at Brown University, and with her mother. They had little success trying to calm her down. 'Michelle is really upset with Barack,' Marian Robinson confided to an old family friend, 'and you know she's not shy about telling him off.'

Barack acknowledged his shortcomings. 'I leave my socks around,' he conceded. 'I'll hang my pants on the door. I leave newspapers lying around. But she lets me know when I'm not acting right.'

For the most part, he felt he was being treated unfairly. 'Whenever I could, I pitched in,' he later wrote. 'All I asked for in return was a little tenderness.' Instead, he when he got home he would find post-it notes (PLEASE PICK UP AFTER YOURSELF – YOU LEFT YOUR UNDERWEAR ON THE FLOOR AGAIN!) and endless lists of chores to do and errands to run.

'I remember the lists,' Shomon said. '"OK, Barack, you're going to do grocery shopping two times a week. You're to pick up Malia. You're going to do blah, blah, blah and you're responsible for blah, blah, blah." So he had his assignments, and he never questioned her, never bitched about it.'

Occasionally, Barack struck back with a reminder that she had racked up more than her share of parking tickets, but for the most part he just asked her to be patient. He was still finding his way as a politician, he reminded her, and things would improve once he'd settled into the job. 'After all,' he said, 'it isn't as if I'm out carousing with the boys every night . . . As far as I was concerned, she had nothing to complain about.'

For Michelle, the final straw came with Barack's decision to challenge incumbent Democratic US Congressman Bobby Rush for his party's nomination. The former Black Panther, Student Nonviolent Coordinating Committe member and Stokely Carmichael follower had just been trounced by Richard Daley in Chicago's mayoral primary, and Barack interpreted that defeat as meaning that Rush was vulnerable.

'You are *so* wrong,' Michelle would later say she told her husband. As a daughter of the South Side, she knew just how popular Rush was with the voters in his district, regardless of how he played city-wide. Barack was still inexorably linked in the minds of South Side voters with the University of Chicago and Hyde Park's academic elite. 'There is just no way,' she warned him, 'that you are going to beat Bobby Rush.'

'Michelle put up no pretence of being happy with my decision,' he later wrote. 'Leaning down to kiss Michelle goodbye in the morning, all I would get was a peck on the cheek.'

'Michelle was not a happy camper,' said Barack's friend and fellow senator Denny Jacobs. 'She felt he was wasting his time in Springfield, but she also felt that running for Congress just wasn't worth the trouble. There are plenty of congressman. If he was going to be in politics at all, she wanted him to aim higher.' For his part, Jacobs pushed his friend to seek higher office. 'As far as you're concerned,' he told Barack, 'it's either up – or out.'

Barack wouldn't listen to Michelle, or to advisors who also warned that he faced real resentment from voters for even daring to challenge the popular incumbent. 'The accusations were that Obama was sent here and owned by the Jews,' said Obama campaign worker Al Kindle, 'that he was here to steal the black vote . . . that he didn't know the black experience . . . It was quite deafening.' Added Denny Jacobs's son Mike, also a state senator and an acquaintance of Barack's, 'He had to put up with a lot – being called an Uncle Tom was the least of it. But it just rolled off his back.'

Barack fuelled this perception with remarks that were viewed by many as overtly condescending. 'I gave up a career,' he reminded voters during one stump speech, 'with a high-priced law firm to run for office.'

In terms of connecting on a grassroots level, the best thing Barack had going for him was Michelle. Black voters had no qualms about asking right off the bat whether Barack's wife was white or black. 'Whenever we told them he married a black woman who was born and raised on the South Side,' said a campaign worker, 'you would see a whole different attitude.'

Michelle joked with voters about her bona fides ('You don't get any blacker than me'), but privately she was angry that Barack was being viewed with suspicion. 'I've really had it with that stuff,' she said. 'When you think of all that he's done for the community, it's just insulting.'

Still, Barack was unable to distance himself from the notion that he somehow wasn't black enough to represent Rush's South Side district. It didn't help that Barack's speaking style was decidedly professorial. When he first heard his friend speak at a black church, Abner Mikva was 'completely dismayed. Barack had always appealed to the Hyde Park crowd – the eggheads – and here he was talking to a bunch of African American church ladies as if they were his law students. Frankly, it didn't make any sense to me. I was shocked.' Eventually, Michelle would manage to convince her husband to loosen up in front of black audiences. 'The single most important factor in getting Barack to change his way of speaking in front of black audiences was Michelle,' Mikva said. 'If it hadn't been for her, Barack would never have connected with this core constituency—and he never would have gone beyond the state Senate.'

Unfortunately for Barack, this essential transformation from pedant to folksy orator would not take place until after the congressional campaign. In the meantime, his campaign suffered another blow when Rush's 29-year-old son Huey was shot and killed. Voters were hard-pressed not to sympathise with Rush – a feeling that only intensified when, towards the end of the campaign, Rush's father also died. Even Barack's old South Side friends like Loretta Augustine-Herron knew he was in trouble. 'Bobby Rush had suffered so many tragedies that everybody felt very sorry for him,' she said. 'We are a very tight-knit community. We don't turn our backs on our own.'

When Barack knuckled under to pressure from Michelle and refused to return from his annual family vacation in Hawaii to vote for gun-control legislation, Rush held a press conference to excoriate him. Then, in the final week of the campaign, President Bill Clinton did a series of spots on black radio endorsing Rush. 'I'm President Clinton,' he announced, 'urging you to send Bobby Rush back to Congress where he can continue his fight to prepare our children for the twenty-first Century. Illinois and America needs Bobby Rush in Congress.' At that point, said Obama supporter Toni Preckwinkle, 'It was hopeless.'

Barack lost by a staggering two-to-one margin. Back at the Ramada Inn Lakeshore, where Barack had launched his political career just five years earlier, Michelle stood by her husband's side while he made his concession speech. 'I've got to make assessments,' he told the crowd, 'about where we go from here. We need a new style of politics to deal with the issues that are important to the people. What's not clear to me is whether I should do that as an elected official or by influencing government in ways that actually improve people's lives.'

For the first time in his life, Barack tasted defeat. He took it hard. So did Michelle. 'Michelle is great,' told a Springfield colleague, 'at "I-told-you-so's".'

Ebullient in victory, Barack was incapable of disguising his disappointment in the face of his first loss. 'I am very competitive, but nothing like Barack,' Michelle said. 'He is a terrible loser. It really gnaws away at him.' Barack spent the next few weeks, he later said, 'licking my wounds, and trying hard to figure out what went wrong – and what I could have done differently'.

Barack had been warned by Jesse Jackson that the shooting death of Rush's son was a 'game changer', but Jeremiah Wright told Barack that was only part of the reason he went down to crushing defeat. The reverend told him that he had jumped the gun, that he hadn't taken the time to line up enough party leaders to support him. 'You were,' he said, 'kind of out there on your own.'

That autumn, Michelle learned that she was pregnant for a second time. As happy as they undoubtedly were, the news merely reinforced Michelle's concern about the family's finances. Even though they were taking home combined salaries of $250,000, for some reason it was not enough for them to pay their bills and keep up with payments on their student loans. Occasionally they were, Barack conceded, 'short at the end of the month' – falling behind on various payments and using credit cards to stay afloat.

Michelle worried that, if Barack continued to chase his political dreams at the expense of his family's finances, they were headed for bankruptcy. 'Calm down,' he would tell her. 'Things are going to be fine. You worry too much.' Barack believed differences in both their upbringing and their 'wiring' accounted for the fact that she was rife with worry while he remained unfazed. 'I don't get as tensed or stressed,' he pointed out. 'I'm more comfortable with uncertainty and risk.'

Michelle needed more than just soothing words from her husband. She pleaded with Barack to think more seriously about making what she called 'serious money'.

Instead, he returned to Springfield determined to win over those Democrats who had been reluctant to support him in the past. Chastened, Barack appeared at his first poker game after being trounced by Bobby Rush and, before anyone else could speak, looked around the table, shook his head and confessed, 'I know, I know.' Disarmed by this mea culpa, Barack's colleagues roared with laughter.

In the coming months, Barack turned down a chance to run for Illinois State Attorney General because he did want to subject Michelle to another gruelling campaign schedule so soon after his ill-fated congressional run. But he spent more time than ever in Springfield, shoring up alliances that would prove valuable in the future.

Of these, none was more important than Barack's budding personal relationship with the party's crusty, gravel-voiced Democratic Senate leader, Emil Jones. A contemporary of Michelle's father, Jones had also grown up in the Robinson's old neighbourhood and worked in Chicago's sanitation department. His father, like Fraser Robinson, had been a Democratic precinct captain, and Jones had cut his teeth on South Side politics. Building his own organisation from the bottom up, Jones was a force to be reckoned with – and after 27 years in Springfield, was poised to take over the Senate once control of the legislature returned to the Democrats.

Even though Jones had supported Bobby Rush, he and Barack remained more than just close allies and friends. Although for years he often spoke of Jeremiah Wright as a father figure, he praised Jones as 'my political godfather'. After he heard that, Jones began using the theme from the film *The Godfather* as his cell-phone ring tone. 'I am blessed to be his godfather,' Jones told a reporter at one point during this period, 'and he feels like a son to me.'

With himself strategically positioned in Springfield as Emil Jones's protégé, Barack also carefully tended to his Chicago connections. Already serving on both the Woods Fund board and the board of the billion-dollar, Chicago-based Joyce Foundation, Barack now added the prestigious Saguaro Seminar to his list of obligations. Tackling the amorphous question of how to build 'social capital' by getting people more involved in their communities, Barack was joined at the weekend seminars by the diverse likes of Christian conservative Ralph Reed and George Stephanopoulos.

During these meetings – carved from what little time he had to spend with his family – Barack could not conceal his naked political ambition from the other, better-known participants. According to Saguaro founder Robert Putnam, the Harvard professor who wrote *Bowling Alone*, Obama spoke so openly about his plans for higher office that they began teasing him. 'So we were in the midst of one of our intensive discussions about civic engagement,' Barack's former Harvard Law professor Martha Minow recalled, 'and after one of these discussions, ranging across the political sectors, he did this tour de force summary. We just said "When are you running for president?" It became a joke. We started to nickname him "governor".'

It was no joke for Michelle. The Obamas' second child was born on 10 June 2001, and once again family friend Anita Blanchard was the attending obstetrician. This time, Barack carried Malia into the room and introduced her to her gurgling baby sister Natasha. From this day forward, they would call her, simply, Sasha.

Even though the Senate had once again recessed for the summer and Barack was able to spend more time with his family, Michelle was becoming increasingly agitated. 'It was hard,' she said. 'I was struggling with figuring out how I was going to make it work for me.'

Sasha's terrifying meningitis scare in September of 2001 brought them closer together emotionally than they had been in years. The horrors of 9/11 continued to make it easier to keep things in perspective. 'In the grand scheme of things,' Michelle admitted, 'our problems didn't seem to amount to much.'

Incredibly, 12 September 2001 was business as usual in Springfield, where victorious Democrats gathered in the Stratton Office Building to redraw their legislative districts to give them a demographic advantage over their Republican opponents. 'It was like nothing had happened,' said John Corrigan, an Obama strategist and the man responsible for redrawing the districts of all incumbent Democrats. 'Everybody came in and all they cared about was their districts.'

Barack was not among them; he had attended to this task months earlier, sitting with Corrigan at a computer screen and carefully redrawing his district to include as many influential constituents as possible. 'The exposure he would have to some of the folks on the boards of the museums and CEOs of some of the companies that he would now represent,' Corrigan said, 'would certainly help him in the long run.'

Barack, already mindful of a larger responsibility to history, was hard at work at home in the Hole, writing his own position paper on the 9/11 attacks. 'We will have to make sure, despite our rage,' he wrote in the 19 September issue of the *Hyde Park Herald*, 'that any US military action takes into account the lives of innocent civilians abroad. We will have to be unwavering in opposing bigotry or discrimination directed against neighbours and friends of Middle Eastern descent.

Finally, we will have to devote far more attention to the monumental task of raising the hopes and prospects of embittered children across the globe.'

For a time, it looked as if the 9/11 attacks might also carry with them the seeds of Barack's political ruin. 'My God, Michelle,' he told his wife. 'They're saying Osama Bin Laden planned the attacks. *Osama*. Jesus . . .'

Barack valued Michelle's opinion above all others in part because, unlike many of his other friends, she pulled no punches. 'She's blunt,' he explained, 'so she can tell me things that maybe other people are afraid to tell me.'

In this case, she was not about to reassure him. When she had first heard Barack's name, she thought it sounded 'weird and off-putting'. The similarity between his name and that of a hated international terrorist could not, she told him, be 'a good thing'.

Just days after 9/11, Barack went ahead and had a long-ago scheduled lunch with a leading media consultant for Democratic candidates, Eric Adelstein. Both men had been thinking that Barack should consider making a run for statewide office – maybe the US Senate – but now, in Adelstein's words, the 'political dynamics' had changed. 'Hell of a thing, isn't it?' he told Barack as he held up the front page of the *Chicago Tribune* with Osama Bin Laden's picture on it. 'Really bad luck. You can't change your name, of course. Voters are suspicious of that kind of thing.'

Barack considered the possibility that, at age 40, he had been stopped in his tracks. He looked with envy at younger politicians who, simply by virtue of their names, faced a more promising future.

When Michelle called near tears to say that their babysitter had quit to return to nursing, Barack tried to reassure her. 'Michelle's thinking to herself, "What am I going to do?"' Barack remembered, 'because she had depended so heavily on this person to kind of hold it together. And she was, frankly, mad at me. Because she felt as if she was all alone in this process.'

Barack knew that as long as he stayed in politics the demands on his wife and young daughters would only get worse. Perhaps it was time, he thought, to finally focus on his family – to get that job in the private sector that would finance the cost of childcare, private school tuition and, eventually, college.

It was around this time that he was interviewed for a $300,000-a-year job running the Joyce Foundation, where he had been a board member for seven years. Barack nearly bolted at the last minute; he simply did not want it.

'What the is *wrong* with you?' Dan Shomon asked when Barack told him how he felt. 'This is a dream. You can build up money, build up relationships and run again.' Michelle's reaction to the news was one of quiet resignation. She knew all too well that her husband, despite his recent doubts about ever being able to overcome the Osama–Obama curse, was far too ambitious to quit as a mere state senator.

Barack was no longer certain that his name would keep him from higher office. He had been making inquiries of his powerful, well-connected friends in Chicago – chief among them Mayor Daley – and he was convinced that Illinois's incumbent Republican senator, Peter Fitzgerald, was vulnerable.

The Dartmouth-educated scion of a wealthy banking family, Fitzgerald had unseated one-term senator Carol Moseley Braun in 1998. He repeatedly ran afoul of his own party's leadership on a wide range of issues, including the authorisation of federal funds to build an Abraham Lincoln Presidential Library in Springfield and the $15-billion post-9/11 airline bail-out. Fitzgerald was, in fact, the only US senator to vote against the bail-out.

Because of his maverick, go-it-alone stance both in Washington and in Illinois, Fitzgerald's approval ratings were approaching record lows. GOP leaders were threatening to put up candidates to challenge him in the primaries. Barack was convinced that Carol Moseley Braun's Senate seat could be reclaimed for the Democrats in 2004 – and that he was just the man to do it.

'I want to be a senator,' Barack told his friend and Michelle's former boss Newton Minow.

'But you are a senator,' Minow replied.

'I mean a *US* senator,' Barack said.

Minow didn't take much convincing. 'Chief Justice Oliver Wendell Holmes once described Franklin Roosevelt as having "a first-class temperament and a second-class intellect,'" Minow said. 'Barack has a first-class temperament and a first-class intellect. It was a very, very, very long shot. But I told him to go for it.'

Few others were as encouraging. Marty Nesbitt, Valerie Jarrett, Jeremiah Wright, most of his poker-playing friends in Springfield – even the heavy-hitting fundraisers, academics, foundation board member types and Lakefront liberals who for years had been kidding him about running for president – seemed taken aback by his chutzpah. A few, including Nesbitt, actually laughed in his face.

Gradually, however, he managed to persuade them that he could mount an effective campaign – provided he could find a way to raise $10 million. With that kind of backing, which he believed he could raise from the well-heeled friends he had cultivated for years, he insisted, 'I guarantee you I will win.'

There were those, even among his supporters, who felt the former president of the *Harvard Law Review* might not be enough of a street fighter to win a knock-down, drag-out US Senate race. 'I've seen a lot of tough guys get knocked down and stay down,' Denny Jacobs said. 'I'll take the resilient guy who gets knocked down and gets right back up. It's going to be the hardest thing in the world to defeat Barack Obama. He just keeps getting right back up.'

While nearly everyone thought Barack was at best a long shot ('I remember thinking he had a snowball's chance in hell,' Toni Preckwinkle said), several friends appealed to him to reconsider for strictly personal reasons. Dan Shomon knew that Barack already felt 'tremendous guilt' over not spending more time with his children. 'It burns a small hole in his heart,' he said, 'every night when he is not with them.'

'You will destroy your marriage,' another friend told him. 'Look what you've put Michelle through already. She is really pissed off at you as it is. Don't do this.'

Barack turned steely. 'I've made up my mind,' he said. 'I'm running.'

He would, of course, be far more diplomatic when broaching the subject with his wife. 'Politics has been a huge strain on you,' he told Michelle, 'but I really think there is a strong possibility that I can win this race . . . If you are willing to go with me on this ride and if it doesn't work out, then I will step out of politics.'

Michelle studied his face. 'Just this one last time,' he pleaded. 'I think I can do this . . . Just give me one more shot. It'll either be up – or out.'

At this point, Michelle was primarily concerned with one thing: 'How are we going to make it – I mean, financially?' she asked. They were still deep in debt – in part due to his failed congressional race two years earlier. If he lost, that debt would deepen. In the unlikely event that he won, then they would have two residences to maintain – one in Chicago and one in the nation's capital. 'It's just killing us,' she told him. 'How will you afford all this?'

'I guess,' Barack replied matter-of-factly, 'I'll just have to write another book.'

Michelle, aware that his first book had taken Barack five years to write and ended up selling a modest ten thousand copies, shook her head in disbelief. 'Oh, another *book* . . . Snake eyes there . . . yeah, you just go ahead write that book, Jack.'

Then Michelle collected her thoughts and sighed. 'OK,' she said. 'Whatever.'

Barack looked at her quizzically. 'OK?' he asked.

'Yeah, we'll figure it out,' she said with a shrug. 'We're not hurting. Go ahead.' Barack waited for the inevitable zinger. 'And,' she said, grinning, 'maybe you'll lose.'

Michelle had, in fact, found a way to come to terms with the 'huge strains' Barack's political ambition had taken on their marriage. 'This was the epiphany,' she later recalled. 'I am sitting here with a new baby, angry, tired and out of shape. The baby is up for that four o'clock feeding and my husband is lying there, sleeping.' It was then that she realised if she simply left the condo at 4.30 a.m. and went to the gym for her workout, Barack would have 'no choice but to get up'.

The first time she disappeared after Sasha's 4 a.m. feeding, Barack didn't notice until 8 a.m., when he finally stumbled out of bed and realised he'd been left in charge of the kids. From that point on, whenever Barack was in town, Michelle tiptoed out of the apartment before sunrise and headed for a workout with her personal trainer. 'I would get home from the gym, and the girls would be up and fed,' she recalled. 'That was something I had to do for me.'

It was then that Michelle made the conscious decision that she would be the one to adjust to the circumstances he created – and not vice versa. 'The big thing I figured out was that I was pushing to make Barack be something I wanted him to be for me,' she explained. 'I believed that if only he were around more often, everything would be better. So I was depending on him to make me happy. Except it didn't have anything to do with him. I needed *support*. I didn't necessarily need it from Barack.'

Michelle decided to approach the problems in her marriage the way she would approach the problems she faced daily at work. 'I had to change,' she said. 'So, how do I stop being mad at him and start problem solving, and cobble together the resources? I also had to admit that I needed space and I needed time. And the more time that I could get to myself, the less stress I felt.'

Her husband was more than happy to oblige, giving the nod to hiring a full-time live-in housekeeper. Michelle also took her mother up on her long-standing offer to help her take care of Malia and Sasha.

No longer quite as stressed-out as she had been, Michelle felt free to consider yet another job switch. When University of Chicago Hospitals President Michael Riordan offered Michelle a job as executive director of community affairs, she showed up with Sasha in a car-seat carrier and breast-fed her in the ladies' room. 'It was probably the most unique interview I've ever had,' Riordan conceded.

With a starting salary of around $110,000, Michelle set out to accomplish at the University of Chicago Hospitals what she had accomplished at the main campus and, before that, at Public Allies. She wanted to build bridges between the medical centre's staff and the surrounding neighbourhood. Towards that end, she placed volunteers from the hospital in the community, and volunteers from the community in the hospital.

Periodically, Michelle would visit South Side health clinics, sometimes with Sasha in tow, and simply ask the administrators, 'What do you need?' Within a matter of days, a volunteer from the hospital would show up and pitch in. 'She was getting down with us . . . She really wanted us to tell her right then and right there, how can I help?' said Berneice Mills-Thomas, who runs several healthcare centres in Chicago. 'We'd never really seen that before.'

Michelle's superiors were no less impressed. 'I have seen her in a meeting with the board of trustees giving a presentation,' said her boss, Susan Sher. 'I have seen her with angry patients and community residents. I have seen her talking down a two year old in the middle of a temper tantrum. She can handle them all.'

Now that Michelle had given him the green light to run for the US Senate, Barack set out to collect as many IOUs as he could from party leaders. Part of his strategy was to get squarely behind his party's nominee for governor. Barack backed Illinois's African American Attorney General, Roland Burris. But when Burris lost to mop-topped Congressman Rod Blagojevich – thanks largely to the machinations of Blagojevich's powerful alderman father-in-law – Barack joined Blogojevich's inner circle of advisors. According to then Congressman Rahm Emanuel, he and Barack 'participated in a small group that met weekly when Rod was running for governor. We basically laid out the general election, Barack and I and two other advisors.'

On 27 June 2002, Barack appeared on a local TV news show to push Blagojevich's candidacy. 'Right now, my main focus is to make sure that we elect Rod Blagojevich as governor, we—'

'You working hard for Rod?' host Jeff Berkowitz interrupted.

'You betcha,' Barack answered.

'Hot Rod?'

'That's exactly right,' Barack shot back.

When Blagojevich became governor in November of 2002, Barack was one of the first people he thanked. Behind the scenes, Blagojevich was in awe of his new political ally – not because of Barack's vision, but because of his political savvy. He was particularly impressed with the finesse Barack had displayed in gerrymandering his district. 'Barack is a classy guy,' he told a member of his staff, 'but beneath it all he's a real street fighter. He knows how to work the system . . . You'd never guess it to look at him.'

Along with his new friend and colleague Rahm Emanuel, Barack was emerging as something of a political mastermind. 'He thinks strategically,' Emanuel observed. 'He sees the big picture.'

As a campaigner, however, Barack needed work. The measured, intellectual approach that had gone over so well with his fellow academics and foundation board members had been no match for Bobby Rush's earthy, booming delivery.

Once again, he could count on Michelle to tell him the truth. 'You take too long to answer questions,' she told him, 'and sometimes you just sound snooty, like you're talking down to your audience. If you're going to get through to people in the community, then you've got to speak their language.' She suggested he emulate the most effective speaker they knew – Jeremiah Wright.

On 16 September 2001 – the first Sunday after 9/11 – millions of Americans went to church to share their grief and pray for the victims and their families. At Trinity United Church, Wright offered a very different take on the terrorist attacks that had taken nearly 3,000 American lives. 'We bombed Hiroshima, we bombed Nagasaki, and we nuked far more than the thousands in New York and the Pentagon,' he thundered, 'and we never batted an eye. We have supported state terrorism against the Palestinians and black South Africans, and now we are indignant because the stuff we have done overseas is now brought right back to our own front yards. America's chickens,' Wright said, jabbing the air with his finger, 'are coming home to roost.'

That day, Barack and Michelle were at home caring for Sasha, who was still recovering from viral meningitis. But they were hardly surprised when they learned of Wright's incendiary remarks a few days later. The reverend's rants against so-called American imperialism, especially as it related to Palestine, South East Asia and Africa, were standard fare at Trinity United.

'Michelle and Barack were there practically every Sunday, with Malia and Sasha,' said one long-time church member. 'Nobody walked out when Reverend Wright was saying those things – they were cheering.' The Obamas were also apparently enthusiastic participants in the tradition of call and response that is the hallmark of black churches throughout the US.

Barack carefully studied Wright's oratorical flourishes, as well as his gestures and his pacing. He employed all these devices, liberally sprinkled with down-home aphorisms and gritty street vernacular, when addressing predominantly black audiences.

'There's going to be a certain rhythm you feel from the audience,' he told reporter David Mendell. 'An all-black audience is going to respond in a different way. They are not going to just sit there.'

Barack tried out his new, more laid-back, more rhythmic and idiom-filled style in the same South Side churches and meeting halls where, just three years earlier, he had been putting his audiences to sleep. He began every speech with the same nod of gratitude to his mentor and revered father figure: 'I bring you greetings from my pastor, the Reverend Jeremiah Wright.' It would be the same greeting Michelle would use when, in future campaigns, she spoke at churches on behalf of her husband.

Between speeches, Barack and Michelle focused on raising the $10 million that would, Barack insisted, make him an unbeatable candidate. Since Marty Nesbitt owed the existence of his airport-parking empire to one of the richest women in the country, Penny Pritzker, Barack asked Nesbitt if he would set up a meeting.

A granddaughter of Hyatt Hotel founder Abram Nicholas Pritzker (as well as one-time chairman of Superior Bank, which was closed by federal regulators because of the subprime mortgage crisis in 2001), Penny Pritzker shared in a family fortune estimated at over $20 billion. She had met Barack and Michelle socially, but was by no means convinced he was a viable candidate for the US Senate. Still, that August she invited Barack, Michelle and the girls up to the Pritzkers' sprawling lakefront summer 'cottage' about 50 miles outside Chicago.

When they arrived, Obama sauntered coolly up the front steps, slipped off his black sunglasses, took Pritzker's hand and leaned down to kiss her on the cheek. At that moment, it seemed unlikely that the billionairess would deny him the support he sought.

Pritzker and her husband, Bryan Traubert, were equally impressed with Michelle and their attractive, well-behaved offspring. After the Obamas departed for Chicago, Pritzker and Traubert went for a run and spent the whole time talking about Barack. In the end, they concluded that while he may lack a thorough knowledge of some important issues, he was so confident and so persuasive that he might just pull it off. 'Michelle was also an enormous part of the equation,' Pritzker said. It was right after their weekend meeting with Barack and Michelle, Pritzker said, that she decided she would support '*them*'.

Once Barack was anointed by the Pritzkers, one major contributor after another fell into line. Playboy Enterprises chairman and chief executive officer Christie Hefner, daughter of *Playboy* founder Hugh Hefner, came on board after Barack's friend Bettylu Saltzman brought him to meet the 'Ladies Who Lunch' – 19 well-to-do Chicago women with an interest in backing liberal candidates and causes. Christie then introduced him to *New York Times* columnist Thomas Friedman, and to TV producer Norman Lear, who in turn put Barack in touch with his powerful entertainment-industry friends in Los Angeles and New York.

Suddenly, money was no longer a problem. Throughout 2002, the biggest obstacle to Barack recapturing Carol Moseley Braun's old Senate seat was Carol Moseley Braun. The former senator toyed with the idea of running herself, and Barack knew that he stood no chance of getting his party's nomination if the popular Moseley Braun entered the race.

Frustrated that he could not announce his candidacy for the US Senate as long as Braun vacillated, Barack decided to attend the annual Conference of the Congressional Black Caucus in Washington. Michelle encouraged the trip; perhaps, she said, he could garner support from some of the bigger names in Congress.

What he discovered was something quite different. When he returned, he was so shaken by what he had encountered that he felt obliged to tell his pastor. Wright had attended the Black Caucus weekends before, so he was well aware of what went on there. Barack, Wright told writer Manya Brachear, 'had gone down there to get support and found out it was just a meat market. He had people say, "If you want to count on me, come on to my room. I don't care if you're married. I am not asking you to leave your wife – just come on." All the women hitting on him. He was like, in shock. He's there on a serious agenda, talking about running for the United States Senate. They're talking about giving him some pussy.'

Wright looked at Barack in amazement. 'Barack, c'mon, man. Come on!' the reverend said. 'It's just a non-stop party, all the booze you want, all the booty you want. That's all it is.' According to Wright, Barack went to meet Washington's African American congressmen and congresswomen 'with this altruistic agenda, trying to get some support. He comes back shattered. I thought to myself, "Does he have a rude awakening coming his way."'

While he waited impatiently for Moseley Braun to make up her mind, Barack was invited in October of 2002 to speak at a rally against US military involvement in Iraq. The invasion of Iraq would not take place until the following March, but Barack was already lining up with others in his party to oppose it. While future presidential hopefuls like senators John Kerry and Hillary Clinton would be persuaded that only US military action could prevent Saddam Hussein from unleashing his 'weapons of mass destruction', Barack thought otherwise.

As he was poised to run for the Senate, he had to think long and hard about whether this was a gamble worth taking. Sentiment in the country was running two-to-one in favour of a US invasion of Iraq, and President George W. Bush's approval ratings were at 65 per cent.

Once again, he turned to Michelle for advice. She had nodded in agreement when Jeremiah Wright preached that young black men were being used as fodder for 'another unjust war'. She also knew that that message resonated with South Side voters.

Besides, she reminded her husband, the very people he was counting on to fund his campaign were the ones that had invited him to speak at the rally.

'Let me begin by saying that although this has been billed as an anti-war rally,' he told the crowd, 'I stand before you as someone who is not opposed to war in all circumstances. The Civil War was one of the bloodiest in history, and yet it was only through the crucible of the sword, the sacrifice of multitudes, that we could begin to perfect this union . . . I don't oppose all wars. My grandfather signed up for a war after Pearl Harbor was bombed . . . What I am opposed to is a dumb war . . . a rash war. A war based not on reason but on passion, not on principle but on politics.'

The speech would serve Barack well as the American public gradually soured on the war; he would be one of the few leaders of either party who could claim he opposed the invasion from the beginning. At the time, however, he wasn't so sure his stance would pay off politically. 'What if,' he asked Michelle, 'it turns out like the Persian Gulf War and everybody comes home a hero?'

'It won't,' she told him. 'And even if it did,' she went on, 'you've got to say what you believe.'

By this point, Barack had managed to persuade one of Chicago's top campaign strategists to join his team. A long-time pal of Clinton advisor turned Congressman Rahm Emanuel, and one of Mayor Daley's most trusted advisors, the endearingly dishevelled, mustachioed David Axelrod was a seasoned practitioner of Chicago's take-no-prisoners brand of politics.

At the same time, Axelrod fancied himself a 'progressive', and it was that same streak of practicality mixed with idealism in Barack that most appealed to him. For her part, Michelle viewed all Chicago politicos with no small degree of suspicion – and Axelrod was no exception. 'Barack,' she would tell her husband repeatedly, 'this is not a noble business.'

Periodically, Michelle still found herself harbouring doubts about the wisdom of Barack's decision to pursue a life in politics – and what it was costing her family in terms of financial security. When he called home from the campaign trail ecstatic about the response he was getting from crowds, the response he got from Michelle was frosty at best.

'They're drinking the juice,' he told her immediately after delivering one of his rafter-rattling speeches. 'I feel like I'm inspiring people.'

'You don't even have enough money,' she shot back, 'to drink your own juice.'

As he did every December, Barack took the family to Hawaii for Christmas. Still stymied by Moseley Braun's indecision, he told Toot that maybe this was the end of his political career. But on Christmas Eve, things changed. Instead of trying to regain her Senate seat,

Moseley Braun, who was even more cocky than Barack, announced that she was making a run for the White House.

It was just the first of several breaks – some lucky, some calculated – that would go Barack's way in the coming months. In April of 2003, Republican incumbent Peter Fitzgerald announced that he was relinquishing his seat for family reasons. 'I thought I could beat him, and still think I could have beaten him,' Barack later said. 'But the fact that he did not end up running, obviously, left the field wide open.'

That same month, Jeremiah Wright was delivering one of his most incendiary sermons to date. 'The government gives them the drugs, builds bigger prisons, passes a three-strike law and then wants us to sing "God Bless America",' he bellowed as church members shouted 'amen' in reply. 'No, no, no, God *damn* America – that's in the Bible, for killing innocent people. God *damn* America for treating our citizens as less than human. God *damn* America for as long as she acts like she is God and she is supreme.'

For Barack, who according to several church members was present at Trinity United with Michelle and the girls when Wright gave his infamous 'God Damn America' sermon, such comments were hardly surprising. It was the kind of over-the-top rhetoric that Wright had indulged in for years. Moreover, downstaters and white liberal voters who had already succumbed to Barack's considerable charms would remain unaware of his ties to Wright, and there was essentially no chance that Wright's sermons would ever be covered in Chicago's mainstream press.

Now that the Democrats had finally wrested control of the state senate from the Republicans, Barack approached his political godfather with a proposition. 'You're now the Senate President,' he told Emil Jones. 'You have a lot of power.'

'I do?' Jones replied coyly.

'Yes.'

Jones continued to play along. 'Tell me,' he said, 'what kind of power I have.'

'You have the power to make a US senator,' Barack said.

'I do?'

'You do,' Barack answered with a nod.

'If I've got that kind of power,' Jones said, 'do you have anyone in mind?'

'Yeah,' Barack answered brightly. 'Me!'

Over the coming months, Jones ushered through several pieces of legislation crafted by Barack and aimed squarely at his core African American constituency. Among them: a bill that increased the number of poor children covered by Illinois's health-insurance programme, a law that forced the videotaping of criminal confessions, and, in response to complaints of African American motorists being harassed for 'driving while black', a law that required police to collect data on the race of every driver they pulled over as a way to monitor racial profiling.

Just as important, Jones's backing meant that other Democratic Party heavyweights – most notably Mayor Daley – would refrain from endorsing any other candidates in the primary. (Because Barack was so instrumental in getting Blogojevich elected, the governor was one of his earliest and most enthusiastic supporters.) And while Barack sold himself as an anti-machine politician, at the same he took Michelle's advice and privately approached not only Daley but also Daley's brother Michael asking for their support if he won the primary. 'Barack had some chameleon in him,' Mike Jacobs observed. 'He'll be what he has to be to garner support, but in the end you get the sense that he'll try to do the right thing.'

In addition to his political savvy, David Axelrod would soon provide Obama with some valuable ammunition for use against his most formidable Democratic adversary. Before he was hired by Barack, Axelrod was being wooed by Blair Hull, a flamboyant Las Vegas card player who turned his skills into a fortune on Wall Street. Hull had sold his company to Goldman Sachs for more than half a billion dollars and was now willing to spend whatever it took to get elected to the US Senate. He wanted Axelrod on board – at any price.

As tempting as the offer was, Axelrod never felt comfortable with the idea of taking on Hull as a client. Over the course of several meetings the previous year, Axelrod had learned some disturbing things about Hull – namely, that the court records from his third divorce had been sealed because of allegations of spousal abuse.

Axelrod warned Hull that this information would somehow be leaked during the campaign and doom his chances of ever being elected.

Once Axelrod was on board with Barack, he shared what he knew with his new boss and with Michelle. All three agreed that, even though Hull's media blitzkrieg had made him the Democratic front-runner, it was only a matter of time before the contents of Hull's sealed divorce records would be leaked, sinking Hull's candidacy. In the meantime, Hull would draw votes away from the other Democrat in the race, the popular state comptroller Dan Hynes.

With Barack's main rival in the primaries self-destructing, the other candidates in the race – all white – spent most of their time attacking each other. 'Nobody,' said a media advisor to one of the candidates, 'wanted to risk looking racist by slamming the only black candidate in the race. And Obama didn't seem like much of a threat, anyway.'

Barack's team, meanwhile, was delighted that none of the other candidates were forced to drop out. 'As long as they're competing for the same middle-class white votes,' one advisor said, 'that leaves the rest for us.' This divide-and-conquer strategy, predicated on the belief that the minorities, white liberals and some downstaters would vote for Barack, would be key to the success of the Obama campaign.

If he was going to stitch together this kind of coalition, Barack 'needed to be in about ten places at once', an advisor pointed out. To help ease the burden, a reluctant Michelle agreed to stand in for her husband at a few fundraisers and rallies. Occasionally, she introduced him – a task that, increasingly, she seemed to relish. 'I am tired,' she told an enthusiastic crowd packed into a South Side church, 'of just giving the political process over to the privileged. To the wealthy. To people with the right daddy.'

Michelle spoke passionately to anyone who would listen about her husband's qualifications, but she was determined that he not let her words go to his head. As he headed out the door to a candidates' forum one Saturday morning, Michelle stopped him in his tracks. 'Where do you think you're going?' she asked. 'Oohhh, no. You've been gone all week and I've got stuff to do today and you're taking the kids.'

When Barack arrived at the forum with Malia and Sasha in tow, his opponents, said Dan Hynes, 'felt a little sorry for the guy . . .

There he was, trying to herd these two little kids, and they're knocking things over and taking pamphlets and throwing them. And here he is trying to be this dignified Senate candidate.'

By the spring of 2004, Barack, who had been holding back on his own campaign ads, was ready to unleash his own barrage of TV commercials. But when Axelrod proudly unveiled the campaign's new slogan, Barack was decidedly underwhelmed.

'"Yes we can?" "Yes we *can*?"' he said between drags on a cigarette. 'I don't like it. Come on . . . I'd like a slogan that actually means something.'

But Axelrod argued forcefully for the 'Yes We Can' message. It was catchy, inspirational; it conveyed a sense of optimism, of hope. And most importantly, like any great advertising slogan, it was almost annoyingly simple and to-the-point – like 'Where's the beef?' or 'Head On!'

'Yeah, but I don't want to talk down to people,' Barack objected. '"Yes we can." Yes we can what? What does it mean?' Unswayed by the arguments of Axelrod and his media experts, Barack told his staff to come up with another. '"Yes we can,"' he said, 'just seems childish to me.'

Axelrod would not budge, so Barack tried it out on Michelle. She had always resented the fact that in the black community she had to 'dumb down' so that her South Side friends wouldn't think she'd turned her back on them. Michelle understood Barack's initial objects to 'Yes We Can'. But she also knew on a gut level that the phrase would resonate in Chicago's black neighbourhoods. Jesse Jackson, who had thrown his support to Barack, agreed. And when Barack tried the phrase out on Jeremiah Wright, the reverend shouted it to the rafters as if he were at the climax of one of his hell-raising sermons: 'Yes . . . we . . . *can*.'

In the end, Michelle's was the deciding vote. 'I like it,' she said, trying it out again and again, each with a different inflection. 'The brothers and sisters will get it, Barack.'

'I don't know,' he said, shaking his head. 'It's so corny . . .'

Michelle grew impatient. 'I am telling you,' she said, 'it will work. Trust me.'

In the end, Barack deferred to Michelle, as he always did when it came to what would appeal to African American voters. 'OK,' he told her at one meeting. 'You know more about that sort of thing than I do.'

As he looked over the rest of the field, Barack realised that, more than ever, much of his appeal as a candidate hung on his squeaky-clean image. He fostered the image of himself as a devoted family man and as a clean-cut fitness fanatic who worked out daily ('like a gladiator' said Gibbs), ran and played basketball whenever he could – despite the fact that, following a number of minor injuries on the court, Michelle was now pressuring her husband to give up basketball for something 'less punishing for a man your age – you know, like golf'.

That Barack veritably glowed with health belied the fact that he smoked – a lot. Like Jackie Onassis, who despite a life lived in front of the cameras was almost never photographed indulging her lifelong smoking habit, Barack went to great lengths to conceal his smoking from the public. He did so, he explained to one reporter who agreed not to write about his smoking habit, because he believed it would cost him votes. People who smoked, he said, were 'no longer cool. People think you lack personal discipline if you smoke.'

Driven to and from campaign stops in a chauffeured black SUV, he would hunker down in the back of the car and sneak a few drags while he talked on his cell phone. As the SUV sped along down the highway, he rolled down the window and tossed one glowing cigarette butt after another out the window. In the side-door pocket, where he also stashed a dog-eared copy of the Bible for quick reference, Barack kept gum to mask the smell on his breath.

Barack, who preferred Marlboros, felt free to smoke at home – although Michelle occasionally railed against him for exposing their daughters to second-hand smoke – in closed-door meetings with his staff, on the chartered plane that he used to barnstorm the state. But as the pace of the campaign quickened and the stress mounted, he found himself becoming increasingly testy – particularly when he was unable to duck out of sight for a cigarette.

'Having to hide it is killing him,' Michelle conceded to a co-worker, adding that he seemed to be spending 'half the time' looking for a stairwell or an alleyway where he could light up without being spotted by a reporter or a photographer.

In the closing weeks of the campaign, the 'Yes We Can' spots Barack had so vehemently opposed turned him into a statewide media star. Giggling girls and middle-aged women alike mobbed him on the street. Even the wife of one of his opponents looked like a smitten schoolgirl when he leaned in to kiss her on the cheek after a candidates' debate. Meanwhile, volunteers – again overwhelmingly female – were flocking to the campaign. 'People call it drinking the juice,' Dan Shomon said. 'People start drinking the Obama juice. You can't find enough for them to do.'

Michelle had always been aware that her husband was attractive to the opposite sex and that his long absences from home had given him ample opportunity to be unfaithful. But, unlike many of his fellow politicians, Barack had never been linked with other women. 'He's never given me reason to doubt him,' she told her friends more than once. 'Not once.'

Now that women were mobbing him on the street, even pushing Michelle out of the way to get to him, she began to confide to a few close friends that it was all getting to be 'a real pain in the ass'. According to a college friend, Michelle joked that 'she wasn't going to let all the adulation "go to his head". But you could tell it wasn't entirely a laughing matter to her. They have a trusting relationship – he's a totally devoted husband and father – but no wife wants to see other women pawing her man.'

Eventually, Michelle would resign herself to the fact that Barack would attract his share of political groupies. When asked if she worried that Barack might some day cheat on her, Michelle did not hesitate to answer. Obviously, she had given the issue plenty of thought. 'First of all,' she said, 'I can't control someone else's behaviour. I'm not worried about some woman pushing up on my husband. With fidelity – with Barack and me – if somebody can come between us, we didn't have much to begin with.'

Those who knew them took Michelle's laid-back answer with a grain of salt. 'He has a huge ego, but he loves his girls too much to ever put his marriage in jeopardy,' said one advisor. Valerie Jarrett agreed that Barack had always been more than a little intimidated by Michelle. In their marriage, Jarrett observed, 'there is a subtle element of fear on his part, which is good'.

On primary night in March, everyone waited at the Pritzker-owned Hyatt Regency Hotel for election results to roll in. As Barack posed for photos with Malia and Sasha, Michelle assured everyone that her preternaturally calm husband was 'really pretty excited' that he had won a staggering 53 per cent of the vote in a four-way race. 'They like you!' she told him, in a take-off on Sally Field's famous Oscar speech. 'They really like you!' Then, when he finally stepped onstage to address his cheering supporters, Barack delivered the kind rafter-ringing stemwinder they had come to expect.

Behind the scenes, however, Barack was battling feelings of melancholy. Now that he was stepping onto the national stage, he knew he would be spending even less time with his family. He broke down on several occasions when he started talking about the girls. 'God,' he admitted after one emotional moment, 'I'm starting to remind myself of my mom.'

In a dramatic turnabout, Michelle now reassured Barack that whatever sacrifices he made were well worth it – that as a US senator he would have the opportunity to influence the lives of millions. She also promised that she would do 'whatever we have to do' to make sure that he would get to spend plenty of time with Malia and Sasha.

First, he had to win the general election. The Republicans had fielded a formidable candidate in Jack Ryan, an articulate, movie-star handsome, Dartmouth-educated millionaire who had actually left Wall Street to become an inner-city high school teacher. Ryan was also a moderate with strong support outside Chicago, and early polls indicated he stood a good chance of eking out a narrow victory over Barack.

Once again, fortune would smile on Barack. In the wake of Blair Hull's troubles with sealed divorce records, the press quickly took note of the fact that Ryan had divorced TV star Jeri (*Star Trek: Voyager, Boston Public, Boston Legal*) Ryan, and that portions of those records were also sealed. The *Chicago Tribune* sued to have the files opened.

Barack was campaigning downstate in mid-June 2004 when a Los Angeles court ordered Ryan's divorce records unsealed. In sworn affidavits taken while the couple vied for custody of their young son, Jeri Ryan had accused her husband of taking her to sex clubs in New York and Paris where he demanded that she have sex with him in front of strangers. Ryan 'wanted me to have sex with him there with another couple watching,' his ex-wife claimed. 'I refused . . . I was very upset.'

Michelle was as dumbfounded as her husband. 'Are you seeing this?' he asked when he called in from the road.

'I know, I know,' she replied. 'Crazy stuff. Can you believe this is happening *again*?'

Barack and Michelle were both amazed that Ryan had run in the first place. 'What was he thinking?' he mused. 'I mean, he must have known it would get out.'

Michelle agreed with David Axelrod and Barack's other advisors that right now Barack should take the high road and say nothing. It was only a matter of time, they believed, before Ryan would be forced by his own party to bow out of the race.

They were right. Ryan pulled out of the race on 25 June 2004. Once again, before the contest could begin in earnest, Barack's main opponent had fallen victim to a sordid sex scandal. 'You really have got to wonder,' he said to Michelle, 'why these guys get into a race like this when they must *know* it's going to bite them in the ass.'

Now there was speculation that the Republicans would field a high-profile candidate with instant name recognition – someone like former Chicago Bears coach-turned-TV personality Mike Ditka. When she heard Ditka's name mentioned, Michelle, who appreciated just how much Chicagoans loved their hometown sports heroes, grimaced. 'He could be trouble,' she murmured.

With Republicans holding a 51 to 48 edge in the US Senate, the Democrats needed something to help their young candidate capture the Illinois seat. As the Democratic National Convention approached that July, Axelrod, Obama communications director Robert Gibbs, Pritzker, Abner Mikva and virtually dozens of other well-connected party members were urging officials to pick Barack to give the keynote address. Their argument: that like such keynote speakers as Texas Congresswoman Barbara Jordan, New York Governor Mario Cuomo and Texas Governor Ann Richards, Barack knew how to fire up a crowd.

The man who would make the ultimate decision – presumptive presidential nominee John Kerry – had seen that quality in Barack at first hand. Barack had appeared in June at a fundraiser for the Massachusetts senator, and later at a factory where the two men discussed on-the-job training programmes with workers. Both times Kerry, who realised that others perceived him as stiff and humourless, was impressed with how effortlessly Barack worked the crowd. Nor did it hurt that Barack was a fellow Harvard graduate and had taken an early stand against the war in Iraq.

As he was driving from Springfield to Chicago, Barack got the call from Kerry campaign manager Mary Beth Cahill. Clicking off his cell phone, he quickly called Axelrod with the news that he had been picked to deliver the keynote address. It was, the two men agreed, a 'game changer'.

When he hung up the phone, Barack leaned back in his seat. 'I guess,' he said to his driver, Mike Signator, 'this is pretty big.'

'You could say that,' Signator agreed.

No sooner had Barack told Michelle that he was the convention's keynote speaker than she was sharing the news with relatives and friends. Although Barack's staff sent him previous keynote addresses by Jordan, Cuomo, Richards and others, Michelle knew that Barack's speech would have a distinct tone of its own. 'They were great speakers,' she said, 'but Barack is unique.'

Still juggling his duties as a state senator with the rigours of a US Senate campaign, Barack organised his thoughts in the car as he drove back and forth between Chicago and the Illinois capital. Then, sitting in a hotel room in Springfield, he spent hours crafting the speech on yellow legal pads in his distinctively loopy, left-handed scrawl. Later the inveterate night owl would return to the Obamas' Chicago condo and retire to the Hole, where he stayed up until 2 a.m. transcribing the handwritten copy onto his computer.

Barack made endless revisions to the speech, which he then emailed to staffers at virtually any time of the day or night. The Kerry staff also had a hand in editing the address, but Michelle, who was being shown drafts as the process proceeded, urged her husband to resist their changes. 'Stick to your guns,' she told him. 'You're the only one who knows what's right for you.'

When Kerry's people excised the lines 'I am my brother's keeper, I am my sister's keeper', Michelle and Barack's staff insisted that it be put back in. 'Are they kidding?' she asked, knowing that black audiences had gone wild every time Barack had uttered those words in the past. 'That stays, definitely.'

More than 15,000 reporters were in Boston to cover the Democratic National Convention, and a sizable chunk of them descended on Barack when he arrived in town. Without ever having uttered a word on the national stage, he was already a media star, squeezing dozens of radio and print interviews in between appearances on NBC's *Meet the Press*, CBS's *Face the Nation* and ABC's *Nightline*.

Michelle was unimpressed. 'All of this is very flattering,' she told a reporter, 'but he will not get a big head. We have a six year old and a three year old who couldn't care less about all of this, and he comes home to that every night.'

In reality, Michelle worried that her husband was being pulled in too many directions. On Tuesday, 27 July – the day of his keynote address – Barack was looking haggard as he practised the speech surrounded by Axelrod, Gibbs and a dozen other aides. Although he had whittled it down to his allotted time of seventeen minutes, leaving out much of his own history so he would have time to sing the praises of the candidate, his aides were still eager to put in their two cents.

There were added pressures: Barack had never addressed a crowd as large as this (5,000 delegates on the floor at Boston's Fleet Center and, even though it was not being broadcast at prime time, a cable TV audience of millions). Nor had he ever used a TelePrompter. And, after talking to so many reporters since his arrival in Boston, Barack now had a seriously sore throat.

The rehearsals took on a more urgent tone as the appointed time for the keynote address approached. At one point during one of these practice sessions, Barack grew visibly angry as he was peppered with suggestions for last-minute changes. 'We were spending intense sessions tinkering with wording and commas,' said a senior member of Obama's team. 'It was pretty tense, because everybody was picking at Barack and making suggestions. He was getting a little irate.'

To say the least. Mr Unflappable gazed in amazement at Axelrod and the others. 'Why the hell are you bringing this up *now*?' Barack demanded, shaking as his head.

It was then that he locked eyes with Michelle, who had been sitting calmly, watching him and digesting what the others had to say. 'She was kind of handling him as well as some of the speech,' the handler said. 'She was listening intently and, without being overly directive, was somebody that he could glance over to, almost a telepathic kind of relationship, he was clearly looking to her for her reaction.'

'So,' he asked after yet another run-through, 'what do you think?'

'I think,' she said with a wry smile, 'that you're not going to embarrass the family.'

Unless, she added, he didn't change his tie. Although Michelle often pointed out with some irritation in her voice that Barack 'is thin so he looks good in everything', she decried his lack of fashion sense. 'He just doesn't care about clothes,' she observed. 'Buy him a black shirt for Christmas and he is a happy man.'

Now that he was to appear before a national audience for the first time, she gave him one last once-over. The dark suit was perfectly acceptable, but not the rust-coloured tie with the geometric patterns. 'Now that,' she said, pointing to his communications director's new powder-blue tie, 'is very nice.'

That afternoon Barack, looking particularly handsome in his new powder-blue tie, attracted a crowd as he and Marty Nesbitt walked down the street towards the Fleet Center. 'This crowd was building behind us,' Nesbitt said, 'like it was Tiger Woods at the Masters.'

Nesbitt was astonished at his friend's overnight fame – and even more surprised at how none of the attention seemed to faze the Illinois state senator.

'Barack, man,' Nesbitt told him, 'you're like a rock star.'

'Yeah,' Barack replied without missing a beat, 'if you think it's bad today, wait until tomorrow.'

Nesbitt paused for a moment as Barack quickened his step. 'What do you mean?' he asked.

'My speech,' Barack replied with a wink, 'is pretty good.'

Michelle had faith in the speech, but even more so in the man who was giving it. She told Axelrod and the others that she had total confidence that Barack, whose skills as an orator had grown exponentially over the past few years, would make history with his keynote address. What concerned her that night wasn't the prospect of failure but the likelihood of success – and how it might transform her little family for ever. In an unguarded moment, she shared her doubts with the others. 'I'm just kind of worried,' Michelle said wistfully, 'that things will never be normal again, you know?'

I'm the badass wife who is sort of keeping it real.

Michelle

———◆◆◆———

If I ever thought this was ruining my family, I wouldn't do it.

Barack

———◆◆◆———

I always told Michelle to step out of her comfort zone in life.
But I never thought she was going to step this far out.

Marian Robinson

———◆◆◆———

No, no, no. I would never cheat. Michelle would kick my butt.

Barack

———◆◆◆———

My sister doesn't suffer any fools. If there was any foolishness to him,
they wouldn't be married right now.

Craig Robinson

7

He had been too busy honing his speech to concentrate on all that was hanging in the balance. Now, as her husband was about to step onto the national stage for the first time, Michelle could tell that he was showing unmistakable signs of stage fright. Was he OK? she asked.

'I'm just feeling a little queasy,' he confessed.

Then Michelle leaned in, gave her husband a reassuring hug and said sweetly, 'Just don't screw it up, buddy!'

They both laughed and, with the tension broken, waited for Illinois Senator Dick Durbin to introduce him to the crowed. Then Barack calmly walked up to the podium to deliver the speech that would make or break his political career.

'Tonight is a particular honour for me because, let's face it, my presence on this stage is pretty unlikely,' he began. 'My father was a foreign student, born and raised in a small village in Kenya. He grew up herding goats, went to school in a tin-roof shack . . . While studying here, my father met my mother. She was born in a town on the other side of the world, in Kansas.'

Over the next 17 minutes, cheering delegates jumped to their feet again and again as Barack exhorted them to join in the crusade to elect John Kerry president. Attacking the 'spin masters and negative-ad peddlers' and the 'pundits who like to slice and dice our country into Red States and Blue States', Barack insisted that 'there's not a liberal America and a conservative America – there's a United States of America. There's not a black America and white America and Latino America and Asian America; there's the United States of America!'

As he ended his speech, Barack turned to the words of Jeremiah Wright to invoke hope as an underlying theme: 'the hope of slaves sitting around a fire singing freedom songs; the hope of immigrants setting out for distant shores; the hope of a skinny kid with a funny name who believes America has a place for him, too. The audacity of hope!'

Michelle, elegant in a white satin suit and pearls, watched from the wings. Struggling to maintain her composure, she reached up at one point to wipe the tears from her eyes. When it was over, she joined Barack onstage and, arm in arm, the couple waved to the rapturous crowd.

Barack knew he had electrified the crowd – a point that would be driven home with hyperbolic glee by the very pundits he had accused of dividing the nation. Literally overnight, Barack's stirring keynote address propelled him from relatively obscure state legislator to political megastar. During the next few days, he was mobbed wherever he went at the convention, upstaging everyone – including Kerry and his running mate, John Edwards.

When he returned to Illinois to resume his Senate campaign, Barack was now mobbed wherever he went. Women, not surprisingly, continued to be his most enthusiastic fans. They pushed their bodies up against his, slipped phone numbers in his pockets and, on rare occasions, whispered untoward suggestions in his ear as if none of the surrounding multitude could hear.

For the first time on the campaign trail, Barack now found himself the victim of groping by some of his more ardent female admirers. On more than one occasion, Barack tried not to look startled when some random woman in the crowd would grasp him firmly by the derrière – and sometimes try hard to hold on.

'Jesus,' he said after sliding into the back of his SUV after an appearance in Peoria, 'I wish they'd stop grabbing my ass!'

At an Illinois Dental Society Dinner, one comely guest sidled up to the senator. 'If you were my husband,' she purred, 'I wouldn't let you go around alone.'

Michelle, understandably, was not amused. Now that her husband's career was in overdrive, his would-be groupies were becoming more aggressive – a fact that had not gone unnoticed by her friends or by the press. Political cartoons already poked fun at Barack's obvious sex appeal, depicting starry-eyed female delegates swooning over him at the convention. As for the women who insisted on what amounted to full-body contact with her husband, Michelle was in no mood to be charitable. 'I want to tell these women, "Back off. Get a life,"' Michelle admitted. 'It's just embarrassing, that's all.'

Moreover, Michelle knew that all this unseemly fawning nourished Barack's admittedly already oversized ego. 'He's loving it,' she muttered at one point. 'He's a man, isn't he?' Once again, she resorted to giving him the silent treatment. He, in turn, complained that she was being 'unfair' and had no appreciation of the 'incredible stress' he was under. 'The tension between Michelle and her husband,' said *Chicago Tribune* reporter David Mendell, 'was palpable.'

There were, in fact, rumours afoot that it was more than just the random flirting from strangers that was getting to Michelle. Her husband, it would later be reported, had grown close to an attractive young African American member of his campaign named Vera Baker.

Born and raised in San Francisco, Baker attended Mills College for Women, where she received dual bachelor's degrees in political, legal and economic analysis and African American studies. She later earned her master's in political science from Howard University and her master's in African American studies from Columbia.

In 2000, Baker teamed up with another Howard alumnus, Muthoni Wambu, to start Baker, Wambu & Associates, a firm that would go on to raise over $3 million for the congressional campaigns of African American candidates. While Wambu would later become an advisor to Delaware Senator Joe Biden, Baker allied herself with Barack's Senate campaign.

According to Federal Election Commission records, Baker was paid a hefty fee for her services as finance director for the Obama Senate campaign. But in fact, Claire Serdiuk was officially and repeatedly referred to as Obama's finance director throughout the Senate campaign.

When Baker suddenly and inexplicably vanished from the campaign and resurfaced on the Caribbean island of Martinique, tongues reportedly began wagging. A jealous Michelle, it was suggested, had engineered Baker's departure.

'No,' Baker would later insist, 'Nothing happened. I just left . . . at the end of the campaign.' If Michelle had complained that she and Barack were getting too cosy, Baker wasn't saying. 'I have no comment on anything,' she told writer Sharon Churcher. 'I switched careers. That's it. I'm a Democrat and I support Senator Obama. I don't have anything to say.' Baker did add, however, that it was love that brought her to the Caribbean in the first place – she moved there, she said, to live with the man she had fallen in love with. (In a strange twist, Baker later went to work for Alta Capital Group, a municipal bond brokerage founded by Michelle's long-time friend Adela Cepeda.)

Rumours aside, tensions between Barack and Michelle ran especially high during a five-day, one thousand six hundred-mile, thirty-three-county campaign tour the Obamas embarked on right after the convention. The whirlwind tour was originally designed as a leisurely SUV trip with the family, including stops in small downstate communities where voters would get a chance to see Barack, Michelle, Malia and Sasha up close and personal. There would, Barack and Michelle were told, be plenty of time for ice cream, picnics, visits to zoos and country fairs, swimming, boating and even some fishing.

Instead, the campaign staffer who organised the tour, Jeremiah Posedel, had loaded up the schedule with an average of seven campaign stops *per day*. With Barack's new-found fame, hundreds of people flocked to see him at every appearance, making it impossible for him to spend any quality time with his family. 'Like an idiot,' Posedel conceded, 'I neglected to plan for the huge crowds.'

So while the girls were whisked off to local amusement parks by staffers and her husband shook thousands of hands and signed countless autographs, Michelle spent much of her time alone in the SUV.

Some of her time was spent reassuring Posedel that Barack, despite his grumblings to the contrary, would not hold it against him for devising such a punishing campaign schedule.

Back at the very beginning of the Senate campaign, Posedel had hosted several Obama events in his living room. 'People would say, "Are you crazy? This guy hasn't got a chance." I'd have to scour 26 counties to find 25 people who were willing to come and listen to him.' Ever since, the two men had enjoyed an easy rapport – until now. 'We would normally be joking around with each other,' Posedel said, 'but now he spoke to me only when he had to. I knew he was angry.'

What Barack could not forgive Posedel for was the fact that he was spending virtually no time with Malia and Sasha – family time that he had been looking forward to for weeks. While he gave Posedel the silent treatment, Michelle would occasionally sneak away with Posedel to grab a Big Mac. 'Barack would never, ever eat at McDonald's or any fast-food place,' Posedel said, 'unless maybe it was some veggie sandwich at Subway. He was incredibly careful about what he ate.'

Michelle, on the other hand, enjoyed the occasional hamburger. 'He's not around!' she told Posedel at one point during the tour. 'We can eat what we want!' At a later stop, Michelle took Posedel to celebrate his birthday at a nearby Friday's. 'It was just nachos and a couple of drinks,' he said, 'but she was so upbeat and nice that I almost forgot her husband was still mad at me.'

When it was all over, Barack took Posedel aside and thanked him for all the hard work he had put into the tour. Then, without ever raising his voice, Barack added, 'Now, don't *ever* do that to me again. Understand?'

Incredibly, Barack was once again campaigning unopposed. Because he had not faced a strong opponent since the 2000 congressional primary race against Bobby Rush, Barack had never really been the victim of anything approaching a political attack. Nor, conversely, had he had to come out swinging against a political foe.

All that changed that August when, with only three months left before the election, former radio talk show host and two-time presidential candidate Alan Keyes agreed to replace Jack Ryan on the Illinois ballot. A flamboyantly outspoken African American conservative with a taste for the jugular, Keyes did not actually live in Illinois. A long-time Maryland resident, he established his Illinois residency by moving into the upper storey of a Calumet City 'two-flat' (duplex).

No sooner had he set foot in the Land of Lincoln than Keyes blasted Barack for his 'anti-Christian' support of abortion rights.

Employing his trademark hellfire-and-brimstone technique, Keyes kept hammering away at his opponent, accusing Barack of advocating policies that condemned thousands of unborn black babies to death every year.

'My God,' Barack complained to Michelle, 'have you heard the stuff he's saying about me?'

She was not surprised; Keyes was merely living up to his hard-line reputation. When Barack, who was confident that he could win over anyone, told her that he was going to try and reason with Keyes, she laughed. 'Yep, OK,' she cracked. 'You just go ahead and do that thing.'

If anything, Barack's overtures merely provoked even stronger attacks from Keyes. Not that it mattered. Keyes was widely viewed as both a token and carpetbagger – certainly no match for the promising young man who had captivated the nation with his soaring rhetoric and the beautiful Michelle at his side.

What Barack hadn't expected was persistent criticism from radical factions that saw him as a traitor to the African American cause. After he gave speech at Liberty Baptist Church on the South Side, Michelle walked out the back door and into what former Black Panther Party associate Ron Carter called 'a bunch of hoodlum thugs'.

Michelle, who at 5 ft 11 in. towered over most of them, put her hand on her hip and glared at the men. 'Y'all got a problem or something?' she asked.

'They all froze,' Carter recalled, 'guys who would slap the mayor, who would slap Jesse Jackson in the face, even.' In that moment, Carter said, Michelle proved herself to be 'a very strong woman. She knows how to stand up for herself, to put on her street face. I was very impressed.'

On 2 November 2004, the Obamas were ensconced with friends and family members in a suite at the Chicago Hyatt Regency watching election results on television. While Barack coasted to a comfortable 70 per cent to 27 per cent victory over Keyes – the largest margin for a statewide race in Illinois history – he and Michelle posed for photos with Malia and Sasha.

As TV camera crews and photographers were trooped in for the inevitable photo op with the family, the girls grew more and more impatient. 'Can we stop taking pictures now?' Sasha asked as she fidgeted in Daddy's lap. 'I want to go home.'

The smiles, like the enthusiasm for a victory that had been all but assured for months, were forced. That night, Barack's uncharacteristically low-key acceptance speech reflected the reality of his situation: while Barack Obama had been elected to the US Senate, the Kerry–Edwards ticket had gone down to defeat.

The next day, reporters asked Barack if he intended to make a run for the White House in 2008. 'I can unequivocally say,' he replied, 'I will not be running for national office in four years.' Later, Michelle sidled up to him. 'I will hold you to that,' she said.

As he was sworn in, with a third of the Senate, as a member of the 109th Congress – Barack had already been told he would be assigned the same Senate desk used by Robert F. Kennedy – the Illinois freshman marvelled at what he would call 'my almost spooky good fortune'. Having won every one of his state senate primary contests (and even the 2002 general election) unopposed, Barack sat back during the US Senate race and watched as one formidable opponent after another self-destructed. Then he was handed the opportunity of a lifetime – the chance to deliver the keynote address at his party's convention before a TV audience of millions. 'It seemed like a fluke,' Barack had to concede. On his arrival at the Capitol, he felt like a rookie in a spotless uniform surrounded by 'mud-splattered' players who 'tended their wounds'.

Michelle would have none of it. After they took the children to watch Daddy replay the swearing-in ceremony with Vice President Dick Cheney for the cameras – six-year-old Malia shook his hand properly, but Sasha, three, slapped the veep's palms – Michelle reminded her husband that he had worked hard to get here. As they walked out of the Capitol towards a reception at the Library of Congress, Michelle grabbed Barack's hand and kissed him on the lips. 'Congratulations, Mr Senator,' she said. 'Congratulations, Madame Senator.'

Not to be outdone, Malia blurted out, 'Daddy, are you going to be president?'

Careful not to answer his daughter in front of the reporters who were trailing them, Barack merely smiled. Michelle's usual poker face was set firmly in place.

At the reception, Barack and Michelle greeted family members and friends from Africa, England, Hawaii, Illinois, Boston and New York. All the Jacksons – Jesse, Jesse Jr and Santita – were there, as were Valerie Jarrett, Marty Nesbitt and his wife, Dr Anita Blanchard, Emil Jones and the Reverend Jeremiah Wright. Toot, who was suffering from a variety of medical problems at age eighty-four, couldn't travel from Hawaii, but Barack's sister Maya made the trip with her husband of two years, University of Hawaii Assistant Professor of Creative Media Dr Konrad Ng. Half a dozen relatives from Kenya were also on hand, celebrating the fact that one of their own had become only the second black man (after Massachusetts Senator Edward Brooke) elected to the United States Senate since Reconstruction.

After the hugs and handshakes were over, Barack had to face the sobering fact that his family would be returning to Chicago without him. 'I want you and the girls to move with me to Washington,' he had told Michelle. 'I've been apart from Malia and Sasha for too long as it is. I'll just miss you all too much.'

But his long-time pal Illinois Congressman Rahm Emanuel was among the many who urged him to leave his family behind. Michelle remained close to her mother, who still lived in the same tiny apartment where Michelle and her brother Craig had grown up. Besides Marian Robinson and the built-in support network of relatives and friends that Chicago offered, Michelle still had her job at the University of Chicago Hospitals. While Emanuel tried to convince Barack that it would be best for him to simply divide his time between Washington and Chicago, Rahm's wife, Amy, told Michelle she knew from experience that such a plan was workable.

What eventually persuaded Michelle to remain in Chicago was the fact that her children were already enrolled in school there – both at the Lab School, a private school affiliated with the University of Chicago. The girls were also extremely close to their grandmother, who often took care of them when Michelle was working, on the campaign trail with her husband or standing in for him. 'With all the crazy stuff going on,' she said, 'the best thing right now is not to disrupt their lives.'

Reluctantly, Barack rented a one-bedroom apartment in a high-rise complex not far from Georgetown Law School. He stayed there from Tuesday night through Thursday night before flying back to Chicago on Friday afternoon. Saturdays were taken up with meetings and other business, leaving all day Sunday to catch up with his wife and their little girls. In between, Michelle kept a journal of the girl's activities that she emailed him each day.

Trying to adjust to the proverbial joys of bachelorhood – takeaway food, hours watching sports on TV, settling in with a good book – Barack soon found himself calling home several times a day just to hear the sounds of his wife's and daughters' voices. He also admitted that he was so 'domesticated, soft, and helpless' that he forgot to buy a shower curtain.

At age 45, Senator Obama was in the throes of separation anxiety. 'I am just lonely as hell for my wife and kids,' he told a Senate colleague after just a few weeks. 'It's really getting to me.'

Not that he had that much time to himself. With an eye towards positioning Barack for either a vice presidential or presidential run as early as 2008, his team had devised a plan – actually referred to by Axelrod and Gibbs as 'the Plan' – to keep him front and centre on the national scene and build his reputation as a potential leader.

Towards that end, the freshman senator's agenda in Washington was packed with meetings – he promptly landed a plum assignment on the career-burnishing Foreign Relations Committee – and he was soon planning tours to Eastern Europe, Russia and the Middle East. Back at home in Illinois, Barack conducted at least one town hall meeting a week as part of an ongoing effort to shore up grassroots support. When he wasn't there, Michelle took up the slack. 'There is no better stand-in for Barack,' said an aide, 'than Michelle. Frankly, they can connect with her in a way that they can't connect with him. And she can sing his praises until the cows come home, and everybody accepts it because she's his wife.'

In addition to their elevated public profile, the Obamas were discovering that Barack's meteoric rise was having a substantial impact on their family finances. When Barack was selected to give the keynote speech at the Democratic National Convention, his loyal agent and friend, Jane Dystel, looked into reclaiming the rights to *Dreams from My Father* and selling it to a new publisher. But Random House's Crown division, which still owned the book, had moved quickly to reissue it in paperback.

Obama's convention speech and the frenzy of interest it spawned propelled *Dreams from My Father* onto the *New York Times* Best Seller List; eventually it would sell an estimated two million copies in the United States and earn Barack more than $2 million in royalties.

Following his election to the Senate, Barack signed a new two-book deal with Crown for more than $2 million. But this time, Michelle urged Barack to repay Dystel's loyalty by replacing her with high-powered Washington lawyer Robert Barnett. According to former Times Books publisher Peter Osnos, who signed up *Dreams* back when Obama was a law student, the reason was obvious. 'Whereas agents take a flat percentage of all the client's earnings – usually 15 per cent these days,' Osnos said, 'Barnett charges by the hour, which means that the bill is substantially smaller.'

Dystel, whom Osnos described as 'a feisty sort', was furious. 'I have no idea about the details of the interaction between Barnett, Dystel and Obama,' he said, 'but I would bet it was not warm and fuzzy.'

The entire episode left a sour taste in Osnos's mouth. 'I just wish that this virtuous symbol . . . did not move quite so smoothly into a system of riches as a reward for service,' he said, 'especially before it has actually been rendered.'

In the immediate wake of her husband's Senate victory, Michelle reaped a financial windfall of her own. She returned to full-time work at the University of Chicago Hospitals – and a promotion to Vice President for External Affairs that nearly tripled her salary to $316,962 from $121, 910.

In justifying the dramatic and curiously timed pay hike, hospital officials pointed out that over two years Michelle had transformed a two-person part-time office to a full-time staff of seventeen and quadrupled the total number of volunteers to nearly one thousand eight hundred. 'I wanted to send a strong message to our community that I was committed to it,' said Michelle's boss Michael Riordan, 'so I wanted to make this a vice presidential position.'

Riordan laughed off the suggestion that Michelle's promotion was aimed at currying favour in Washington. 'She was hired before Barack was Barack,' Riordan insisted. 'Michelle is the real deal and really earned every bit of her promotion on her own.' In what was probably an unfortunate choice of words, Riordan added, 'She is worth her weight in gold, and she is just terrific.' (Conflict-of-interest allegations would arise months later when Senator Obama tried and failed to earmark $1 million in federal funds for a new pavilion at the hospital.)

Michelle's fortunes would improve even further in early 2005, when she began searching for companies eager to increase minority representation on their boards. By June, she was appointed to the board of TreeHouse Foods, one of Wal-Mart's principal suppliers. For attending a few meetings a year, she was paid $45,000, with stock options that after the first full year would total $60,000.

Now able to pay off those college loans and settle their other long-standing debts, Michelle and Barack were in the market to move to a nicer home. In the spring of 2005, his controversial low-income-housing-developer friend Tony Rezko called with the news that the doctor who lived across the street from Rezko in the South Side's Kenwood enclave had put his home on the market.

When real-estate agent Donna Schwan of MetroPro Corporation and Rezko took Michelle to see the property, she could not conceal her enthusiasm. The 6,400-square-foot, 96-year-old red-brick Georgian Revival occupied a double lot on the corner of South Greenwood Drive and East Hyde Park Boulevard. The house stood not far from the home of Muhammad Ali and directly across from the street from the Byzantine KAM Isaiah Israel Temple, with its immense dome and tiled minaret.

The three-storey structure at 5046 South Greenwood Drive boasted six bedrooms, six bathrooms, four fireplaces and a wine cellar capable of storing more than a thousand bottles. The price for the house: $1.95 million. To complicate matters further, the doctor was insisting on selling the separately listed $625,000 building lot at the same time.

Michelle called her husband in DC and told him about Rezko's find. 'So, Tony really thinks it would be great for us,' Barack said. 'What do you think?'

'I'm in,' Michelle told him. 'I love this house. But,' she quickly added, 'it's more than we were talking about paying for, but I really think it's a great house, you should go take a look at it.'

A few days later, Rezko took Barack on a tour of the house. Barack was as 'blown away' as Michelle had been, but he told Rezko that at nearly two million dollars, the asking price was just beyond the range he could afford.

Rezko, who had pumped some $250,000 into Barack's various campaigns, was already working on a plan to bring the house within his friends' reach. If his wife, Rita, bought the vacant lot for the full $625,000 asking price, that would give the Obamas the leverage they needed to negotiate a better deal on the house.

It was already widely known that Rezko was under investigation by the FBI for corrupt business dealings (he would eventually be convicted on 16 counts of paying – and taking – kickbacks). Barack asked his most trusted advisor – Michelle – if she thought Rezko's plan might at least give the appearance of impropriety.

Michelle was indignant. 'He's a good friend,' she told him. 'There's nothing wrong with what he's suggesting.' Michelle, who now owned a mink coat, several designer dresses and more than one pair of $500 Jimmy Choo shoes, knew that money and trappings of success meant little to her husband. But she also felt they deserved a Chicago residence befitting the family of a United States senator. More to the point, Michelle wanted their girls to grow up in a house with a big back yard where they could play with their friends.

'Barack wanted his family to be comfortable,' said a friend, 'but he would have been satisfied with three spoons, a fork and a dish. It was an issue for her.' The bottom line, Barack would later say, was that Michelle was 'determined to have that house'.

Barack called Rezko up and told him that Michelle was on board with his plan. With Rita Rezko agreeing to purchase the 'garden lot', the Obamas were able to shave $300,000 off the asking price and buy the house for $1.65 million. Rita Rezko and the Obamas closed both deals on the same day in June 2005.

Not long after the Obamas moved into their new house, they inexplicably decided to buy a ten-foot-wide strip of the adjacent lot from Rita Rezko for $125,000, or $84,500 above the $40,500 appraisal. The purchase aided the Obamas because it rendered the adjacent lot unbuildable. (Later, when he was being pilloried in the Chicago press for dealing with a notorious slumlord who was headed for federal prison, Obama confessed that the property purchases had been 'a bonehead move . . . I consider this a mistake on my part,' he added, 'and I regret it.')

Consumed with town meetings, working on his new book and making campaign appearances for fellow Democrats around the country, Barack had little opportunity to enjoy his spacious new digs. But when he was at home, he did what he could to please his wife. 'I try to be more thoughtful,' he said of this period in their marriage. 'Sometimes it is just the little gestures that make a big difference. Just me putting the dishes in the dishwasher. Making sure I come home for dinner, even if I have to go back out.'

Barack also boasted that he would occasionally do the laundry – but without folding it. 'Which is pretty useless,' Michelle hastened to point out. What Barack's wife appreciated most was that he was her 'biggest cheerleader, as a mother, as a wife and as a career person. He's always telling me how great I'm doing. That helps keep you going when you realise that you have someone who appreciates all the hard work that you are doing – even if they don't do enough to help!'

Michelle was equally insistent that he make time for the children – no matter what. 'You'll be there,' she often told him when there was a school pageant or a game that was too important for him to skip. 'You're doing this. Period.'

On those occasions when she did not prevail, Michelle made her displeasure known. When Barack missed one of Malia's basketball games to campaign for New Jersey Governor John Corzine on Sunday – the one day they had agreed to strictly reserve for the family – Michelle, in the words of one aide, 'blasted him'. Later, she facetiously remarked, 'It's a tough choice between, "Do you stay for Malia's basketball game on Sunday or do you go to New Jersey and campaign for Corzine?" Corzine got it this time around, but it's a constant pull to say, "Hey guys, you have a family here."'

Still, Barack attended parent–teacher conferences and, at Michelle's insistence, always played some role in putting together the children's birthday parties. On the eve of Sasha's June birthday, Barack was instructed to go to the store and bring back pizza, ice and balloons. When he volunteered to get goody bags for the 20-odd party guests, Michelle pulled him back from the brink.

'You can't *handle* goody bags,' she said, imitating Jack Nicholson's marine colonel character on the stand in *A Few Good Men*. 'You have to go into the party store and choose the bags. Then you have to choose what to put in the bags, and what is in the boys' bags has to be different from what is in the girls' bags.' After wandering around the store for an hour, Michelle told him, 'Your head would explode.'

The girls' birthday slumber parties had become, in Daddy's words, such 'big productions' over the years that Barack and Michelle made it clear there would be no birthday presents from Mommy and Daddy. 'We spend hundreds on their parties,' Daddy explained, 'and we want to teach some limits.'

The same went for Christmas: none of the presents under the tree were officially from Mommy and Daddy. 'I know there is a Santa,' Malia once told them, 'because there's no way you'd buy me all that stuff.'

That Halloween, Malia and Sasha both dressed up as witches and Barack took them trick-or-treating around their Kenwood and Hyde Park neighbourhoods. During the holidays, when Michelle noted that Barack's staff had scheduled him for a Democratic Party fundraiser in Florida on the same day as Malia's *Nutcracker* recital, she glowered at her husband. 'You *don't* miss it,' she said pointedly. Somehow, he managed to catch Malia's afternoon performance, dash to a private plane that waited for him at Chicago's Midway Airport and arrive in Tampa just in time for the fundraiser.

Not even the Obamas' annual holiday in Hawaii was sacrosanct. Instead of flying out with the family the week before Christmas, the senator stayed behind in Washington. He was to join them later, but the idea that Michelle and the girls had headed west without him hit Barack hard. In the middle of a meeting, he looked at his watch, gazed out the window and sighed. 'We'd be over the Pacific now,' he said.

When he did join them in Hawaii, Barack turned off his ever-present BlackBerry and returned, however briefly, to the soul-recharging business of being a full-time dad. He and Michelle swam and snorkled with the girls at Sandy Beach Park, body-surfed at Kailua Beach and spent long hours visiting Toot.

On this particular visit, Barack was even more concerned than usual with his grandmother's deteriorating physical condition. The woman who had for all intents and purposes raised him was now suffering from a wide range medical problems, from osteoporosis to cancer. Yet she continued to drink more than the family would have liked – and to smoke. Whatever damage he might have thought the latter was doing to the health of his beloved grandmother, Barack was in no position to lecture her. In fact, in Hawaii the two often unwound at the end of the day by sharing a smoke together as Michelle watched disapprovingly.

By 2006, the Plan to bolster Barack's credentials as a national leader was in full swing. In April, he appeared with actor and activist George Clooney at the National Press Club to speak about the ongoing conflict in the Darfur region of Sudan.

While photographers at the Press Club event swarmed around Clooney, no one paid much attention to AP photographer Mannie Garcia as he crouched down, snapping photos of the junior senator from Illinois. Later, artist Shepard Fairey would transform the photo into a Warholesque portrait that would become an icon of the 2008 campaign. Later, when they noticed the image popping up again and again at events, Michelle wondered aloud when the photo was taken. Barack didn't know. Besides, he said, he wasn't quite sure yet if he liked it.

That summer, he and Michelle embarked on a 15-day trip to Africa with a small army of reporters and photographers trailing behind them. 'I offered him a ride,' his new friend Oprah Winfrey would later reveal. 'He wouldn't take it on my plane.' Instead, Barack and his entourage flew commercial.

In South Africa, Obama struck a pose for photographers inside the cell where Nelson Mandela had spent 18 of his 27 years in prison. Barack condemned the genocidal violence in Darfur, and in Kenya, where he joined Michelle and the girls, spoke to the cheering thousands who clogged the streets just to catch a glimpse of the man they regarded as a native son.

With an eye towards bolstering both Barack's standing abroad and his image as an inspiring, almost messianic figure at home, Axelrod, Gibbs and the rest of Obama's team were thrilled by the wild, worshipful crowds that materialised wherever they went in Kenya. Barack, as self-possessed as ever, appeared to accept this undiluted adulation as his due. 'He has a regal bearing, don't you think?' said a top advisor with a self-satisfied grin. 'Make that "presidential".'

But there were moments, if only fleeting, that brought Barack down to earth. As he began to speak to a crowd gathered at the state house in Nairobi, Malia pleaded loudly, 'Daddy, Daddy! Look at me!'

Michelle, who had already confessed to being 'totally freaked out' by the crowds her husband could attract back in the US, was nonplussed by their reception in Kenya. 'What was *that*?' she asked when the crowd waiting outside their hotel roared their approval as Barack stepped into view. 'I mean,' she said with a look of dismay on her face, 'do they *know* him?'

Over the next two years, Michelle would take it upon herself to remind the adoring multitudes back in the US that her husband was all too human. But for now, in Kenya, she was willing to do whatever was asked of her. When Barack wanted to draw attention to Africa's AIDS epidemic by taking an HIV blood test, Michelle volunteered to take one too. 'It's really a couples issue,' she explained, 'so it doesn't matter if one half of the couple is tested and the other isn't.'

The same logic would apply to their next challenge. With his new book, *The Audacity of Hope*, climbing up the *New York Times* Best Seller List and the Democratic Party poised for sweeping victory in the 2006 congressional elections, Barack now admitted to Tim Russert on NBC's *Meet the Press* that he was no longer ruling out a run for the White House in 2008. 'I don't want to be coy about this,' Barack said. 'Given the responses I've been getting over the past several months, I have thought about the possibility, but I have not thought about it with the seriousness and the depth that is required.' If Barack did decide to run, he said, 'I will make a public announcement and everybody will be able to go at me.'

Far more important than that television appearance – or for that matter any TV interview that year – was the Obamas' joint 19 October 2006 appearance on *Oprah*. Oprah, who had shared a pew with Barack at Jeremiah Wright's Trinity United Church back in the 1990s, was now an outspoken supporter.

Winfrey had actually begun to see Barack as something more than just another politician back in 2004 when he gave his convention keynote address. When she decided to interview him a few months later for the November 2004 issue of *O, The Oprah Magazine*, her friends asked the usually apolitical Winfrey, 'What's happened to you?' She replied that in Barack she saw 'something above and beyond politics. It feels like something new.'

On 25 September 2006, Oprah had said on *Larry King Live* that she hoped Obama would run for president. Now, three weeks later, she was chatting with Michelle and Barack about whether or not she sometimes felt like a single mother ('You know, you always feel that way . . . That's always the nature of the beast') and the fact that once when he called home to report that he was working on an important nuclear non-proliferation bill, Michelle asked him to buy ant traps on the way home from the Senate.

'She says we have ants,' he recalled. 'I said, "Ants?" She said, "Yes, we have ants and I need ant traps. We have ants in the bathroom and ants in the kitchen. So on your way home, can you pick up some ant traps, please?" You know, so I'm thinking, you know, "Is John McCain stopping by Walgreens to grab ant traps on the way home?"'

'If he's not,' Michelle shot back, 'he should be.'

Oprah asked Barack to consider running for president, but he declined to answer. With good reason. He may have had the backing of the most powerful woman in the country, but he had not yet persuaded the only woman whose opinion really mattered.

In the immediate wake of their Oprah appearance, *The Audacity of Hope* rocketed to number one on the *New York Times* Best Seller

List. It, too, would go on to sell more than two million copies, boosting the Obamas' household income in 2007 alone to $4.2 million. (In the meantime, his audio book recording of *Dreams from My Father* had earned him a spoken-word Grammy.) The week following the Obamas' bow on *Oprah*, Barack was on the cover of *Time* magazine with the heading 'Why Barack Obama Could Be the Next President.'

Despite the groundswell of support for a presidential run, Michelle was not yet ready to hop aboard the Obama bandwagon. When his former Senate rival Dan Hynes, now a friend and backer, urged him to run, Barack replied, 'Well, Dan, I'm flattered – but Michelle will never forgive you.' He said much the same thing to *Cleveland Plain Dealer* columnist Connie Schultz. 'You know,' he confided to Schultz in late 2006, 'Michelle really does not want me to do this.' And without her blessing, he told Schultz, there would be no run for the presidency.

It was part of a larger tug of war between Barack and Michelle that had gone on ever since he had pleaded with her to let him run for the US Senate. 'We haven't had a lot peace and quiet over the last four years,' he conceded. 'Michelle's always had veto power, and always will, over decisions that have a direct impact on her.'

Michelle's first concern, recalled Axelrod, was that running shouldn't be 'a crazy, hare-brained idea. Because she's not into crazy, hare-brained ideas.' Michelle, who like everyone else believed that Hillary Clinton had the inside track, wanted reassurance that they could really defeat the powerful Clinton machine. She also wanted details on how the campaign was going to be funded. 'Where's the money going to come from?' she asked point-blank. 'She didn't want Barack,' Axelrod added, 'to launch some kind of empty effort here.'

During a series of marathon meetings – two of which lasted over four hours – her husband's team of advisors and trusted long-time friends like Valerie Jarrett, Abner Mikva and Newton Minow gradually persuaded Michelle that victory was achievable. 'Granted, it was a long shot,' said a participant in several of the meetings, 'but we showed her how, if all the pieces fell into place, Barack could win enough delegates to secure the nomination.'

Not surprisingly, a major concern was her husband's safety. 'It only takes one person and it only takes one incident,' Michelle told writer David Mendell. 'I mean, I know history too.'

Ever since the keynote address in Boston, Michelle had commented on some of the odd characters who seemed to be among the faces in the crowds that engulfed her husband. She wondered about the obsessed 'crazies' who, like John Lennon's assassin, Mark David Chapman, might seek to harm the very person they idolised.

Like Alma Powell, whose concern for her husband's safety led Colin Powell not to seek the Republican presidential nomination, Michelle faced the added realisation that as an African American her husband made a particularly attractive target. Conversely, she would also use her husband's race to banish her fears. 'I don't lose sleep over it,' she would say when asked if she worried about the danger to her husband. 'Because the realities are that as a black man Barack can get shot going to the gas station, you know, so you – you know, you can't make decisions based on fear and the possibility of what might happen.'

In any event, Axelrod brought in security experts to go over the plans they had for protecting Barack during a campaign that would take him back and forth across the country for two years. 'Mrs Obama was very realistic,' said one. 'She knew there were no guarantees, but she wanted to know *precisely* what it was we could to keep her husband safe.'

As for the children, Michelle wanted to make sure that their lives would not be disrupted any more than they already were. Daddy's absences were inevitable, but Michelle promised herself that she would be home every night by six – to make sure they did their homework, eat dinner with them, tuck them into bed and be there when they woke up the following morning.

Not that Michelle actually woke Malia and Sasha up in the mornings. Like her mother, Michelle supplied the girls with their own alarm clocks with the understanding that they were responsible for getting themselves ready for school, making their beds and being down in the kitchen in time for breakfast. Mom was there. So was the Obamas' full-time 'family caregiver', Marlease Bushnell, and a full-time housekeeper charged with 'things I don't fully enjoy,' Michelle said, 'like cleaning, laundry, and cooking'.

Marian Robinson – the person Michelle unhesitatingly referred to as 'my best friend' – had already proven herself to be the family's indispensable backstop. Michelle's mother, who ran a senior marathon at age 60 and was strongly in favour of her son-in-law's presidential aspirations, reassured Michelle that she would continue to take care of Malia and Sasha whenever Mommy and Daddy were on the stump.

Michelle had even come up with a new way for the candidate to keep in touch with his family during the campaign. She purchased webcams for Barack and the girls, so that each evening they could connect via their respective Macs and recap the day's events.

In making her own list of needs for the coming campaign, one demand was non-negotiable – that she be allowed to spend Saturdays with Malia and Sasha. For years, Michelle had taken the girls to spend Saturdays with her friends Yvonne Davila and Sandy Matthews and their daughters. The drill was usually the same: ballet, then soccer practice or perhaps tennis lessons, lunch at California Pizza Kitchen or Pizza Capri, and then a movie – something along the lines of *Harry Potter* or the latest offering from Disney. If there was time, they might take the kids to browse the children's stacks at 57th Street Books. Even if it meant dodging reporters and travelling with a phalanx of bodyguards – which it eventually would – Michelle insisted on preserving the family's Saturday routine.

At the time, polls showed that New York Senator Hillary Clinton was the overwhelming favourite to win her party's nomination for president. Given the quixotic nature of her husband's candidacy, the next question Michelle asked embarrassed even her. 'I know it's crazy, guys,' she asked, 'but what happens if we *win*?'

Michelle and the girls had remained behind during the nearly two years since her husband had been elected to the US Senate. They would obviously be living in the White House if he somehow managed to emerge victorious in 2008, but where would the girls go to school? Would they be able to have anything approaching 'normal' lives in the White House? How could they make the prospect of leaving their family and friends in Chicago less wrenching for Malia and Sasha?

'It will be a hard transition for these little girls,' she said in one of the meetings. 'They'll be leaving the only home that they've known. Someone's got to be the steward of that transition. And it can't be the president of the United States. It will be me.'

Barack, meanwhile, had agonised about what a presidential run might mean for him as a father. Indeed, at one of the many book parties celebrating the publication of *The Audacity of Hope*, Barack broke down while apologising for all of the time he had spent away from his children. He was crying so hard, Valerie Jarrett remembered, 'he couldn't continue'.

In December, Barack met with Newton Minow and Abner Mikva in Minow's offices at Sidley Austin. 'I just don't want to be away from my little girls,' he told them. 'They need their father to be there for them now.'

'Look,' Minow replied, 'I'm no psychologist, but if you're going to be away from your girls, now is the time to do it – when they're small and adaptable. It's far more important to be around them when they're teenagers – that's when you'll have the most impact.'

Barack was sceptical.

'Abner and I have raised six daughters between us – three each,' Minow continued. 'We were away a lot when they were little, and they all turned out great.'

By the time Barack left his office, said Minow, 'I think he was looking at things differently. We helped ease his concerns enough so that he felt free to move forward. But of course, it still all hinged on whether Michelle was willing to go along.'

As he had done so many times before during their Christmas holidays, Barack used this time together to convince his wife to let him make just one more run. There were long walks on the beach and 'we just talked it through,' Barack recalled. 'It wasn't as if it was a slam dunk for me.'

It was during this quiet family time away from the pressures of their public lives that Michelle seriously considered whether this was a quest they could afford to embark upon. She decided it was.

'When you're in Hawaii, on a beach,' Michelle explained, 'everything looks possible.'

The fact that her husband had delivered on so many impossible-sounding promises in the past had a lot to do with her decision to give Barack the green light. 'Look, he's done everything he said he would,' she told a friend. 'He's written bestselling books, he's built this successful political career . . . I need to get on board.'

'I think part of the reason she agreed to do it,' Barack said, 'was that she knew that she had veto power, that she and the girls ultimately mattered more than my own ambitions . . . and if she said no we would be OK.'

Michelle's about-turn also had much to do with her own sense of mission. She had long felt – even more strongly than her husband – that it was time to wrest power from the 'trust-fund brats' and 'people with the right daddies' she had had to deal with at Princeton and Harvard.

'To me, it's now or never,' she said. 'We're not going to keep running and running and running, because at some point you do get the life beaten out of you. It hasn't been beaten out of us yet. We need to be in there now, while we're still fresh and open and fearless and bold.'

In the coming weeks and months, Michelle would admonish Barack and his inner circle to 'not forget what we're fighting for'. For Michelle, Axelrod recalled, it was important that any campaign remained 'consistent with what he is and what he thinks, and we wouldn't distort that'.

Michelle's blessing came with two caveats. First, she made her husband vow that he would follow through on the pledge that he had never managed to keep in all the years of their marriage: that at long last he would quit smoking. While they were still on vacation, he began chewing Nicorette gum.

Michelle made it clear that she was willing to put herself and their children on the line 'once and only once. This is it,' she told Barack. 'If it doesn't work this time, don't think we're doing this again in another four years.'

The next step: explaining it all to the girls. Barack and Michelle sat their daughters down and, as plainly as they could, told them that Daddy was going to be away even more than usual – and that, while Mommy was going to help him out, she would still be there for them most of the time.

While they stressed that becoming president was a great honour, and that as president Daddy could do a great deal of good for a great many people, Michelle and Barack knew what it would take to seal the deal.

Ever since they had seen President Bush's pet Scottie Barney scampering around the South Lawn during a visit to the White House ('They were so bored until Barney showed up,' Michelle said, 'and they started running with him'), the Obama children had been lobbying for a puppy. But Malia's asthma – which, incidentally, occasionally flared up when Daddy smoked inside the house – made her parents reluctant to bring a dog into their home. Now the girls were so adamant about getting a dog that Michelle decided it was time to begin researching hypoallergenic breeds. 'They're such good girls,' she said. 'I can't deny them this one thing that they want so badly.'

'Win or lose,' Michelle told them, 'when the election is over – and if you've been good – we're getting a dog.'

'Promise?' Malia asked.

'Promise,' her father answered.

Malia wanted to know one more thing. 'Are you going to try to be president?' she asked. 'Shouldn't you be vice president first?'

It was enough for Malia to hit the Internet and begin her own thorough search of breeds that are considered hypoallergenic. Over the course of the next two years, she and Sasha would periodically bring up a candidate so the family could weigh the pros and cons of that particular breed. 'At this point I think they know more about dogs,' said a Hyde Park neighbour, 'than your average vet.'

In January, Barack announced on his website that he was forming a presidential exploratory committee. Around this time, Michelle suggested that, by way of heading off any future criticism, Barack pay $375 to clear up the delinquent parking tickets he had racked up years earlier while a law student at Harvard.

Of more concern to Barack's advisors were the rumours that Obama was Muslim. The campaign issued a statement that Barack had 'never been a practising Muslim'. Yet the candidate himself saw no problem with making known his affection for Muslim culture or to disguise the fact that it had been part of his life as a child in Indonesia. During an interview with Nicholas Kristof of the *New York Times*, Barack suddenly began reciting the opening lines of the Arabic call to prayer – *Allah-u Akbar, Allah-u Akbar* ('God is the greatest, God is the greatest') – with what Kristof called a 'first-rate Arabic accent'. Barack called the Muslim call to prayer 'one of the prettiest sounds on Earth at sunset'.

A few weeks later, Michelle would pull back to a part-time position at the University of Chicago Hospitals so that she could campaign for her husband. It was not the only career concession Michelle would make. In light of the fact that Barack was a vocal critic of Wal-Mart's labour practices, Michelle's position on the board of Wal-Mart supplier TreeHouse Foods became problematic. After TreeHouse closed its pickle plant in La Junta, Colorado, displacing 150 Hispanic workers, pressure mounted on Michelle to resign. She resisted, in part because she felt she would need to be able to earn a living if 'something unexpected or unfortunate' happened during the campaign.

If her husband were to fall victim to an assassin – something she had thought about long and hard – Michelle said, 'I need to be able to take care of myself and my kids.' She allowed that any such tragedy would trigger 'great sympathy and outpouring. But I have to maintain some level of professional credibility . . . I need to be in a position for my kids where, if they lose their father, they don't lose everything.'

On 10 February 2007, 15,000 people waited in the cold outside the flag-draped Old State Capitol Building in Springfield. It was here where, in 1858, Abraham Lincoln issued his famous warning that 'a house divided against itself cannot stand'.

Barack had wanted the Reverend Jeremiah Wright, who was still railing against America as 'a Eurocentric wasteland of lily-white lies', to give the convocation. His advisors, fearful that the slumbering press would soon latch onto Wright's incendiary opinions, wanted Barack to withdraw the invitation to speak.

For the Obamas, who had given $22,500 to Wright's church in 2006 alone, it was a tough call. 'Barack got the title for his book from Pastor Wright talking about the "Audacity of Hope" in his sermons,' said a church member. 'But it was Michelle who really wanted him to give the blessing when Barack announced for president. She didn't like it when they kind of "disinvited" the reverend, but I guess there wasn't a whole lot she could do about it.'

That frigid morning in Springfield, Barack and Michelle, both clad in long black overcoats, strode hand in hand to the wooden podium that had been set up on the capitol steps. Against the backdrop of the pillar-ringed state-house rotunda and with Michelle looking on, Barack drew parallels between himself and the Great Emancipator. 'As Lincoln organised the forces arrayed against slavery, he was heard to say, "Of strange, discordant, and even hostile elements, we gathered from the four winds, and formed and fought to battle through,"' Barack told the crowd. 'That is our purpose here today. That's why I'm in this race. Not just to hold an office, but to gather with you and transform a nation.'

Michelle nodded in agreement. 'And that is why,' he continued, 'in the shadow of the Old State Capitol, where Lincoln once called on a divided house to stand together, where common hopes and common dreams still live, I stand before you today to announce my candidacy for the presidency of the United States.'

With that, the crowd exploded in chants of 'Obama! Obama!' as the handsome couple and their beautiful children, wrapped in wool caps and scarves, waved from the capitol steps. After the speech, Barack headed straight for Iowa, where the first votes in the Democratic primary process would be cast a year later. By this time, he had adopted a new greeting as he shook the hands of voters that was as cloying as it was awkward. 'I,' he would say with conviction, '*appreciate you.*'

The day after Barack formally announced his candidacy, the Obamas' joint interview with Steve Croft aired on CBS's *60 Minutes*. Michelle and Barack, both mindful of the fact that it was Croft whose questions back in 1992 about Bill Clinton's alleged infidelity prompted Hillary Clinton to say she wasn't 'some Tammy Wynette standin' by her man', waited for a gotcha moment that never came.

Instead, Michelle reiterated that one of the prerequisites for the race was that Barack 'couldn't be a smoking president. Please, America, watch,' she joked into the camera. 'Keep an eye on him and call me if you see him smoking.'

It was in this role as the great leveller that Michelle found her groove. That March, at a fundraiser in New York, Michelle rolled out the crowd-pleasing shtick that would serve as her mantra throughout the campaign. Just as Barack could be guaranteed a laugh when he claimed people usually referred to him as 'Alabama' or 'Yo Mama', Michelle riffed on his shortcomings as a husband.

'He's a man who's just awesome,' she began, 'but he's still a man . . . There's Barack Obama the phenomenon, Barack Obama the genius, the editor of the *Harvard Law Review*, the constitutional-law scholar, the civil rights attorney, the community organiser, the bestselling author, the Grammy winner. This Barack Obama guy's pretty impressive.

'Then,' she added with a wry smirk, 'there's the Barack Obama that lives in my house. That guy's not so impressive. He still has trouble putting the bread up and putting his socks actually in the dirty clothes and he still doesn't do a better job than our five-year-old daughter, Sasha, making his bed. So you have to forgive me if I'm a little stunned by this whole Barack Obama thing.'

Often, Barack was there to take Michelle's good-natured needling. 'Hey, you left the butter on the counter this morning,' she would say as he shook his head and grinned sheepishly. 'You're just asking for it. You *know* I'm giving a speech about you today.'

Barack loved it. 'I'm often reminded by events, if not by my wife,' he would say, 'that I'm not a perfect man.'

Soon she was drawing crowds almost as big as her husband's – in some cases 10,000 or more. More importantly, after each appearance she collected more signed commitment cards than Barack. When Axelrod and others complimented Michelle on her speechmaking ability, she was taken aback. 'Why,' she asked indignantly, 'is everybody so surprised?'

Soon Barack's staff had a new nickname for Michelle. They called her 'The Closer'.

On the national stage, however, stories of Barack's failings – his snoring, his morning breath, his odd penchant for leaving his underwear on the kitchen floor – did not play quite so well. Some critics believed Michelle's good-natured ribbing diminished the first black man seeking to occupy the White House.

New York Times columnist Maureen Dowd went further, accusing Michelle of making 'emasculating' remarks about her husband that only served to make him look like an 'undisciplined child'. Dowd began calling Barack 'Obambi'.

When asked to comment, Michelle shrugged off Dowd's comments. 'She obviously,' the candidate's wife said, 'doesn't know who I am.' But privately, Michelle expressed anger at what she saw as an attempt to cast her as 'just another angry, castrating black woman beating up on her husband. That's the stereotype, right? The mould I'm supposed to fit?'

Later, with Barack's blessing, she addressed the issue head-on. 'Somehow I've been caricatured as his emasculating wife,' she said at one point. 'Barack and I laugh about that. It's just sort of like, do you think anyone could emasculate Barack Obama? Really now.'

As for toning down her remarks: 'I know who I need to be,' Michelle declared in answer to her critics. 'I'm a grown-up. I've seen it up and I've seen it down, and I know who I need to be to stay true to who I am.'

During the campaign, Michelle, who never resorted to notes, would seldom deviate from her standard 45-minute script. In addition to pointing out her husband's accomplishments and his harmless, endearing foibles, Michelle spoke of her Chicago roots. '*Ozzie and Harriet* – South Side working-class version,' she said of her childhood. 'My favourite mental images are of family. Summertime images of barbecues and folks sitting around, kids playing. Of just being with the people you've loved your entire life, and feeling a sense of security and comfort and safety – the feelings and emotions, for me, of what it means to be an African American.'

For Michelle, life on the road – even though she was never away from Sasha and Malia for long – quickly took its toll. On the hustings, she devoted part of her spiel to talking about how she still managed to juggle campaigning and motherhood. 'I get them to a neighbour's if I can't get them to school,' she said of her children. 'I get on a plane. I come to a city. I do several events. I get on a plane. I get home before bedtime. And by doing that, yeah, I'm a little tired at the end of the day, but the girls, they just think Mommy was at work. They don't know I was in New Hampshire. Quite frankly, they don't care.'

Marian Robinson's decision to retire in the summer of 2007 so she could pitch in more with the grandchildren would prove to be a 'godsend' for Michelle. Robinson, in turn, had nothing but 'total admiration' for her daughter's commitment to the campaign. 'I think supporting her husband is what is necessary,' Robinson said. 'For her to dive into it the way she does is just the way she does everything.' But, Michelle confided to a small group of women volunteers in Las Vegas, 'This is hard. This is really a hard thing. This isn't a natural choice to be made in your life. It's strange, all this.'

Then why do it? she was asked. 'I took myself down every dark road you could go on, just to prepare myself before we jumped out there,' she said. 'The bottom line is, man, the little sacrifice we have to make is nothing compared to the possibility of what we could do if this catches on.'

Besides, she admitted that Barack made it hard for her to complain. 'It's harder for him, being on the road,' she said. 'I've got my girls and our routine. I am feeling their love. He is missing that.'

Through it all, Michelle tried to maintain something resembling a normal home-life for her children. After returning from a campaign event in Minnesota, she squeezed in a workout and then stopped off at Target in her gym clothes to buy toilet paper. The next day, she was off again – this time to give speeches in New York and Connecticut before heading home to take Malia and Sasha to ballet classes and a performance of *Disney on Ice*. In the few spare moments she could spare for herself, Michelle might sit back and watch reruns of two of her favourite TV programmes – *Sex and the City* and *The Dick Van Dyke Show*.

Whenever Barack managed to break away from the campaign for a few days and return to Chicago, Michelle insisted 'that he be part of this life, real life. He doesn't come home,' she insisted, 'as the grand poohbah.'

Even when he did manage to steal a day or two to spend with his family, Barack was distracted by endless phone calls, text messages and emails. Axelrod was accustomed to getting midnight calls from his boss; he always knew when Obama was calling by his ringtone – 'Signed, Sealed, Delivered I'm Yours' by Stevie Wonder.

Increasingly, Michelle would wake up in the middle of the night to discover that her husband had sneaked out of bed and into the study, where he was frantically scribbling notes. That is how, Michelle told a friend, she could tell Barack was 'really stressed out. When he is writing small notes late at night. When he's really sort of brooding about something, it's late at night, and there's a lot of little note writing going on. That's when I know.'

That's also when Michelle would put on her robe and join him in the study. 'What's happened?' she would find herself asking again and again. 'What's going on?' Barack never hesitated to share his problems with her. 'Michelle is his sounding board,' Valerie Jarrett said. 'There is not a problem he would hesitate to share with her, because he knows she'll never hold back.' Unlike other advisors who might be less than forthcoming, Michelle is 'very direct. She'd tell him exactly what she's thinking' before returning to bed.

Much later, Barack would join her and fall fast asleep, only to be jostled by Sasha and Malia as they climbed under the covers with their parents just after dawn. Michelle would turn on the lights: 'So we're sort of waking up. And we talk. We talk about Daddy being president, about adolescence, about the questions they have.' Through it all, Daddy would lie there, motionless. 'A dead body,' sniffed Michelle. Eventually, the girls stopped joining them in bed if Barack was there because, said Michelle, 'Daddy is too snorey and stinky.'

Such lines drew the expected laughs when Michelle delivered them on the stump. But many people were surprised to discover that the overall tone of her message was decidedly downbeat. While Barack travelled the country spreading his generally optimistic message of hope and change, his wife seem to relish the role of bad cop – especially when talking to African American audiences.

Black church ladies made up Michelle's most receptive audiences, and she took great care to speak to them in their language. 'On behalf of my church home and my pastor, Reverend Jeremiah Wright,' she invariably began, 'I bring greetings.'

Then, to establish her working-class African American credentials, she spoke of the Robinson Family's South Carolina roots, of her South Side girlhood and the relatives who saved up enough money to buy nice furniture just to wrap it in plastic. To those who feared for Barack's life were he to be elected – following a series of threats, he had already been assigned Secret Service protection – Michelle implored audiences not to 'wrap us in plastic just because you're afraid'.

Relaxing into the black vernacular, Michelle instructed her listeners to get 'ten other triflin' people in your life' to volunteer for her husband or to contribute to his campaign. She wanted them to do this now, she said, because America under George W. Bush was a divided nation 'guided by fear', a country that is 'downright mean'. We are 'cynical' and 'lazy . . . We just don't care about each other any more.'

Healthcare? 'Let me tell you,' she warned, 'don't get sick in America.' College? 'Who can afford it? We just got out of debt ourselves.' Retirement? 'Pensions are drying up. People have to work longer than they ever thought they'd have to.' The bottom line, according to Michelle: 'We have become a nation of struggling folks who are barely making it every day. Folks are just jammed up, and it's got worse over my lifetime. And, doggone it, I'm young!'

Michelle's unremittingly bleak view of America actually played well in these venues. But once again, on the larger national stage, Michelle's caustic observations made her look . . . bitter.

Indeed, once she was no longer playing to an audience, Michelle seemed oddly detached. 'Her bearing is less royal than military: brisk, often stone-faced . . . mordant,' commented the *New Yorker's* Lauren Collins. 'Her winningly chipmunk-cheeked smile is doled out sparingly, a privilege to be earned, rather than an ice-breaker or an entreaty.'

Barack's minders considered Michelle's candour to be something of a double-edged sword. 'Occasionally it gives campaign people heartburn,' allowed Axelrod, who complained to Barack that his wife's comments might alienate white voters. 'She's fundamentally honest – goes out there, speaks her mind, jokes. She doesn't parse her words or select them with an antenna for political correctness.'

It was a problem shared by at least one of the seven other Democrats running for president at the time. When asked in February 2007 what he thought about newcomer Barack Obama, long-time Delaware Senator Joe Biden said, 'I mean, you got the first mainstream African American who is articulate and bright and clean and a nice-looking guy. I mean, that's storybook, man.'

No sooner had African American leaders expressed indignation over Biden's use of the word *clean* to describe Barack than Biden called Barack to apologise. He also issued a statement and spoke to reporters trying to clarify what he meant. 'My mother has an expression: clean as a whistle, sharp as a tack,' he explained. 'That's all I was trying to say.'

Barack brushed it off. 'He was very gracious,' he said of his fellow senator. 'I have no problem with Joe Biden.'

But Michelle did. '"The first African American who is articulate and bright and *clean*,"' she said as she read Biden's comments in the *New York Times*. 'Gee, go figure. He's black and he's articulate and he's *clean*. So typical – I've heard things like that all my life. "My, you're so well-spoken – you sound just like a white girl!"' According to one acquaintance, 'Michelle was furious with Joe Biden. It rolled off Barack's back, but not hers.'

Ignoring her critics, Michelle criss-crossed the country with her 'something's wrong with America' message. 'We are our own evil,' she said at one campaign event, claiming at another that, because of its inherent racism, the US was the only country 'on the planet' where 'a man with the credentials and the commitment and the ability of Barack Obama' would have difficulty being elected president. To supporters in Iowa, she stated flatly that, while her husband was prepared to be president, it remained to be seen if Americans were worthy of him. 'Barack cannot lead a nation,' she said, 'that is not ready to be led.'

To be sure, the Obama campaign faced an uphill battle. Despite a state-of-the-art Internet operation devised in part by 24-year-old Facebook co-founder Chris Hughes, and a hit 'Yes We Can' YouTube video by hip hop artist will.i.am, Barack lagged far behind Hillary in the polls.

The situation only got worse in April, when Barack squared off against Clinton, Biden, former North Carolina Senator John Edwards, Connecticut Senator Christopher Dodd, New Mexico Governor Bill Richardson, Ohio Congressman Denis Kucinich and former Alaska Senator Mike Gravel in the first of 17 nationally televised Democratic primary debates. When asked how he would respond to a surprise terrorist attack, Barack waffled. In comparison with Hillary, who promised to 'move as swiftly as is prudent to retaliate', Obama stammered a vague response that made him sound, said *Time*'s Karen Tumulty, 'like a candidate to head the volunteer fire department'.

From the outset, Hillary did not hesitate to charge that Barack's inexperience and immaturity made him 'unelectable'. Barack, however, was reluctant to strike back. 'I am not interested in tearing into Hillary Clinton,' he replied when asked why he wasn't taking a more forceful stand. 'I think she is an admirable person, a capable senator.'

In an attempt to offset criticism that Barack appeared 'detached' and 'aloof' during the first debate, the Obamas hauled out their biggest gun. On 2 May 2007, Oprah appeared on CNN's *Larry King Live* to announce that, for the first time, she was endorsing a candidate for president. 'What he stands for,' she told King, 'is worth me going out on a limb for.' Her endorsement of Barack, she added, 'doesn't mean I'm against Hillary. I haven't got anything negative to say about Hillary Clinton.'

Like her husband and Oprah, Michelle had also long admired the Clintons. Bill had been so popular in the African American community that he was often affectionately referred to as the country's 'first black president', and it seemed only fitting that, after leaving the White House, he would establish his post-presidential headquarters in Harlem.

Yet, after Hillary sniped that Barack had done nothing to prove he was worthy of the nomination, Michelle, in the words of a friend, 'lost respect for the Clintons'. She now joined with Obama's inner circle of advisors – whom Gibbs described as 'panicked' – in urging Barack to 'punch harder'.

Barack resisted. 'That's not,' he said, 'who I am.'

After he stumbled during the second debate, Michelle told him point-blank that he was going down to defeat if he did not 'take off the gloves'.

Chimed in Axelrod: 'Michelle is right: You have got to engage.'

The Hillary juggernaut continued through the summer months. As late as September 2007, polls put her 23 points ahead of Barack; 37 per cent of voters did not even know who Obama was.

It was then that Barack finally decided to strike back. During the subsequent debates and in interview after interview, he charged that it was Hillary who was unelectable. She was a polarising figure, a symbol of politics as usual and, Barack pointed out repeatedly, an early supporter of the war in Iraq – a war that he had opposed from the beginning.

'I am not convinced the Obamas have any sense of how hard the Clintons fight,' said Al Gore's former presidential campaign manager Donna Brazile, 'when they feel their birthright is being challenged.'

Even though his wife boasted a double-digit lead in the polls, Bill Clinton was telling friends in Arkansas that he feared Obama would be able to run away with the nomination. One reason for this was the complicated new Clinton-endorsed system of delegates and 'superdelegates' – elected officials and party bigwigs that made it possible for a candidate to lose the popular vote and still walk away with the nomination.

Now Bill jumped into the fray. Over the next nine months, he would accuse the Obama campaign of everything from playing the race card to personal attacks on his wife's character to using union members to intimidate voters. When the former president claimed Obama was exaggerating his opposition to the war – Clinton called Barack's account of his position 'a fairy tale' – Michelle called her husband's advisors and demanded that the campaign fire back. 'You can't let him get away with that,' she told them. 'Barack opposed the war when they went right along with Bush. How dare they.'

For the most part, Michelle refrained from publicly lashing out against her husband's adversaries. But now her speeches seemed to be salted with not-so-subtle references to the Clintons' marital troubles ('Our view is that if you can't run your own house, you certainly can't run the White House') and sly remarks about people who had simply been in power too long.

Michelle let her guard down one afternoon when someone asked what she thought about the broadsides Bill Clinton was levelling against her husband. 'I want to rip his eyes out!' she said, clawing with her fingernails. When a campaign staffer cast a disapproving look in her direction, she demurred. 'Kidding!' she said. 'See, this is what gets me into trouble.'

That summer of 2007, all the Obamas were out in force in Iowa. While the girls ran across the green grass in their summer dresses, Michelle kicked off her shoes and told a few dozen Iowans gathered for a garden party in Sioux City why they should vote for her husband. On her ninth birthday, a poised Malia was warmly applauded when she gave a speech about the meaning of freedom to a small Fourth of July crowd. A few weeks later, she and Sasha were screaming as they rode alongside Dad on Big Ben, one of the scarier rides at the Iowa State Fair. Then Sasha and Dad teamed up against Malia and her mom playing several carnival games.

Michelle was more irreverent than other aspiring first ladies who had had to make the requisite pilgrimage to Iowa in primary season. 'We're here for the State Fair,' Michelle would tell crowds with a straight face. 'I just want some stuff on a stick – a corn dog, a Snickers bar . . . doesn't matter what it is. Just has to be on a stick.'

The Obamas did not always have the media coverage to themselves; in several instances on the stump, they found themselves looking on as Daddy shared a platform that included Hillary. At this time, as Daddy's battle with his arch-rival was building to fever pitch, Malia suddenly turned serious. 'You know, this is a pretty big deal,' the ten year old said. 'If Daddy wins, he'd be the first African American to be a nominee.'

Michelle was surprised at her daughter's out-of-the-blue comment, and pleased. 'Do you realise how important that is, how significant?'

'Oh, yeah,' Malia answered confidently. 'Because there was slavery, and there were people who couldn't do things because of their race.' Then she paused. 'But it would also be a big deal if a woman won. Because there was also the time when women couldn't vote. So it would be a big deal either way.'

'This,' Michelle said when later recounting the exchange, 'is *her* talking . . . Amazing.'

While the more free-spirited Sasha provided much of the comic relief, spinning around until she dizzily plopped to the ground and giving everyone from the vice president on down high-fives, Malia proved time and again that she was one of the more thoughtful members of the family. When asked what it felt like to appear in front of large crowds with her parents, Malia replied, 'Well, I realise the people aren't here to see me. I'm just a kid.

'I can do my part,' Malia continued. I can recycle. I can pick up the trash. But I can't pass any laws to make anybody do anything. They just think I'm cute. I just wave and I smile and I'm outa there.' Barack's nickname for his elder daughter: 'Little Miss Articulate.'

Sasha, on the other hand, managed to throw Mommy with her questions about a particular video that was suddenly causing a sensation on the Internet. In the less-than-completely-wholesome 'I Got a Crush . . . On Obama', bikini-clad self-proclaimed 'Obama Girl' Amber Lee Ettinger sang of her love for Michelle's husband against the backdrop of Barack running on the beach.

'Wow,' Michelle said when she first clicked on the video. 'That's weird . . . but I guess nobody's really gonna hear about that.' But in June, Sasha declared, 'Daddy has a girlfriend. It's you, Mommy.'

Michelle suddenly realised that Sasha was talking about Obama Girl, but for some reason had confused Ettinger with Mommy. 'Oh, shhhii . . . Yeah,' Michelle replied, stopping just short of uttering an expletive. 'Yeah, Mommy is Daddy's girlfriend, all right.' (Ettinger would later make a video in which she pleaded with Hillary Clinton to 'stop the attacks'.)

As kind as Malia had been about Hillary Clinton, one high-profile member of the Obamas' inner circle proved to be considerably less charitable. 'Barack knows what it means to be a black man in a country and a process that is controlled by rich white men,' said the Reverend Jeremiah Wright, apparently not imbued with the spirit of the holidays, said during his Christmas sermon. 'Hillary can never know that, Hillary ain't never been called a nigger!'

On 3 January 2008, nearly one year after his first campaign stop in Iowa, Barack scored a decisive victory in that state's caucuses. On election night in Des Moines, Michelle, wearing a black dress and jawbreaker-sized pearls, stood by her husband and their two daughters and waved to the cheering crowd. 'It was,' wrote *Washington Post* columnist Eugene Robinson, 'one of those moments that give you goosebumps.'

'They said this day would never come,' Barack said, adding that his victory was a 'defining moment in history'. Perhaps. But just five days later, Hillary rebounded with an upset win in New Hampshire. The polls had predicted that Barack would ride a wave of momentum to victory in the Granite State. Instead, women who felt Hillary had been unfairly treated by the media – a sentiment that was reinforced when Hillary choked back tears during a discussion in a Portsmouth, New Hampshire, coffee shop – turned out in force to support her.

Over the next few weeks, the lead see-sawed between Hillary and Barack as she won in Michigan and Nevada and he scored an impressive victory in South Carolina. Announcing his endorsement of Obama in late January, Senator Ted Kennedy compared Barack to his brother John, and even drew parallels between Bill Clinton's sniping at Barack and former President Harry Truman's early criticism of JFK's candidacy. 'And John Kennedy replied: "The world is changing. The old ways will not do. It is time for a new generation of leadership,"' Ted boomed. 'So it is with Barack Obama!'

A few days later, on the eve of the 5 February 2008 Super Tuesday contest, when voters in more than 20 states and protectorates cast their ballots, Michelle was joined onstage at a rally in Los Angeles by Caroline Kennedy, Kennedy cousin Maria Shriver and Oprah. Beneath her cool exterior, Michelle later confessed to being 'completely star-struck. I mean, Caroline Kennedy – come on! She's part of history.'

Even when the inevitable comparisons were made between the

tall, stylish, immaculately tailored Michelle and Jacqueline Kennedy, Michelle was more impressed with Jackie's abilities as a parent than her status as legendary style icon. 'If you botch raising your children,' Jackie had famously said, 'nothing else you do matters very much.' Michelle agreed. Given the media microscope Caroline and John Jr grew up under – not to mention the assassinations of their father and their beloved uncle Bobby – the two Kennedy children ended up as 'wonderful, well-balanced adults. That doesn't happen by accident,' Michelle said. 'Jackie was obviously an incredible mom.'

If the Clintons justifiably felt betrayed by their long-time political allies the Kennedys, Hillary got some modicum of revenge on Super Tuesday. Although Barack won thirteen states, Hillary's eight wins included the Kennedys' home state of Massachusetts and the biggest prize of all – California.

Five days later, Barack won his second spoken-word Grammy, this time for *The Audacity of Hope*. 'I'm almost more impressed by that,' Michelle cracked to a friend, 'than by this whole running-for-president thing.'

Wisecracks aside, Michelle took each victory – and each defeat – to heart. As tensions mounted, she became increasingly irritable. When a TV reporter physically brushed aside her press secretary, Michelle asked angrily, 'Did you place your hand on my staff? You do not touch my team.'

Barack was feeling the pressure, too. But he turned increasingly to the one thing that had helped him stay calm in times of crisis: cigarettes. Despite Michelle's tongue-in-cheek plea for Americans to report to her if they caught him smoking, Barack was lighting up more than ever in restrooms, stairwells and the back of his SUV. The only difference from earlier in the campaign was that he indulged his habit under the watchful eyes of the Secret Service agents assigned to protect him.

Still, the rigours of the campaign seemed to be taking a greater toll on Michelle than on the candidate himself. 'Barack will say she's more driven than he is,' a campaign staffer observed, 'and in the sense that she does not really let things roll off her back as easily as he does, he's right.' As the momentum shifted from her husband to Hillary

Clinton and back again, Michelle was perhaps most responsible for insisting that her husband 'not equivocate. When he was weighing his words carefully, she told him to come out swinging.'

During a conference call before a debate in early February, Michelle had dialled in to listen as he brainstormed with his advisors. Exasperated with the all the varying opinions being offered, Michelle finally cut in. 'Barack,' she told him, 'feel – don't think! You've been over-thinking, and Hillary just cuts right to the point. Don't get caught in the weeds. Be visceral. Use your heart – and your head.'

Silence. Michelle had spoken. 'Nobody's opinion matters more to Barack,' said one participant in the conference call. 'And, of course, she was absolutely right.'

Unfortunately, no one was minding Michelle on 18 February when she told Obama supporters in Madison, Wisconsin, that 'for the first time in my adult life, I am proud of my country because it feels like hope is making a comeback'. Later that same day at a rally in Milwaukee, she said it again. Only this time, there were TV cameras there to record her remarks.

Understandably, Michelle's claim that in her entire adult life she had never been proud of America unleashed a torrent of criticism. While Cindy McCain, the wife of presumptive Republican nominee Senator John McCain, proclaimed she had always been proud of her country, Laura Bush unexpectedly sprang to Michelle's defence. What Michelle meant to say, the First Lady suggested, was that she was 'more proud' of her country now that an African American was in striking distance of the presidency.

Touched by these unsolicited words, Michelle dashed off a note of thanks to Laura. 'There's a reason people like her,' Michelle later said. 'She doesn't add fuel to the fire.'

Good intentions aside, Laura's interpretation of what Michelle 'meant to say' wasn't entirely accurate, either. 'What she meant was,' Barack told an interviewer, 'this is the first time she's been proud of the politics of America. Because she's pretty cynical about the political process, and with good reason, and she's not alone.'

Cast in the classic 'angry black woman' mould, Michelle would draw fire for months. But as a campaign issue, Michelle's comments would be all but totally eclipsed by another, potentially far more damaging controversy.

For over a year, David Axelrod and his senior staff had been wringing their hands in anticipation of the moment when the press would wake up to Jeremiah Wright and his offensive rhetoric. In March of 2008, that moment arrived when ABC News aired excerpts from Wright's more provocative rants.

The ensuing outrage over the reverend's racist and blatantly anti-American rhetoric ('God bless America? No, no, no. God *damn* America!') threatened to capsize the Obama campaign. (Wright also had choice words for the Clintons during the campaign: 'Hillary is married to Bill and Bill has been good to us. No, he ain't! Bill did us, just like he did Monica Lewinsky. He was riding dirty.')

Frantic, Axelrod and Barack's other staff advisors unanimously urged him to get out in front of the issue and disavow Wright in unequivocal terms.

Mrs Obama thought otherwise. 'Pastor Wright is like a father to us,' Michelle told her husband. 'You are not going to turn your back on him just because some people don't like what he has to say.'

In reality, Barack did not need much coaxing. Instead of denouncing Wright, he seized the opportunity to address the divisive issue of race at a televised news conference in Philadelphia on 18 March. In a moving and wide-ranging speech, Barack condemned Wright's comments. But, he went on, 'as imperfect as he may be, Reverend Wright has been like family to me. He strengthened my faith, officiated at my wedding and baptised my children.' And, he neglected to mention, helped save his marriage.

'I can no more disown him,' Obama continued, 'than I can disown the black community. I can no more disown him than I can my white grandmother . . . a woman who loves me as much as anything in this world, but who once confessed her fear of black men who passed by her on the street, and who on more than one occasion has uttered racial or ethnic stereotypes that made me cringe.'

Like others in the audience that day, Michelle grew visibly emotional as her husband spoke movingly of America's legacy of slavery and the wounds that still needed to be healed. After he was finished, Barack found Michelle backstage, weeping. While others tried to look away, they shared a quiet, intensely difficult moment together. Once his wife seemed comforted, he turned to no one in particular. 'What's next?' he asked.

The speech would be lavishly praised by Democrats and Republicans alike, although Barack was roundly criticised in some quarters for, in the words of more than one commentator, 'throwing Grandma under the bus'.

Apparently neither Barack nor Michelle, who had been given an advance copy of the speech, considered the possibility that Toot would be hurt by his comments. He had, after all, written about his grandmother's prejudices years before in *Dreams from My Father*. At Michelle's suggestion, Barack called his grandmother to smooth things over. 'It's OK,' she told him. 'Do what you have to do. It's OK.'

It would not be the last time Barack and Michelle would have to deal with the Reverend Jeremiah Wright. In the meantime, Barack's own unguarded words would threaten to cost him the election. Talking to fundraisers in San Francisco, he spoke of bitter whites whose frustrations caused them to 'cling to guns or religion or antipathy to people who aren't like them . . . as a way to express their frustrations'.

The remarks, widely condemned on both sides of the aisle as elitist, did not play well in the working-class neighbourhoods of Pennsylvania. Once again, Barack's advisors scrambled to find a way to get out the message that Barack had not lost touch with the common man.

Michelle had the answer. She urged her husband not to back down or 'be all wishy-washy'. He took her advice. 'No, I'm in touch,' he said at a rally in Pennsylvania. 'I know *exactly* what's going on. People are fed up, they're angry, they're frustrated.'

It was too little, too late. On 22 April, Pennsylvania voters handed Hillary Clinton a decisive win. But once again, because of the new delegate rules that had been promulgated by the Clintons, she would receive only a few more delegates than Barack.

For all the flak Barack drew for what many perceived as his

disparaging remarks about working-class whites, there were still elements in the black community that insisted he was really not one of them. This was one thing Michelle, who was now usually more cautious about the statements she made, was not willing to let slide. 'We're still playing around with the question of "Is he black enough?"' Michelle told a Women for Obama group. 'That's nonsense. Stop it! If a man like Barack isn't black enough, then who is?'

The Obamas were still licking their wounds from the Pennsylvania defeat when their old friend and mentor Jeremiah Wright resurfaced unexpectedly. This time Wright, who had retired as pastor of Trinity United, was delivering a speech at the National Press Club in Washington. 'This is not an attack on Jeremiah Wright,' Wright said of his critics, 'this is an attack on the black Church.'

Wright then went on to defend his earlier comments blaming the US for starting the AIDS epidemic and for 9/11, and to defend his friend Louis Farrakhan. As for Barack's speech condemning some of the minister's comments, Wright argued that Obama 'had to distance himself because he's a politician . . . Politicians say what they say and do what they do because of electability.'

This time, Barack's advisors implored him to publicly denounce Wright and resign from Trinity United Church. Wright had betrayed their friendship, they argued, and handed Obama's political enemies a weapon that could end his candidacy.

But when Barack talked it over with Michelle, she defended Wright. 'Your pastor is like your grandfather, right?' she had said. 'There are plenty of things he says that I don't agree with, that Barack doesn't agree with . . . You can't disown yourself from your family because they've got things wrong.'

Now Barack and Michelle were meeting with Wright's successor at Trinity United, the Reverend Otis Moss III, and, in Obama's words, 'praying on what to do'. In these discussions, Michelle's opinion prevailed. 'You stand by your family, the people you love, no matter what,' she insisted, 'and Reverend Wright is family.'

It would be another month before the Obamas finally resigned from the church, and then only after Father Michael Pfleger, a visiting Catholic priest, gave a sermon at Trinity United that mocked Hillary

Clinton. 'I really believe she always thought,' Pfleger said, '"This is mine. I'm Bill's wife. I'm white, and this is mine . . ." Then out of nowhere came, "Hey, I'm Barack Obama," and she said, "Oh, damn! Where did you come from? I'm white! I'm entitled! There's a black man stealing my show!"' Then Pfleger, who was white, pretended to wipe tears from his face, mimicking Hillary's emotionally charged remarks before the New Hampshire primary. 'She wasn't the only one crying,' Pfleger said. 'There was a whole lot of white people crying.'

Once again, Barack and Michelle talked over what to do about Trinity United. This time, since the culprit was not Jeremiah Wright but a white priest, they agreed that they could leave the church without appearing to turn their backs on their pastor and the black community.

'I am deeply disappointed in Father Pfleger's divisive, backward-looking rhetoric,' Barack said, making no reference to Wright's similarly inflammatory statements. Submitting the Obamas' formal letter of resignation from the church, Barack said, 'This is not a decision I come to lightly. We do it with some sadness . . . We don't want to have the church subjected to the scrutiny that a presidential campaign legitimately undergoes.'

In the end, Barack and Michelle never repudiated or abandoned Wright per se – only certain sentiments he expressed, sentiments they insisted they had never actually hear him express in church. According to an acquaintance of the reverend, 'Since they left the church, both Barack and Michelle have spoken to Reverend Wright several times. He is still a part of their lives.'

In the meantime, Barack and Hillary continued to battle it out for the nomination. On 6 May, Hillary won in Indiana but lost the all-important North Carolina primary to Barack. 'You did it,' Michelle told Barack as the results came in, assuring his nomination. 'You did it.'

As she had for every victory and defeat, Michelle, this time clad in a pumpkin-coloured dress and her trademark pearls, clasped hands with Barack and joined him onstage in North Carolina. 'This fall, we intend to march forward as one Democratic Party, united by a common vision for this country,' he told the cheering crowd. 'Because we all agree at this defining moment in history . . . we can't afford to give John McCain the chance to serve out George Bush's third term.'

Hillary, however, was not about to concede. Obama maintained his usual cool, but behind the scenes Michelle was seething. 'Why doesn't she just do the right thing and bow out gracefully?' Michelle asked. 'There's no reason for her to keep hangin' on.'

It would be a month before Barack's 3 June win in the Montana primary would trigger a mass migration of superdelegates to Obama's camp, formally clinching the nomination for Barack. Even then, Hillary would refuse to admit defeat until her supporters told her the race was over in a conference call. Two days later, Hillary conceded via email.

Now faced with defeating John McCain, Barack joked with Michelle about his chances. 'Oh great,' he said about how the match-up would be touted in the press, 'war hero against snot-nosed rookie.'

In truth, Barack had been treated with kid gloves by the mainstream press – and he knew it. Over the course of the campaign, Barack – either with or without Michelle – would end up on countless magazine covers, from *Time* (no fewer than 15 times before the end of 2008), *Newsweek*, *Vanity Fair*, the *New Yorker* and *The Atlantic* to *People*, *GQ*, *Men's Vogue*, *Ladies' Home Journal* and *Men's Health* to *Vibe*, *Parade*, *Esquire*, *Ebony*, *Rolling Stone* and *Tiger Beat*. With the rare exception, nearly every article portrayed him in glowing, almost messianic terms.

Michelle was not so fortunate. While her coverage was overwhelmingly positive, she came in for far more criticism than her husband. Columnist Michelle Malkin called Michelle 'Barack's bitter half', while the conservative *National Review* ran a picture of a scowling Michelle on the cover under the heading 'Mrs Grievance'.

Even Obama-friendly *Time*, in an article entitled 'The War Over Michelle Obama', speculated that Barack's wife 'could be a liability as well as an asset. Her speeches can sound stark and stern compared with her husband's roof-raisers. He's all about the promise; she's more about the problem.'

None of this came as a surprise to Michelle's brother, Craig, now the head basketball coach at Oregon State University. 'When you get to the Final Four,' he said, 'you aren't going to run up against guys who say, "Well, we are happy to have got this far; you can have it."'

Craig had no qualms about his sister's ability to weather the storm. 'In a funny way, she was raised to be in this position,' he said. 'To be political, you have to care about what people think about you. We were raised the complete opposite.'

Still, it hardly helped matters when Fox News anchor E.D. Hill jokingly referred to the fist-pound greeting the Obamas used – taught to them by some of their younger staffers – as some sort of 'terrorist fist-jab'. In the context of the lighthearted piece Hill was doing on the candidate's body language, the offhand comment was clearly meant to be funny. Essentially an updated version of the high-five, the fist-pound (also known as the 'bump' or 'dap'), was a staple on softball and soccer fields as well as basketball courts across the country.

Nevertheless, the strange 'terrorist fist-jab' line gained traction, and soon the Internet was abuzz with rumours that videotape existed of Michelle railing against 'whitey'. Michelle's reaction to this particular fable was predictable. 'Whitey? *Whitey*?' she said, utterly dumbfounded. 'What is this, the '70s? I mean, come on. It's not a word I would ever use.'

Barack was incensed. 'If they think they're going to make Michelle an issue in this campaign,' he said, 'they should be careful because I find that unacceptable, the notion that you start attacking my wife or my family. These folks should lay off my wife.'

Righteous indignation aside, by June the campaign was casting about for new ways make over Michelle's image. Six months earlier, Michelle had turned down an invitation to appear on ABC's popular daytime talk show *The View* because she would not cross a picket line during a lengthy writer's strike. After Cindy McCain co-hosted *The View* in April, Michelle told the show's executive producer, Bill Geddie, that she wanted to do the same.

Now, two months after McCain's appearance, Michelle needed the kind of exposure to a largely female audience that only a show like *The View* could provide. On 18 June – the same day the *New York Times* ran a front-page cover story on Mrs Obama's perceived gaffes and ongoing efforts to 'soften' her image – Michelle appeared on the show. Just as she had kidded with her husband not to 'screw it up' right before his 2004 convention keynote speech, Barack called her up to offer words of advice before her debut on *The View*. 'Be good,' he said.

No sooner had she been greeted with a standing ovation from the studio audience in New York than Michelle abruptly halted the proceedings. 'I have to be greeted properly,' she said with a straight face. 'First-bump, please.' She then pressed knuckles with co-hosts Barbara Walters, Whoopi Goldberg, Elizabeth Hasselbeck, Joy Behar and Sherri Shepherd.

When Walters asked her to address her critics, Michelle was eager to set the record straight about her claim that for the first time in her adult life she was proud of her country. 'I am proud of my country, without a doubt,' she said. 'I'm a girl who grew up in a working-class neighbourhood in Chicago, and let me tell you, of course I'm proud. Nowhere but in America could my story be possible.'

Asked why she thought there were as many negative stories about her in the press as there were positive stories about her husband, Michelle replied, 'I wear my heart on my sleeve. There's a level of passion there . . . that's the risk that you take.' Another reason for all the controversy, she said, was the media's appetite for controversy. 'I fill up some space,' she said.

For the remainder of the hour-long show, a charming and relaxed Michelle talked about her marriage and her children, her fashion sense ('I stopped wearing pantyhose a long time ago – it's painful . . . put 'em on, rip 'em, it's inconvenient') and the many comparisons to Jackie Kennedy. She conceded that Hillary had been the victim of sexism ('People aren't used to strong women. We don't even know how to talk about 'em'), and even praised Hasselbeck, an outspoken supporter of John McCain, as 'solid. She has great kids, she's funny.'

Members of Barack's staff who were watching the show live as it aired in New York burst into applause. If poll numbers were any indication, her *View* appearance and the mountain of press it received did much to improve the public's perception of the woman who aspired to be America's first black First Lady. Michelle's turn on *The View* was also a boost for New York designer Donna Ricco. Even before the show was over, women were rushing out to buy Michelle's off-the-rack, sleeveless black-and-white print Ricco sundress. The price: $148.

For the next few weeks, Michelle, now sensitive to the fact that any verbal misstep could cost her husband support in a tight election, tossed aside her usual doom-and-gloom script. It wasn't long, however, before the intemperate remarks of another Obama supporter were making headlines.

On 8 July, the Reverend Jesse Jackson, unaware that his microphone was on as he waited to do a TV interview, whispered to his fellow guest that he was fed up with Barack 'talkin' down to black people. I wanna,' he added, 'cut his nuts off.' To drive home his point, he clenched his teeth and made a slashing gesture with his right hand.

Jackson's tasteless remark ignited a firestorm of controversy, and the reverend immediately called a televised news conference to apologise for what he conceded were his 'hurtful' comments. His daughter Santita also apologised to her pal Michelle, although it was hardly necessary. 'Hey,' Michelle cracked to another friend, 'it's not something I haven't considered doing myself.'

As it turned out, that July both Barack and Michelle would find themselves taking more friendly fire. As her husband was about to depart on a long-planned tour of Europe and the Middle East designed to bolster his foreign policy credentials, Michelle's favourite magazine – the *New Yorker* – ran a cover story on the Obamas that would unintentionally revive some of the old fears about them.

On the cover of the magazine's 21 July 2008 issue, a cartoon by Barry Blitt depicted an Afro-topped, camouflage-wearing, AK-47-toting Michelle and her turbaned husband fist-bumpng in the Oval Office while the American flag burned in the fireplace. Above the mantlepiece: a portrait of Osama Bin Laden.

Although it was clearly a satirical swipe at some of the strange rumours that had swirled around the Obamas throughout the campaign, many failed to get the joke. Outraged readers of the liberal publication wrote in saying they were cancelling their subscriptions. Both the Obama and McCain camps condemned the cover, claiming most readers would find the cartoon 'tasteless and offensive'.

For their part, Barack and Michelle could only shrug their shoulders. 'Why would they do this?' asked Michelle, who knew that many would mistakenly interpret the cover as an endorsement of the charges of anti-Americanism that had been levelled against them in some quarters. 'Unbelievable.' Still, it was not nearly as offensive as a website posting – also by someone who was apparently sympathetic to the Obamas – that showed Michelle being lynched. Under pressure, the website took it down.

Leaving Michelle and the kids at home, Barack headed off on his whirlwind five-day international tour, which included meetings with Afghanistan's President Hamid Karzai, Prime Minister Nouri al-Maliki of Iraq, King Abdullah II of Jordan, Palestinian President Mahmoud Abbas, Israeli Prime Minister Ehud Olmert, German Chancellor Angela Merkel, French President Nicolas Sarkozy and British Prime Minister Gordon Brown. The climax of the tour was Barack's speech to a cheering crowd of 200,000 at the Victory Column in Berlin. The comparison's to JFK's stirring 'Ich bin ein Berliner' speech were inevitable.

Back in Chicago for a couple of days, Barack made the most of this sliver of time he could carve out for his wife and children. He and Michelle clapped as the girls re-enacted *Kung Fu Panda* on the living room floor and listened patiently as seven-year-old Sasha practised 'Li'l Liza Jane' on the piano.

They ate a takeaway lunch from Subway, played a quick game of Uno and took time out of the day to pose for pictures on the living room couch. (When Sasha teased him about his thinning hair, Daddy shot back, 'Well, you have no teeth!') This was also the time when the kids would hit Daddy up for their one-dollar weekly allowance. 'I'm out of town,' Barack explained, 'so Malia will say, "Hey, you owe me ten weeks!"'

Of course, things were not entirely as they once were at 5046 South Greenwood Drive, where a discreet blue-and-white 'Obama for President' sign had been placed on the front lawn. As a barefoot Sasha scampered outside, a Secret Service agent watching unobtrusively from the dining room whispered into the tiny walkie-talkie on his wrist: 'Front porch.'

Barack had appointed his vice presidential search committee two days after clinching the nomination in June. But now, in the final few weeks leading up to the Democratic Convention in Denver, the most pressing question was: would Barack pick Hillary to be his running mate?

Michelle, who had long insisted she was no policy wonk ('Please, I don't have the time'), publicly insisted that she would have 'nothing to do with' picking her husband's running mate. 'I don't want it. A nominee gets to pick who he thinks will best complement him.'

In fact, according to a New York Democratic State Party official who was close to the selection process, 'Michelle certainly played a role' in selecting her husband's vice president.

For all the talk of party unity, there were those in the Obama camp who still did not entirely trust the Clintons. But there was also a feeling that, given the fact that her husband would certainly be one of her chief counsellors, Hillary could bring experience and no small degree of foreign policy credibility to the table.

The same could be said for 35-year Senate veteran Joe Biden, chairman of the Foreign Relations Committee. Although the names of Indiana Senator Evan Bayh, Virginia Governor Tim Kaine and Kansas Governor Kathleen Sebelius were floated as possible vice presidential picks, Hillary and Biden were always at the top of the list. At one point, the Obama camp mulled over the idea of Hillary as vice president with Biden as Secretary of State. When asked what he thought of such an arrangement, Biden made it clear that he was interested only in the vice presidential slot. Hillary, on the other hand, let it be known that she would rule nothing out.

In what may have been the deciding factor, Michelle sided with those who felt Hillary would make a better Secretary of State than a vice president in an Obama administration. 'Do you,' Michelle asked her husband at one point, 'really want Bill and Hillary just down the hall from you in the White House? Could you live with that?'

On 23 August 2008, Barack announced his selection of Biden as his running mate via text message, email and on his website. Five days later at Denver's Invesco Field football stadium, against a stylised Grecian temple backdrop (instantly dubbed 'the Temple of Obama' by the McCain camp), Barack accepted the nomination before eighty-four thousand screaming supporters and a record-breaking television audience of forty million.

When he was finished, Michelle, dressed in a red-and-black shift, leapt onstage with Malia and Sasha. While the girls smiled and waved in their pink dresses, Michelle wrapped her arms around her husband. And, while the crowd roared, Barack nuzzled her cheek and kissed her.

I can't believe you pulled this off.

Michelle to Barack

Michelle is my chief counsel and advisor. I would never make
a big decision without asking her opinion.

Barack

Michelle is *totally* in control. She is friendly but very stern
and sharp – stern is the only way I know how to say it –
and she is *very* involved in is decision making.

Kim Lightford, Barack's friend and former state senate colleague

---

They don't seem to be fazed by anything.

Barack on Malia and Sasha

Our girls are just complete comic relief.

Michelle

8

'Oh, come on,' Michelle said when she heard the news. 'He's got to be kidding.' It had been just 12 hours since her husband made history by accepting his party's nomination. Now, on his 72nd birthday, John McCain was making some history of his own by picking Alaska Governor Sarah Palin as his running mate – the first woman ever to appear on a Republican ticket.

Michelle's stunned reaction to Palin's selection was shared by Barack, his senior staff and a sizable chunk of the American public. In fact, McCain had wanted to pick Connecticut Senator Joe Lieberman, a lifelong Democrat and Al Gore's running mate in 2000, but was stopped by party leaders who felt Lieberman was too liberal. Instead, McCain, known for taking political risks, hastily picked the virtually unknown Palin.

The feisty 44-year-old self-described 'average hockey mom' did manage to energise the GOP's conservative base – something that McCain had failed to accomplish thus far – and to pique the nation's curiosity. Four days after McCain introduced Palin to the nation, it was revealed that her seventeen-year-old daughter, Bristol, was unwed and pregnant. Even conservatives acknowledged that this was an embarrassment for the candidate whose appeal was based in part on upholding traditional Christian values.

Understandably, there were those on Barack's team who delighted in Bristol's predicament. Michelle was not one of them. Aware that Palin was also raising a four-month-old son of her own suffering from Down's syndrome, Michelle told Barack that she had 'nothing but sympathy' for the governor. Barack agreed, issuing a statement defending the Palin family's right to privacy and warning his own campaign staff not to make any comments about Bristol's pregnancy.

Five days after Barack's electrifying acceptance speech in Denver, Palin gave an acceptance speech of her own at the Republican Convention in Saint Paul, Minnesota. The Alaska governor's address, which electrified Republicans and engrossed a TV audience even larger than the one Barack had drawn, was aimed at squarely at white working-class voters – some of whom had supported Hillary. Palin was not shy about praising Clinton and reminding Hillary's supporters that there was still a woman they could vote for in the general election.

Palin managed to hold her own against Biden in the sole vice presidential debate on 2 October, but a series of disastrous TV interviews chipped away at the public's desire to put her a heartbeat away from the presidency. Palin would be the topic of several phone calls between Barack and Michelle, who admitted to being 'fascinated by this woman'.

The presidential candidates themselves, meanwhile, went toe-to-toe in three debates. During the second debate, a town hall-style event in Nashville, McCain pointed to Barack and referred to him as 'that one' to make a point. Later, McCain joked that he was simply taking a cue from Oprah. 'She called him "The One". I just called him "That One". What's the big deal?'

Michelle got the joke. For the foreseeable future, whenever she wanted to bring him down a peg, she took special pleasure in calling her husband 'that one'.

For the remainder of the campaign, it often seemed as if both candidates would take a back seat to Samuel J. Wurzelbacher, a plumbing contractor who confronted Barack as he campaigned door-to-door in Ohio. When Wurzelbacher demanded to know if Barack's tax plan would cost him as a small-business owner, Obama replied offhandedly, 'I think that when you spread the wealth around, it's good for everybody.'

The comment was captured on video and soon Wurzelbacher – now simply known as 'Joe the Plumber' – was being touted by Republicans as a working-class hero who had dared to expose Barack's tax-and-spend, share-the-wealth agenda. During the final presidential debate, at Hofstra University in New York, McCain invoked Joe the Plumber's name no fewer than nine times.

Away from reporters, Michelle and Barack joked about Joe the Plumber. While Barack had cautioned everyone associated with the campaign to avoid taking personal shots at McCain, his wife could not disguise her contempt for Joe the Plumber – especially when it was revealed that he was not a really a licensed plumber and had actually not paid all his taxes. (In fairness, even McCain saw the humour in his Joe the Plumber rap when South Carolina's Republican Senator Lindsey Graham started calling their old Senate pal 'Joe the Biden'.)

While Sarah Palin and Joe the Plumber seemed to be dominating the airwaves – along with a worsening economic crisis that looked increasingly impossible for the Republicans to overcome – an Obama family drama was unfolding half a world away. On the eve of the 7 October presidential debate in Tennessee, Barack's grandmother had fallen in her Honolulu apartment and broken her hip. She was treated at Kaiser Permanente's Moanalua Medical Center and returned home.

Over the next two weeks, her conditioned deteriorated. On 20 October, Barack's sister Maya, who now taught at Honolulu's La Pietra-Hawaii School for Girls and cared for their grandmother, called to tell him that Toot, who was also battling a recurrence of cancer, might die at any time.

'I never saw self-pity or fear,' Maya said of their grandmother. 'She was clear about wanting to stay at home, protective of us, dignified and determined to be herself to the very end.' Toot kept her sense of humour, too. 'Oh, my,' she told Maya as flowers flooded in from well-wishers. 'With all this hullabaloo, it's going to be embarrassing if I *don't* die.'

Three days after Maya called, Barack broke away from his campaign, boarded a plane and flew nine hours to be by his beloved Toot's side.

For Barack, who had always regretted not being there when his mother died, it was important to say goodbye to the woman who had raised him. 'One of the things I wanted was to have a chance to sit down with her and talk to her,' he explained before departing for the islands. 'She's still alert and she still has all her faculties and

I wanted to make sure that I don't miss that opportunity right now.' He and Michelle decided that it would be best if Malia and Sasha stayed behind in Chicago with their mother.

As soon as he landed in Honolulu, he went by motorcade straight to her Beretania Street apartment building. That night, he stayed at the Hyatt Waikiki Hotel before returning the next morning at eight fifteen to spend the day with Toot.

At one point, Barack, wearing a T-shirt, went out for a stroll along Young Street – and, if he could avoid being spotted, a smoke. While the Secret Service kept a discreet distance, he got only so far as Times Supermarket before a crowd began to gather. 'Everybody was screaming and running,' recalled local resident Josef Werner. 'Everybody was yelling, "Barack, Barack is here! Obama is here!"'

Two days later, Barack was back on the campaign trail in Nevada. 'She's gravely ill,' he told ABC's *Good Morning America*. 'We weren't sure and I'm still not sure she'll make it to Election Day. We're all praying and we hope she does.'

It would not be long before another relative – this time on his father's side of the family – was making news. On 30 October, it was reported that Barack's 'Auntie Zeituni', Barack Obama Sr's half-sister Zeituni Onyango, was living in a Boston public housing project despite the fact that a federal judge had denied her political asylum from her native Kenya in 2002 and two years later ordered her to leave the country.

Barack had written extensively about his beloved Auntie Zeituni in *Dreams from My Father*, and she had even attended the swearing-in ceremonies when he became a US senator in 2005. But Auntie Zeituni's nephew claimed he was unaware of her immigration problems.

Calling it 'a family matter', the McCain campaign chose not to pursue Auntie Zeituni's illegal status as an election issue. In a bizarre twist, however, Homeland Security quietly issued a special directive requiring high-level approval before federal immigration agents arrested fugitives. Federal documents would later show that the Bush administration feared that arresting Obama's aunt might generate 'negative media or congressional interest' – that it would make it appear they were trying to influence the election.

By the same token, new accusations of widespread voter-registration fraud by Obama-friendly ACORN (Association of Community Organizations for Reform Now) fizzled, as did a last-minute TV blitz featuring some of the more outrageous statements by Jeremiah Wright. Asked by a reporter to comment on the latest round of GOP ads concerning the Obamas and Wright, a top Obama official text-messaged his response: 'Zzzzz.'

Just after 8 a.m. on 3 November – election eve – Barack was in Florida when Michelle called from Chicago. 'Toot passed yesterday, Barack,' she told him. 'I am so so sorry.'

After he hung up, Barack went to the gym for his daily hour-long workout, then to a rally in Jacksonville. From there, he travelled to North Carolina. It was in Charlotte, standing before an afternoon crowd of 25,000, that he summoned the courage to talk about Toot. 'She has gone home,' Barack said, his voice beginning to crack. 'I'm not going to talk about it too long because it's hard, a little, to talk about it,' he said. In contrast to the Clintons or the Bushes or so many other politicians who were prone to choking up or crying, Barack rarely indulged in public displays of emotion. But today, he pulled out a handkerchief and wiped away the tears that glistened on his cheeks.

On Election Day, Michelle and Barack voted at 7.35 a.m. at their usual polling place, Chicago's Beulah Shoesmith Elementary School. Michelle lingered so long in the voting booth, savouring the moment, that her husband joked, 'I had to check out to see who she was voting for.'

Malia and Sasha went to school as they normally would and then got their hair done at a local beauty parlour for the night ahead. Daddy, meanwhile, flew off to Indiana for some last-minute campaigning. 'Hey guys!' he said as he dropped into a voter-canvassing centre. Then he picked up a phone and began talking to voters, who stammered in disbelief.

That night the Obamas had a steak dinner at home in Chicago, then the family hied away to a suite at the Hyatt Regency Hotel. There they were joined by the people who had been with Barack from the beginning – Valerie Jarrett, David Axelrod, Robert Gibbs and Obama campaign manager David Plouffe. While they watched the returns on television, a stream of children that included Malia and Sasha, Craig Robinson's son and daughter, Gibbs's son and Biden's grandchildren scurried about.

Ohio had been a toss-up, so when it looked as if Barack had locked it up, he turned to Axelrod. 'So it looks like we're gonna win this thing, huh?' he asked Axelrod. 'It looks like it, yeah,' Axelrod said cautiously.

Around 9.45 p.m., the family repaired to a smaller suite upstairs. Barack plopped on a sofa next to his mother-in-law and held her hand as they continued watching the returns. Michelle's uncle, Steve Robinson, had declared Barack the winner early in the evening, so when it began to look like that victory was in reach, Robinson blurted, 'I *told* you.'

'We had our little laugh when he said it,' Marian recalled of her brother's remark. 'It was like, OK, that means it's true.'

When Barack was officially declared the winner at 11 p.m., the mood was oddly solemn. 'Everybody was quiet,' Marian said. 'I can't tell you how subdued it was. We weren't like the people in the stands – you know, yelling and screaming.' As she continued holding Barack's hand, she turned to him and said, 'I was thinking about what a journey you have to come . . .' Then she fell silent. 'It was almost like,' she said of that moment, 'there weren't any words.'

Of that moment, Michelle would later say, 'I was proud as a wife, amazed as a citizen. I felt a sense of relief, a sense of calm that the country I lived in was the country I thought I lived in.'

Not far away, in Chicago's Grant Park, a crowd of more than 200,000 erupted in whoops and shrieks. Strangers embraced, weeping at the realisation that history had been made with the election of the nation's first African American president. The achievement seemed even more staggering given that Barack had been on the national political scene just four years and, at forty-seven, stood to be the third-youngest (behind Theodore Roosevelt and JFK) president in history.

The euphoria continued unabated, reaching fever pitch when Barack, Michelle and the children appeared onstage at Grant Park.

They had dressed entirely in red and black – Barack in a black suit and red tie, Malia in a red dress, Sasha in a black dress and Michelle in a red-and-black silk Narciso Rodriguez outfit. (She would later be criticised for spoiling her appearance by wearing a plain black cardigan over the designer dress, but Michelle was unapologetic. 'Hey, I was *cold*,' she said. 'I needed that sweater!')

Among the faces in the crowd were Jesse Jackson and Oprah, crying openly as Barack delivered his victory speech behind eight-foot-high plates of bulletproof glass. 'I know my grandmother is watching,' he said at one point, 'along with the family that made me who I am.'

Back in Hawaii, Barack's sister was sitting in the apartment where he had spent his high school years with his grandparents. 'I was too tired to grieve in front of millions,' Maya said of her decision not to accept her brother's invitation to join him in Chicago. That very day, the koa urn containing Toot's ashes was delivered to the apartment, and Maya placed pictures of their mother, Ann, and Toot's grandchildren and great-grandchildren around it. Then she sat back with her husband and their five-year-old daughter, Suhaila, and watched the returns on television. Like many of those in Grant Park that night, Maya wept as she watched her brother give his victory speech.

Barack reserved his most lavish praise for Michelle. 'And I would not be standing here tonight,' he told the cheering throng, 'without the unyielding support of my best friend for the last 16 years – the rock of our family, the love of my life, the nation's next First Lady, Michelle Obama.' As they threw their arms around each other once again, Barack pulled her to him and whispered, 'I love you.'

Afterwards, Michelle and Barack finally let loose, celebrating with friends and supporters. 'They're big huggers,' said one aide, 'so there's a lot of hugs, a lot of thank-yous, a lot of warmth.'

Since the girls were allowed to stay up past midnight, Marian Robinson was convinced their mother would cut them a little slack. 'Well,' she told the girls, 'surely your mother's not going to make you go to school tomorrow after being up this late at night. That would be cruel. Just don't set your alarm clocks.' Malia and Sasha were allowed a little extra time in bed the next morning, but then they were shipped off to school as usual.

Before holding his first press conference as president-elect on 7 November, Barack, properly attired in a dark suit, joined a baseball-capped, jeans-clad Michelle for a parent–teacher conference at the University of Chicago Lab School. When they returned to their waiting SUV, Michelle was cradling a flower arrangement – a congratulatory gift from the girls' teachers. The next day, the Obamas resumed their old date-night routine with an intimate dinner at one of their favourite Italian restaurants, Spiaggia.

On 10 November, the Bushes welcomed the Obamas to 1600 Pennsylvania Avenue. While Laura took Michelle on a tour of the upstairs family quarters and the two women talked about their children, presidents number forty-three and forty-four conferred in the Oval Office. As he walked down the colonnade outside the Oval Office, Barack slapped his hand on Bush's shoulder as they went back inside – as if, said a Bush aide, 'he was the host and President Bush was his guest'.

Even as the country faced its worst economic crisis since the Great Depression, both the outgoing and incoming administrations worked together to make the transition as seamless as possible. To that end, Barack named as his new chief of staff the famously temperamental Rahm Emanuel. The Chicago congressman had once mailed a dead fish to one of his enemies, and his penchant for purple-veined tantrums laced with profanity was legendary. (Barack liked to talk about how, while working as a teenager at Arby's, Rahm had accidentally sliced off a piece of his right middle finger – 'which,' Obama said, 'rendered him virtually mute'.)

There were those within the party who wondered if Emanuel was temperamentally suited to the chief of staff job, and, as he often did when faced with a tough choice, Barack asked for Michelle's input. Michelle reaffirmed what Barack had known all along – that there was no one more loyal than Rahm and no one would pursue the president's agenda with more tenacity. 'He doesn't quit,' Michelle said, 'until he gets it done.'

That December, the Obamas returned to Hawaii to celebrate the holidays and take care of some unfinished family business. Two days before Christmas, the Obamas attended an hour-long memorial service for Toot at a modest two-storey house in Honolulu's working-class Nuuanu neighbourhood, which now served as home to Honolulu's First Unitarian Church.

Following the afternoon service, Barack's motorcade drove along the coast and pulled over at a spot called Lanai Lookout. It was here that Barack had come four months earlier to toss a lei into the surf in memory of his mother. Now, as the wind whipped up the surf along the shoreline, Barack, wearing khakis, a dark-blue Hawaiian shirt and sunglasses, climbed over a stone wall and made his way over the rocks towards the water. Michelle, Malia, Sasha, Barack's sister Maya and more than a dozen friends followed close behind. Then Barack and Maya, who had removed Toot's ashes from the koa urn, scattered them in the Pacific.

When they returned to Washington, Barack and Michelle were eager to see Malia and Sasha settled in at Sidwell Friends School, Chelsea Clinton's alma mater. However, it was unclear where the Obamas would be living during the few weeks prior to the inauguration. When they asked if they could move into Blair House, the president's official guesthouse, the Obamas were told by Bush administration officials that they would have to wait until just five days before the swearing-in ceremony. Blair House, it seemed, had already been promised to former Australian Prime Minister John Howard.

Forced to look for a hotel, the Obamas settled on the historic Hay-Adams. Situated around the corner from Blair House, it offered unobstructed views of the White House directly across Lafayette Square Park.

'Do you see our new house?' Michelle asked her friend André Leon Talley as she drew back the curtains of the Obamas' Hay-Adams suite. From this vantage point, Michelle and Talley could see security officers dressed in black perched on the White House roof. 'They tell me they do that a lot,' Michelle said matter-of-factly.

On 5 January 2009, the Obamas had breakfast in their Hay-Adams suite and then Daddy said goodbye to his daughters as they headed off at 7.10 a.m. with Mommy for their first day at their new school. Making new friends would not be a problem. Joe Biden's grandchildren, with whom fifth-grader Malia and second-grader

Sasha had already had bonded over pizza and popcorn during several sleepovers, attended Sidwell Friends.

The motorcade suddenly appeared from under a security tent that had been put up outside the Hay-Adams and sped off to Sidwell's middle school on Wisconsin Avenue. They arrived at 7.30 – half an hour before school started – and minutes after depositing Malia, Michelle emerged from the school and slipped back into the White House SUV. Then it was off with Sasha, yawning away in the back seat of the SUV, to Sidwell's lower-school campus just outside DC in Bethesda, Maryland. Since Sasha's school day ended at 3 p.m. and Malia's at 3.20, from now on the motorcade would simply pick up Sasha first and stop off for Malia on the way home to the White House. 'I'll try to bring them to school and pick them up every day,' Michelle vowed, but then admitted that 'there's also a measure of independence. And obviously there will be times I won't be able to drop them off at all. I like to be a presence in my kids' school. I want to know the teachers; I want to know the other parents.'

Not long after that first day of school, Barack and Michelle took the girls to see the Lincoln Memorial. After looking up at Lincoln's Second Inaugural Address, which is carved onto one of the monument's walls, Sasha said, 'Looks long.' Malia looked at her father. 'First African American president,' she said. 'Better be good.'

For weeks since the election, Grandma had been mulling over whether or not to accept the Obamas' invitation to have her live with them in the White House. Multi-generational White Houses did not always work out. Harry Truman's mother-in-law publicly disparaged him and frequently questioned his policies. Dwight Eisenhower's domineering mother-in-law nagged constantly and bossed around the White House staff.

But Marian Robinson had already proved herself to be a valuable part of her grandchildren's lives. For 22 months, when their mother wasn't around, she drew the girls' baths, supervised their homework, took them to dentist appointments and chauffeured them to and from ballet lessons and soccer practice.

Grandma had also made only a faint-hearted effort to adhere to Michelle's strict rules governing bedtime (8.30 p.m.), TV (one hour maximum) and food (organic whenever possible). 'I have candy, they stay up late – come to my house, they watch TV as long as they want to, we'll play games until the wee hours,' Marian said. 'I do everything grandmothers do that they're not supposed to.'

Indeed, whenever Michelle caught her mother bending the rules, Marian had a hard time concealing her feelings. 'Mom, what are you rolling your eyes at?' Michelle asked at one point. 'You made us do the same thing.'

'I don't remember being that bad,' she told Michelle. 'I think you're just going overboard.'

Now Marian was baulking at what many would consider the ultimate invitation – to live at 1600 Pennsylvania Avenue. 'I love those people,' she mused, 'but I love my own house. The White House reminds me of a museum. How do you sleep in a museum?'

Her son-in-law understood. 'She doesn't like a lot of fuss around her,' Barack said, 'and like it or not, there is some fuss in the White House.'

Just as important to Marian was the fear that she might be intruding on her daughter's marriage – a marriage that just a few years before had gone through a decidedly rocky patch. 'That, I can do without,' she said of being around whenever her daughter and her son-in-law might be in the middle of a spat. 'When you move in, you just hear a little bit too much.' But isn't the White House big enough for that not to be a problem? she was asked. 'It's never,' Grandma replied, 'big enough for that.'

In the end, Marian decided to move into a guestroom on the third floor of the White House – a floor above the rooms occupied by her son-in-law and his family. She made it clear the move was to be on a trial basis and that she had no intention of giving up her Chicago apartment. 'They're going to need me,' Grandma said, 'so I'm going to be there.'

Marian was on board when, three days before the inauguration, the 'Obama Express' retraced Lincoln's 137-mile whistle-stop tour from Philadelphia to Washington. In Wilmington, Delaware, the Obamas stopped to pick up Joe Biden. 'I like him. I *love* her,' Biden said of the Obamas. 'She is the most impressive person I've met in 35 years.'

Since 17 January also happened to be Michelle's forty-fifth birthday, when the adults got off in Baltimore to give speeches, Malia and Sasha used the time to decorate the interior of the blue 1939 vintage railway carriage with streamers, balloons and banners.

Later, when the train was underway, the girls and a few of their friends went through the other cars distributing noise-makers, party hats and Hawaiian leis. After they sang 'Happy Birthday' to Mommy, she then got up and led all the kids in a stomp dance. 'Nice,' Michelle said as she settled back down in her seat. Then she turned to her husband. 'They've got to clean up!' she told Barack. 'We can't leave this mess for Amtrak.'

Finally settled with his family in Blair House, Barack started 18 January by joining Biden to place a wreath at Arlington Cemetery's Tomb of the Unknowns. Later that day, the Obamas had front-row seats at the star-studded 'We Are One' concert in front of the Lincoln Memorial. An estimated 300,000 people flanked the reflecting pools on the National Mall to hear such superstars as Stevie Wonder, Bruce Springsteen, Beyoncé, Mary J. Blige and Bono perform. For two hours, Malia, who had been diligently taking snapshots with her new digital camera, huddled with her sister against near-freezing temperatures as Mom and Dad bounced, bobbed and clapped to the rhythm in their seats – clearly oblivious to the numbing cold.

There were a few mortifying moments proving that no dad – not even Barack Obama – could really be cool in the eyes of his own children. When Beyoncé was telling the president-elect about her new hit, 'Single Ladies' Dance', he replied 'Oh, I'm trying to learn that.' Malia and Sasha winced in embarrassment (there is no 'Single Ladies' Dance'). 'Oh, Dad,' they groaned in unison.

That night, Barack and Michelle threw a private party for 90 family members and friends, including Michelle's mom and Oprah. Dining on a simple menu of chicken, fish and rice, guests laughed and toasted their hosts as children ricocheted from room to room – 'just kids being kids,' said one of the guests, Charles Fishman. 'It was a very warm, informal evening – a little send-off party.'

On the morning of 19 January, Barack travelled by motorcade to the Sasha Bruce House, a shelter for teens, and helped paint a wall to promote his Day of Service programme. 'Now that I know he can do this,' Michelle cracked after watching her husband paint, 'it's another thing he can do at home.'

At the 'Kids' Inaugural: We Are the Future' inauguration eve concert in Washington's Verizon Center, Malia and Sasha clapped and swayed and bounced in their seats as they and 14,000 others sang along with teen stars the Jonas Brothers. Then Joe Jonas led the girls onstage to dance with the Jonases and fellow teen sensations Miley Cyrus, Keke Palmer and Demi Lovato.

Just hours away from taking the oath of office, Barack stayed up past midnight practising the inaugural address he had been working on for seven weeks with Axelrod and twenty-seven-year-old chief speech-writer, Jon Favreau. Up until the previous day, Favreau had spent hours tinkering with the speech at a local Starbucks.

In addition to running through his address, Barack rehearsed taking the oath itself. There was one other thing he was determined to get right: after consulting a military aide about the proper form, the new president practised snapping off a few crisp salutes in front of a mirror. Michelle, ever the perfectionist, asked him to do it another couple of times before nodding in approval. 'Sharp,' she said.

The next morning – 20 January, Inauguration Day – Michelle and Barack got up at six and squeezed in their customary early morning workout. ('I can go for days without going into a gym,' Michelle said. 'He really can't.')

Then, while Grandma helped the girls get ready for the big day, Dad donned a black suit and red tie. A sobering reminder of the times, Barack's suit was reportedly the creation of Columbian designer Miguel Caballero, who specialised in making bullet-resistant clothing.

The president-elect then waited anxiously in the Blair House foyer as Mom finished dressing in her Isabel Toledo-designed lemongrass-coloured Swiss wool lace coat and sheath, J. Crew jade leather gloves, $585 green Jimmy Choo pumps and $20,000 two-carat diamond stud earrings. 'Barack puts on his suit, tie, and he's out the door,' the compulsively punctual Michelle had said of this ritual. 'I'm getting my hair, make-up, the kids . . . and he's asking, "What's the problem?"'

The couple emerged from Blair House at 8.46 a.m., and Barack held the door of their limousine open for Michelle as she slid into the back seat. Their motorcade then turned the corner and within two minutes arrived at the historic yellow-and-white Saint John's Episcopal Church for an Inauguration Day prayer service.

Joined by their J. Crew-outfitted daughters – Malia in violet-blue and Sasha in pastel shades of pink and orange – as well as the president-elect's sister Maya (whose daughter, Suhaila, called Barack 'Uncle Rocky') and Michelle's brother, Craig, the Obamas settled into the front-row pew next to Joe Biden and his family. Saint John's Church rector Luis Leon welcomed the new First Family – a tradition he had now upheld through ten inaugurations. After a brief invocation by Bishop Charles E. Blake, the choir sang a rafter-rattling rendition of 'This Little Light of Mine'.

An hour later, George W. Bush greeted Barack with a spirited 'Sir!' at the North Portico of the White House, then led the new occupants inside for coffee. Later, President Obama would read the personal note his predecessor had, according to tradition, left inside of the top drawer of his Oval Office desk. While the rest of the note would remain secret, Bush had written that Barack's term signified a 'fabulous new chapter' in American history. For now, however, it was Michelle who presented Laura with a gift – with a white leather journal and pen to encourage the outgoing First Lady, who had just signed a seven-figure book deal, to get to work on her memoirs.

At 11.01 a.m., the 1.5 million people who had come to the nation's capital to witness history being made roared as the Obamas took their places among the dignitaries at the West Front of the Capitol. Only moments before, in a Capitol holding room, Barack had rehearsed the presidential oath with Michelle while her mother watched from the sidelines. Once outside, Malia, still determined to record everything on her new camera, clicked away; later, when her angle was obscured, Malia handed her camera to Vice President Joe Biden and asked if he'd take a few shots for her.

After the Reverend Rick Warren delivered the invocation and Aretha Franklin belted out a stirring rendition of 'America', Biden handed the camera back to Malia and stood to be sworn in as vice president at 11.48 a.m. Twelve minutes later, Michelle lifted up the burgundy velvet-covered Bible Abraham Lincoln had used for his 1861 inauguration and carefully held it out to her husband with two gloved hands. Dad placed his left hand on the volume and, as Malia and Sasha stood by grinning, Chief Justice John Roberts administered the oath of office.

It would not go smoothly. Unlike previous chief justices, Roberts was not reading the 35-word oath from a card and misplaced the word *faithfully* – as in 'faithfully execute the office of president' – in the second phrase. When the Chief Justice botched it yet again, Barack arched an eyebrow ever so slightly. (Later, Michelle joked with her husband, 'That's what you get for not voting for his confirmation.')

Still, when the oath seemed to have been completed, cannons sounded, the multitudes cheered and a smiling Sasha gave Dad an orange-gloved thumbs-up – the first of several. A hush fell over the throng as the new president proclaimed, 'Today we must pick ourselves up, dust ourselves off and begin again the work of remaking America.'

Punctuated with cheers and applause, the 19-minute speech ended with a vow. 'Let it be said by our children's children that when we were tested, we refused to let this journey end,' Barack said, 'that we did not turn back nor did we falter; and with eyes fixed on the horizon and God's grace upon us, we carried forth that great gift of freedom and delivered it safely to future generations.' Afterwards, the president enveloped his predecessor in a warm hug.

Moments later, the Obamas and the Bidens were on the other side of the Capitol, saying goodbye to George and Laura Bush. To underscore the amicable nature of the succession, W hugged Barack yet again before the Bushes boarded the marine helicopter that would carry them off to Andrews Air Force Base and a plane bound for Midland, Texas.

For Barack and Michelle, the day's drama continued at the congressional luncheon for some 200 dignitaries in National Statuary Hall. No sooner had Chief Justice Roberts sidled up to the president to sheepishly whisper, 'It's my fault,' than Senator Ted Kennedy cried out in pain. Collapsing to the floor in a full-throttle seizure, Kennedy, who had been battling brain cancer, was rushed by ambulance to the nearby Washington Hospital Center.

Like everyone else at the luncheon, Barack and Michelle were visibly upset. 'I would be lying to you if I did not say that right now a part of me is with him,' the president later said. 'And I think that's true for all of us. It's a joyous time but also a sobering time.' (Less than an hour later, the president was informed that the senator was chatting with relatives and friends and resting comfortably.)

Memories of her husband practising in the mirror were still fresh when Barack saluted a military colour guard gathered in his honour. Then the First Couple climbed into 'The Beast', the hermetically sealed presidential Cadillac limousine that, among other things, weighs fourteen thousand pounds and boasts five-inch-thick armour plating.

Secret Service agents scrambled as Barack and Michelle emerged from their car near Pennsylvania Avenue and Sixth Street Northwest and strolled hand in hand down the avenue. The Obamas arrived at the White House at 4.40 p.m., freshened up and then re-emerged with Malia and Sasha to walk down the North Driveway towards the enclosed, bulletproof Inaugural Parade reviewing stand. As they walked up to the stand, Michelle yelled to the crowd, 'We're here. We're home!'

After the 1.7-mile-long parade – the most telling moment of which may have been the moment Barack gave the 'hang loose' sign to the Punahou Academy Marching Band – the president and First Lady dashed back into the White House to dress for that evening's ten inaugural balls.

Running more than an hour late, Michelle quickly changed out of the size 10 Isabel Toledo outfit and into her gown. 'Miche, you look beautiful,' Barack said she emerged in flowing white silk chiffon embellished with organza flowers and glittering Swarovski crystals. 'I wanted the dress to reflect hope, fantasy, a dream,' said 26-year-old Tapei-born designer Jason Wu. 'Because this is a pretty surreal moment.' To top it off, Michelle wore rose-cut diamond drop earrings totalling sixty-one carats, white-gold-and-diamond bangle bracelets, and a thirteen-carat diamond signet ring – all of which were lent by the designer, Loree Rodkin, and later donated to the Smithsonian.

With Joe and Jill Biden in tow, the Obamas made the rounds of all ten balls. At the first stop of the evening, the Neighborhood Inaugural Ball, Barack and Michelle were greeted with wild cheers as they stepped onto a dance floor emblazoned with the Great Seal of the United States. Barack was wearing white tie – and his first new tuxedo in 15 years. 'First of all, how good-looking is my wife?' he said proudly.

Michelle allowed that her husband was 'a pretty good dancer – but not as good as he thinks he is'. Tonight, however, as Beyoncé sang Etta James's signature hit 'At Last', Barack and Michelle glided effortlessly across the dance floor as cameras clicked away. 'You could tell that he was a black president,' said Academy Award-winning actor Jamie Foxx, 'from the way he was moving.'

It was a scene the Obamas would repeat ten times – and that included Barack doing a frisky hip bump with fourteen-year-old Victoria Lucas. Among the revellers at one inaugural ball being held in the Mayflower Hotel: Zeituni Onyango. Now living in Cleveland, Barack's Auntie Zeituni was getting ready to fight the government's long-standing order to deport her.

At last, the Obamas took their last spin around the dance floor and returned to the White House around 12.40 a.m. There, with trumpeter Wynton Marsalis supplying the music, they hosted one final get-together with a few of their closest pals from Chicago.

As the First Couple took their friends on an impromptu tour of their new home, Barack stopped to point out some of the masterpieces on the walls – including works by Claude Monet, Mary Cassatt, Childe Hassam and Paul Cézanne. While Valerie Jarrett and the others 'gasped', Michelle said coolly, 'Pretty nice art, dontcha think?'

'It looked as though,' Jarrett said of her old friend, 'she was right where she belonged.'

While all this was going on, Malia and Sasha hosted their own kids' party, watching *Bolt* and *High School Musical 3* in the White House theatre before topping off the evening with a visit from the Jonas Brothers. This time, Mom would not make the first daughters go to school the next day.

The White House they woke up to the next morning bore the unmistakable stamp of its new occupants – a style that, given the fact that they too were moving in with two young children, in some ways reflected that of Jack and Jackie Kennedy. In the Oval Office, Barack decided to keep the historic desk carved from the timbers of the British warship HMS *Resolute* – the same desk where FDR sat to give his famous fireside chats and that JFK Jr ('John-John') loved to hide beneath as a child. Barack also kept the pale-yellow sunburst carpet in the Oval Office that Laura had designed to convey a 'sense of optimism'. He also kept a bust of Lincoln and a portrait of George Washington that hung over the fireplace mantlepiece, but gone were four large paintings by Texas artists and a bust of Winston Churchill.

Since they wanted to maintain their Hyde Park residence as a home away from home ('The South Side of Chicago is our Kennebunkport,' Michelle said), the Obamas brought no furniture at all – just framed photographs, clothes and personal items like Tiger, the stuffed animal Malia had not parted with since age three.

No matter. Like first ladies before her, Michelle soon discovered she enjoyed shuffling antiques from room to room, having walls repainted and unearthing hidden treasures locked away in storage. She was also determined to create a relaxed, homely look – and, since the country was in the middle of a deepening economic crisis, do it for under $100,000.

With that budget in mind, she called on Los Angeles designer Michael Smith, who numbered among his celebrity clients Steven Spielberg, Dustin Hoffman and Cher. 'Michael shares my vision for creating a family-friendly feel for our new home,' Michelle said, 'and incorporating new perspectives from some of America's greatest artists and designers.' She also urged Smith to enlist some of her favourite American retailers to create a new look for the White House – namely Target, Pottery Barn, Crate and Barrel, and Restoration Hardware.

That first full day in office, it became clear that more than just the White House decor was in need of a redo. To quiet constitutional scholars who were claiming that the oath had been read incorrectly and therefore was invalid, Chief Justice Roberts re-administered the oath at 7.35 p.m. in the White House Map Room.

'Are you ready to take the oath?' Roberts asked Barack.

'I am,' he answered. 'And we're going to do it very slowly.'

Only nine people were in the Map Room to witness the redo – four aides, four reporters and a White House photographer. This time, Barack raised his right hand but did not use a Bible.

'Congratulations again,' Roberts said.

'Thank you, sir,' the now duly sworn president replied.

Sensitive to Roberts's feelings, Barack became visibly angry when Vice President Biden poked fun at the Chief Justice during a White House ceremony. Biden later apologised. 'He is always in control,' Abner Mikva said of Obama, 'but you can tell when the president is angry. He clenches his fist. I've certainly seen him clench his fist on occasion.'

Over the next few weeks, America's new First Family would settle into the kind of comfortable family routine that in the past they had only enjoyed sporadically. Now Barack and Michelle exercised together in the Executive Mansion's private gym and then had breakfast with the kids.

Like Laura Bush – and unlike Hillary, who as First Lady operated alongside her husband in the West Wing – Michelle followed tradition by maintaining her offices in the residential East Wing. Rather than texting her husband – the Obamas have two BlackBerrys each – during the day, Michelle would stroll over to the Oval Office to share news about her day.

Now they were having dinners together as a family nearly every night, and for the first time in recent memory, Dad was actually tucking the girls into bed. 'We haven't had that kind of time together for years,' Michelle said, 'so that explains a lot why we all feel so good in this space.'

Realising that hers was the youngest family in the White House since the Kennedys, Michelle borrowed a page from Jackie when it came to child rearing. Like Jackie, who asked the White House staff not to spoil her children and even told Secret Service agents to back off when she took the kids to the beach ('Drowning is my responsibility,' Jackie told them), Michelle also instructed the staff to step back a little.

According to Mrs Obama, the staff want 'to make your life easy' – but 'when you have small kids . . . they don't need their lives to be easy. They're kids.' So Malia and Sasha would have the same chores they always had – tidying up their rooms, clearing their dishes from the table, making their beds ('Doesn't have to look good – just throw the sheet over it,' Mom said). So that the girls would feel right at home, their parents told them they had the run of the White House – including the right to drop in to the Oval Office to see Dad. The novelty wore off quickly. When Michelle asked the girls if they wanted to go outside and see Dad's helicopter land on the South Lawn, Malia shrugged, 'We've already seen it.'

The first daughters were more interested in the new, $3,500 cedar-and-redwood swing set their parents had installed for them on the lawn just outside the Oval Office. While sharpshooters watched from their perch atop the White House roof and Secret Service agents kept a watchful eye from various positions on the grounds of the Executive Mansion, Malia, Sasha and a handful of new friends from school laughed and screamed as they tried out the set's four swings, slide, fort and climbing wall. One detail distinguished theirs from other swing sets: a picnic table featuring brass plates engraved with the names of all forty-four presidents – including Dad.

As much fun as their new made-to-order playground equipment was, it did not succeed in taking the girls' eyes off the ultimate prize: a new puppy. After what amounted to a national poll on what constituted the proper breed for a new First Dog, the Obamas would eventually settle on a spirited six-month-old black-and-white curly-haired Portuguese water dog distantly related to Ted Kennedy's dog, Splash. Malia and Sasha promptly changed their new dog's name from Charlie to Bo.

Within days of moving into the Executive Mansion, Michelle reached out to the surrounding community just as she had in Chicago. Visiting a primary school with her husband, she announced, 'They've let us out!' Later, she dropped in at the Interior Department to meet with Native Americans, read to children at a Washington day care centre and brought a magnolia tree seedling to USDA workers at the Department of Agriculture. Quietly, she got to know her children's schoolmates and teachers.

At dinner every night in the family quarters of the White House, Barack and Michelle kicked off the conversation with a little game they had played for years. It was called Roses and Thorns and involved each member sharing the rose and thorn they had experienced that day. Aware of the mounting crises the president was facing, Malia stopped the proceedings and said, 'Dad, you seem to have a pretty thorny job.'

Her parents laughed. 'Yes,' Barack allowed, 'you could say that.' Michelle, on the other hand, felt her days were overwhelmingly 'rosy'. Ironically enough, winning the presidency had also meant winning something akin to the genuine family life Michelle had always craved. And while she no longer badgered Barack about chores, he was expected to walk Bo at 10 p.m, just as she was expected to walk the dog first thing in the morning.

Of course, none of their lives would ever really be normal again. Among other things, from now on they would be constantly shadowed by the Secret Service. Curiously, the Obamas' romantic-sounding Secret Service code names faintly echoed those given to the Kennedys. Where the Kennedys were Lancer (for JFK), Lace (Jackie), Lyric (Caroline) and Lark (John Jr), the Obamas were Renegade (the president), Renaissance (Michelle), Radiance (Malia) and Rosebud (Sasha).

The comparisons with that other First Family would persist, although Barack and Michelle both chafed at the notion that they were ushering in a new Camelot era. 'Jackie Kennedy was wonderful and I admire her greatly,' Michelle said, 'but believe me, I'm no Jackie Kennedy.'

To be sure, at 45 Michelle was fully 14 years older than Jackie when she became First Lady in 1961. Still, more than any First Lady in recent memory, the tall, leggy, well-put-together Michelle had already established herself as a new kind of style icon – one whose tastes ran from the trendiest designers to clothes plucked off the rack at Target and J. Crew. She's always loved clothes,' said her friend Cheryl Rucker-Whitaker. 'She loves purses, she loves getting a manicure, getting her hair done. She really is a girly girl.' Michelle's favourite drink (Jackie's, too): champagne.

Quick to deny that she was a 'fashionista', Michelle, who routinely showed off her well-toned arms in sleeveless dresses and tops, nevertheless confessed that she liked dressing up in evening gowns and 'feeling pretty for [her] husband'. Her decision to pose for the cover of *Vogue* even before her husband took office was motivated by a desire to set an example for her 'daughters and little girls just like them, who haven't seen themselves represented in these magazines'.

At her first formal function at the White House, the annual ball honouring the nation's governors, Michelle asked for her mother's help in selecting the menu, making sure that they served Barack's favourite dessert – huckleberry cobbler. Michelle also decided to break with tradition by mixing and matching pieces from various sets of china used by previous administrations.

'We laugh at ourselves a lot. We laugh at just the amazement that we're here,' conceded Valerie Jarrett, who as senior advisor and assistant to the president now occupied the second-floor office in the West Wing that once belonged to Hillary Clinton and later to George W. Bush advisor Karl Rove. 'Like, can't you just pinch yourself?' (Not all of the Obamas' old friends were welcome at the White House. Jeremiah Wright complained that 'them Jews' allegedly surrounding the new president were keeping the two men apart. Wright later apologised, explaining that he really should have used the word 'Zionists' instead.)

With her husband away on his first official trip to Canada in February, Michelle invited Jarrett and other female staff members to a girls-only screening of the romantic comedy *He's Just Not That Into You*. 'She just kicked off her shoes and curled up with popcorn and drooled over Ben Affleck like the rest of us,' said one of the guests. 'She has this big, wonderful laugh.'

The Obamas got the chance to unwind with old friends at Camp David, the presidential retreat 70 miles north-west of Washington in Maryland's Catoctin Mountains, where they continued their spring-break tradition of competing in a talent show. Michelle showed off her ability to keep two hula hoops going more or less indefinitely; the president joined with several buddies to belt out a passable rendition of Stevie Wonder's 'You Are the Sunshine of My Life'.

Michelle was equally at ease when, during the Obamas' first official trip to Europe in April of 2009, Queen Elizabeth II shattered precedent by putting her arm around America's First Lady – and then lingered while Michelle reciprocated with a warm hug. Given the fact that the Queen had never been seen indulging in a single display of public affection – not even with members of her immediate family – the embrace between Her Majesty and Michelle set off a media frenzy in Britain.

While several tabloids decried what they viewed as a shocking breach of protocol, the London *Times* called the royal hug a singularly 'touching moment'. Buckingham Palace concurred. 'This was,' a palace spokesman said, 'a mutual and spontaneous display of affection and appreciation between the Queen and Michelle Obama.' The two women would actually forge a bond of friendship in the coming months, sharing their thoughts on everything from child rearing to organic gardening via written correspondence, emails and the occasional phone call. The following June, Michelle, Malia and Sasha would join the Queen for a private tea at Buckingham Palace.

Over the next few days, Michelle was hailed in the press as 'the new Jackie Kennedy' as she and Barack travelled from England to France and then on to Germany. By the time they reached the Czech Republic, Barack decided to forego an official meeting with that country's leaders – who strongly opposed his economic policies – in favour of a 'quiet, romantic dinner with my wife'.

Back at the White House, the president proved to be no less attentive. At least once a day, he took a break and returned to the residence for what he called 'Michelle time'.

As comfortable as Michelle now seemed in her new role as First Lady, even she had to admit that she was 'amazed' at her husband's 'level of calm . . . I see him thriving in this; I don't see the weight.' Amazed indeed, since for starters Barack faced a mind-numbing multitude of issues ranging from the wars in Iraq and Afghanistan to skyrocketing unemployment, proliferating corporate bankruptcies and the threatened collapse of the world banking system.

Publicly Michelle now insisted that she no longer sought to influence her husband's decisions as she once did. 'We'll have conversations, and we'll share our opinions over the course of the conversation,' she told *Time*. 'But I don't want to have a say.'

Yet, according to one of the president's oldest confidants, Michelle 'was one of the strongest voices' arguing for the appointment of federal appeals judge Sonia Sotomayor to replace retiring Associate Justice David Souter on the Supreme Court. Once the field had been narrowed down to two women –Sotomayor and the Obamas' old Chicago friend federal judge Diane Wood – Michelle came down on the side of picking Sotomayor as the Supreme Court's first Hispanic judge. 'The First Lady thought Sotomayor had all those warm empathetic qualities her husband was looking for in an appointee,' the confidant said. 'Barack has always listened to what she has to say. Regardless of what she says in the press, Michelle has strong opinions and she lets the president know what she thinks. She is still his most important advisor.'

Even if the stress of the job was not plainly visible – beyond the fact that Barack's long-time barber now claimed his hair was turning progressively greyer – the president relied more heavily than ever on proven routines to help him cope. In addition to his compulsive need for at least 90 minutes of concentrated exercise every day, Barack had fallen off the wagon and was sneaking cigarettes. Since he had promised repeatedly that he would not break the smoking ban in force at the White House, Barack sidestepped the issue with reporters. Asked during an interview in February 2009 with CNN's Anderson Cooper whether he had had a cigarette since becoming president, Barack said that he hadn't smoked 'on these grounds' and then smiled coyly.

By the summer of 2009, President Obama was, in fact, smoking wherever he could away from the White House and relying on Secret Service agents to keep him covered – either while travelling or at Camp David. Happy that her husband was at least sticking to his pledge not to smoke inside the White House, Michelle gave a tentative thumbs-up whenever she was asked if her husband had managed to quit. 'She's just happy,' an old acquaintance from Chicago observed, 'that he's not setting a bad example by smoking around the girls.'

Personal foibles aside, the first African American First Family seemed almost too perfect for even their most devoted friends to comprehend. Whatever one thought of Barack's liberal philosophy, his sometimes questionable past associations and the lingering taint of Chicago politics, his experience or lack thereof, no one could dispute that his family was a clear reflection of an American ideal.

Like Franklin Roosevelt, who led the nation through a depression and a war, Barack Obama was called upon to prevent one and end the other. Neither man could do it alone: FDR had Eleanor; Barack turned to Michelle.

Where one was firmly rooted in Chicago's South Side, the other was virtually rootless. Where one had known the safety and security of a close-knit working-class family, the other had been abandoned by one parent and seldom saw the other. Where one eschewed politics, the other set out at an early age to acquire political power – and, ultimately, to win the greatest political prize of all.

They did have one important thing in common. Keenly aware of the sacrifices that had been made so that they could make something of their lives, both sought to change the world around them. Michelle gave up her lucrative law career to build bridges between communities; Barack drew on his biracial, multicultural background to tap into the American consciousness in an altogether new way. Together, they shattered a barrier older than the Republic itself – and stunned the world in the process.

Unlike Franklin and Eleanor, Jack and Jackie, or Bill and Hillary – all of whom begged the question – it scarcely seems worth asking whether Barack and Michelle really love each other. They have since that day Michelle realised that the skinny young law student with the big ears and crazy name was something extraordinary.

For all their style and substance – for all the history they have already made – the president and his lady seem anything but regal. They have dealt with tensions in their marriage that at one point threatened it. They have grappled with financial problems, remaining deep in debt well into their 40s. They have fretted about infertility and faced a medical emergency that might have taken the life of their baby girl. They have delighted in their daughters as children and worried about the world they would inherit as adults.

Barack and Michelle have proved themselves to be remarkable – as man and woman, as husband and wife, as father and mother. But it is in those things that make them so accessible, so human, that we recognise ourselves – and, if even for a fleeting moment, like what we see. Theirs is, in every way, an American marriage.

ACKNOWLEDGEMENTS

'We are like two icebergs,' Jacqueline Kennedy once said of her marriage to JFK, 'the public life above the water, the private life submerged.' In my books about Jack and Jackie, Bill and Hillary Clinton, George and Laura Bush, and – saddest of all – Princess Diana and John Kennedy Jr, I found this mainly to be true. All of those books, along with *An Affair to Remember*, my look at the relationship between Spencer Tracy and my friend Katharine Hepburn, were devoted largely to exploring the mysterious forces that draw people to each other and the equally strange forces that hold them together, often against seemingly insurmountable odds.

Like *Jack and Jackie*, *Barack and Michelle* is the biography of a sometimes funny, often inspiring, always spellbinding relationship – a true marriage of hearts and minds that has already begun to shape history. As with so many other great unions, the couple known as Barack and Michelle would turn out to be far more than the sum of its parts.

For the twelfth time, I have the great good fortune of working with one of the finest teams in publishing. I am particularly grateful to my editor Mauro DiPreta, for both his editorial skill and his passionate commitment to seeing that the full story of Barack and Michelle Obama be told. My thanks, as well, to the entire William Morrow/HarperCollins publishing family, especially Michael Morrison, Liate Stehlik, Seale Ballenger, Debbie Stier, Melanie Jones, Chris Goff, Jennifer Schulkind, Richard Aquan, Michelle Corallo, Kim Lewis,

Betty Lew, Dale Rohrbaugh and Lisa Stokes. My continued thanks to two special friends: my very talented jacket designer Brad Foltz and the consummately professional Camille McDuffie of Goldberg-McDuffie Communications.

My agent of 26 years (and as many books), Ellen Levine, must by now be wondering how I could possibly come up with a new way to thank her for her dedication and her friendship. Given the fact that Barack Obama's story begins in Hawaii, it seems only fitting that this time I say, 'Mahalo.' My thanks, as well, to Ellen's top-notch colleagues at Trident Media Group, especially Claire Roberts, Margie Guerra, Alanna Ramirez and Libby Kellogg.

I was fortunate enough to have two remarkable parents – Edward and Jeanette Andersen. I've also had the pleasure of telling my wife, Valerie, in no fewer than 28 books how much she means to me. As Barack said about Michelle, Valerie is my rock – the one who keeps it real. Our daughters, Kate and Kelly – one newly married, the other starting college – have routinely amazed us and, as Michelle said of her two daughters, provided us over the years with no small degree of 'pure comic relief'.

Additional thanks to Newton Minow, Abner Mikva, Laurence Tribe, Senator John Kerry, Jerry Kellman, Clive Gray, Bradford Berenson, Keith Kakugawa, Senator Tom Harkin, Jeremiah Posedel, Mike Kruglik, Toni Preckwinkle, Judson Miner, Denny Jacobs, Mike Jacobs, Maxine Box, Linda Randle, Yvonne Lloyd, Loretta Augustin-Herron, Edward Koch, Leslie Hairston, the Reverend Alvin Love, Wellington Wilson, Chris McLachlin, Judith Hope, Vinai Thummalapally, Lowell Jacobs, Joyce Feuer, Coralee Jacobs, Eric Kusunoki, Alan Lum, Pake Zane, Julie Lauster, Hazel M. Johnson, Cheryl Johnson, Letitia Baldrige, Larry Walsh, Tom Freeman, Yvette Reyes, Kelly Rolf, Danny Taylor, Zarif, Dr Joyce Kenner, Nilda Rivera, Dave Heffert, Amy Barton, Elizabeth Yura, Betsy Vandercook, Janet Allison, Sharon Lorenz, Debra Gage, Everett Raymond Kinstler, Pam Cummings, Dudley Freeman, Paula Dranov, Carlyn Tani, Jeanette Peterson, Liz Miller, the late Irv Kupcinet, Barry Schenck, Bill Diehl, Mary Ann Campbell, Lawrence R. Mulligan, Sophie Gravelat, Larry Klayman, Rosalind Halvorsen, Tobias Markowitz, David McGough,

Elizabeth Loth, Jean Chapin, Hazel Southam, Richard Smart, Lee Wohlfert, Norman Currie, Rosemary McClure, Ray Whelan Jr, Gary Gunderson, David Plotkin, Cranston Jones, Kenneth P. Norwick, Mary Beth Whelan, Larry Schwartz, Tiffney Sanford, Debbie Goodsite, Arturo Santos, the Punahou Academy, the Whitney M. Young Magnet High School, Harvard University School of Law, Princeton University, the *Harvard Law Review*, Occidental College, the New York Public Library, the University of Chicago School of Law, the White House Historical Association, the Bancroft Library at the University of California at Berkeley, the Gunn Memorial Library, the Silas Bronson Library, the *Chicago Tribune*, the *Chicago Sun-Times*, the *Honolulu Advertiser*, Globe Photos, Sipa Press, Polaris Images, Corbis, Getty Images, BEImages, the Litchfield Business Center, Bloomberg News, the Associated Press and Reuters.

SOURCES AND
CHAPTER NOTES

The following chapter notes have been compiled to give an overview of the sources drawn upon in preparing *Barack and Michelle*, but they are by no means all-inclusive. Certain key sources in Washington, Chicago, Hawaii, Indonesia and Kenya – some professional colleagues, close friends and relatives – asked to remain anonymous, and the author has respected their wishes. Accordingly, they are not listed here or elsewhere in the text. Although relatively little was written about Barack Obama prior to his US Senate race in 2004, and even less about Michelle, a virtual tsunami of news reports and articles was generated by the seemingly endless presidential election campaign of 2008. In addition to the non-stop television and Internet coverage, there were thousands of articles published in a wide range of publications including the *New York Times*, the *Washington Post*, *Newsweek*, *Time*, the *Wall Street Journal*, *Vanity Fair*, the *New Yorker*, *U.S. News & World Report*, the *Chicago Tribune*, *Ebony*, the *Chicago Sun-Times*, the *Boston Globe*, the *Los Angeles Times*, *USA Today*, the *Seattle Times*, the *Honolulu Advertiser*, *The Times* (London), *Paris Match* and *Le Monde*, and carried on the wires of Reuters, Gannett, Bloomberg and the Associated Press.

CHAPTERS 1 AND 2

Interview subjects included Newton Minow, Abner Mikva, Toni Preckwinkle, Leslie Hairston, Pake Zane, Julie Lauster, Clive Gray, Maxine Box, Keith Kakugawa, Vinai Thummalapally, Chris McLachlin, Eric Kusunoki, Alan Lum, Janet Allison, Lowell Jacobs, Carlyn Tani and Joyce Feuer. Articles and other published sources for this period included Nicole Brodeur, 'Memories of Obama's Mother', *Seattle Times*, 5 February 2008; Amanda Ripley, 'A Mother's Story', *Time*, 21 April 2008; Janny Scott, 'A Free-Spirited Wanderer Who Set Obama's Path', *New York Times*, 14 March 2008; Barack Obama, *The Audacity of Hope* (New York: Vintage Books, 2006); Jonathan Martin, 'Obama's Mother Known Here as "Uncommon"', *Seattle Times*, 8 April 2008; Dan Nakaso, 'Family Precedent: Obama's Grandmother Blazed Trails', 8 April 2008; Christiane Oelrich, 'Obama the "Curly-Haired One"', *News 24*, 29 April 2008; Johnny Brannon, 'Hawaii's Imperfect Melting Pot a Big Influence on Young Obama', *Honolulu Advertiser*, 10 February 2007; Carlyn Tani, 'A Kid Called Barry', *Punahou Bulletin*, Punahou School, Spring 2007; Barack Obama, *Dreams from My Father* (New York: Times Books, 1995); Ronald Kessler, 'Obama's High School Days: Ran with Bad Crowd', *Newsmax*, October 9 2008; 'The Choice 2008: Barack Obama', *Frontline*, PBS, 14 October 2008; 'Old Friends Recall Obama's College Years', Associated Press, 16 May 2008.

CHAPTERS 3 AND 4

Information in these chapters was based in part on interviews and conversations with Laurence Tribe, Jerry Kellman, Abner Mikva, Bradford Berenson, Mike Kruglik, Yvonne Lloyd, Linda Randle, Loretta Augustin-Herron, Hazel Johnson, Vinai Thummalapally, the Reverend Alvin Love, Cheryl Johnson, Newton Minow and Judson Miner. Published sources included Richard Wolffe, 'When Barry Became Barack', *Newsweek*, 31 March 2008; David Mendell, *Obama: From Promise to Power* (New York: HarperCollins, 2007); 'The Poetry of Barack Obama', *New York Times*, 18 May 2008; Liz Mundy, *Michelle* (New York: Simon & Schuster, 2008); Sally Jacobs, 'Learning to Be Michelle Obama', *Boston Globe*, 15 June 2008; Shailagh Murray, 'A Family Tree Rooted in American Soil', *Washington Post*, 2 October 2008; 'At Harvard, Obama Foreshadowed Presidential Appeal', Associated Press, 26 January 2007; Bob Secter and John McCormick, 'Obama in Chicago: Portrait of a Pragmatist', *Chicago Tribune*, 3 April 2007; Saul Alinsky, *Rules for Radicals* (New York: Random House, 1971); William Finnegan, 'The Candidate', *New Yorker*, 31 May 2004; Rick Pearson and David Mendell, 'Illinois Democrats Praise Obama's Convention Speech', *Chicago Tribune*, 29 July 2004; Joy Bennett Kinnon, 'Michelle Obama: Not Just the Senator's Wife', *Ebony*, March 2006; Gwen Ifill, 'Beside Barack', *Essence*, September 2007; Mike Dorning, 'Employer: Michelle Obama's Raise Well-Earned', *Chicago Tribune*, 27 September 2006; Rosalind Rossi, 'The Woman Behind Obama', *Chicago Sun-Times*, 20 January 2007.

CHAPTERS 5 TO 8

For these chapters, the author drew on conversations with, among others, Senator John Kerry, Senator Tom Harkin, Newton Minow, Jeremiah Posedel, Abner Mikva, Senator Denny Jacobs, Toni Preckwinkle, Judson Miner, Leslie Hairston, Senator Mike Jacobs, Larry Walsh, Zarif, Joyce Feuer, Janet Allison, Letitia Baldrige, Wellington Wilson, Coralee Jacobs, Edward Koch, Rick Lazio, the Reverend Alvin Love, Betsy Vandercook, Mary Ann Campbell and Lowell Jacobs. Published sources include: Lynn Norment, 'The Hottest Couple in America', *Ebony*, February 2007; Christi Parsons, Bruce Japsen and Bob Secter, 'Barack's Rock', *Chicago Tribune*, 22 April 2007; Janny Scott, 'In Illinois, Obama Proved Pragmatic and Shrewd', *New York Times*, 30 July 2007; Holly Yeager, 'The Heart and Mind of Michelle Obama', *O*, November 2007; Richard Wolffe, 'Barack's Rock', *Newsweek*, 25 February 2008; Jay Tolson, 'The Obama Effect', *U.S. News & World Report*, 25 February 2008; Lauren Collins, 'The Other Obama', *New Yorker*, 10 March 2008; Tim Dickinson, 'The Machinery of Hope', *Rolling Stone*, 20 March 2008; Richard Wolffe and Evan Thomas, 'Sit Back, Relax, Get Ready to Rumble', *Newsweek*, 18 May 2008; 'Obama Quits Church, Citing Controversies', CNN, 31 May 2008; Maureen Dowd, 'What's Better? His Empty Suit or Her Baggage?' *New York Times*, 15 March 2006; Nancy Gibbs and Jay Newton-Small, 'The War Over Michelle', *Time*, 22 May 2008; Kathryn Knight, 'Is She the U.S. Cherie?' *Daily Mail*, 26 June 2008; Stefano Esposito, 'Two People Who Love Each Other', *Chicago Sun-Times*, 13 July 2008; Ryan Lizza, 'Making It', *New Yorker*, 21 July 2008; Dave McKinney and Chris Fusco, 'Obama on Rezko Deal: It Was a Mistake', *Chicago Sun-Times*, 5 November 2006; Sandra

Sobieraj Westfall, 'The Obamas Get Personal', People, 4 August 2008; Vanessa Grigoriadis, 'Black and Blacker: The Racial Politics of the Obama Marriage', New York, 18 August 2008; Harriette Cole, 'The Real Michelle Obama', Ebony, September 2008; Liz Mundy, 'Series of Fortunate Events', Washington Post, 12 August 2007; Diane Salvatore, 'The Obamas', Ladies' Home Journal, September 2008; Jon Meacham, 'On His Own', Newsweek, 1 September 2008; Lynn Sweet, 'Role Ayers Played in Obama Political Career', Chicago Sun-Times, 15 October 2008; Drew Griffin and Kathleen Johnston/CNN Special Investigations Unit, 'Obama-Ayers Connection Much Deeper, Ran Much Longer, Was More Political', Anderson Cooper 360°, 6 October 2008; Dan Nakaso and Geraldine Brooks, 'Camelot 2.0?' More, October 2008; James Bone, 'Obama was Unaware 'Aunt Zeituni' Defied Judge's Order to Leave U.S.', New York Times, 3 November 2008; 'The Final Days', Newsweek, 17 November 2008; Jill Smolowe and Sandra Sobieraj Westfall, 'The Obamas' New Life', People, 24 November 2008; Rob Chilton, Delina Dixon and William Reiter, 'Inside Michelle's Private World', OK Weekly, 24 November 2008; David Von Drehle, 'Why History Can't Wait', Time, 29 December 2008; John Feinstein, 'Obama's Brother-in-Law Is a Court Authority', Washington Post, 18 January 2009; Joe Klein, 'A New Destiny', Time, 20 January 2009; 'At Last', Associated Press, 21 January 2009; Christia Bellantoni, Stephen Dinan, and John Ward, 'Obama's Historic Day, Minute by Minute', Washington Times, 21 January 2009; Tom Junod, 'What the Hell Just Happened?' Esquire, February 2009; Jonathan Alter, 'The Confidence Game', Newsweek, 2 March 2009; Carol Felsenthal, 'The Making of a First Lady', Chicago, February 2009; André Leon Talley, 'Leading Lady', Vogue, March 2009; Maureen Orth, 'Enter Obama', Vanity Fair, March 2009.

Select Bibliography

Abramson, Jill, et al. *Obama: The Historic Journey*. New York: New York Times/Callaway, 2009.

Alinsky, Saul. *Rules for Radicals: A Practical Primer for Realistic Radicals*. New York: Random House, 1971.

Andersen, Christopher. *American Evita: Hillary Clinton's Path to Power*. New York: William Morrow, 2004.

———. *Bill and Hillary: The Marriage*. New York: William Morrow, 1999.

———. *George and Laura: Portrait of an American Marriage*. New York: William Morrow, 2002.

———. *Jack and Jackie: Portrait of an American Marriage*. New York: William Morrow, 1996.

———. *Jackie after Jack: Portrait of the Lady*. New York: William Morrow, 1998.

Ayers, Bill. *Fugitive Days: A Memoir*. Boston: Beacon, 2001.

Cone, James H. *Black Theology and Black Power*. New York: Harper & Row, 1969.

———. *For My People: Black Theology and the Black Church*. Maryknoll, NY: Orbis, 1984.

Dougherty, Steve. *Hopes and Dreams: The Story of Barack Obama*. New York: Black Dog and Leventhal Publishers, 2008.

Editors of *Life* Magazine. *Life: The American Journey of Barack Obama*. New York: Little, Brown, 2008.

Fanon, Frantz. *Black Skin, White Masks*. New York: Grove, 1967.

Lightfoot, Elizabeth. *Michelle Obama: First Lady of Hope*. Guilford, CT: Lyons Press, 2009.

Malcolm X, with Alex Haley. *The Autobiography of Malcolm X*. New York: Grove, 1965.

McCain, John, with Mark Salter. *Faith of My Fathers*. New York: Random House, 1999.

———. *Worth the Fighting For*. New York: Random House, 2003.

Mendell, David. *Obama: From Promise to Power*. New York: Amistad/HarperCollins, 2007.

Mundy, Liz. *Michelle: A Biography*. New York: Simon & Schuster, 2008.

Obama, Barack. *The Audacity of Hope: Thoughts on Reclaiming the American Dream*. New York: Vintage Books, 2008.

———. *Dreams from My Father*. New York: Times Books, 1995.

Steele, Shelby. *A Bound Man: Why We Are Excited about Obama and Why He Can't Win*. New York: Free Press, 2008.

Wright, Jeremiah A. *What Makes You So Strong? Sermons of Joy and Strength*. Valley Forge, PA: Judson, 1993.

INDEX